'In language as golden as a freshly cooked pizza, as piquant as a tongue-tweaking aperitif, and as broadly satisfying as an Italian banquet, Johnston lauds the stomach and its gastronomic orgasms with the save loveable attention that Lord Byron lavished on his lady loves ... his language tumbling off the page like a ripened harvest.' David Wood, *Canberra Times*

'Johnston makes good travel writing look easy ... The result is memorable and charming.' Bruce Elder, *SMH*

'One of my favourite reads so far this year ... Johnston's writing is deceptively simple and stylish, and quietly communicates both his wonder and his passion for the food, the people and life on an island that time really does seem to have forgotten.' Keith Austin, *SMH*

'... an evocative portrait of the traditional Sicily tourists rarely get to see ... Don't be put off if you haven't been to Sicily. After reading this you will feel you have, and you will surely want to go again.' James Hall, *Australian*

'Johnston writes deliriously about ice cream and pasta, liver and marzipan, garlic and pastries. He writes of their provenance and history, packing the book full of wonderful anecdotes and insights. A perfect summer read.' *Age*

'Johnston's is a sweet story indeed. and if you're a reader who enjoys burning piety and do
how to chop garlic, then this
Erin O'Brien, *Australian Books*

SICILIAN SUMMER

A story of honour, religion and the perfect cassata

BRIAN JOHNSTON

ALLEN&UNWIN

First published in 2005

Allen & Unwin
83 Alexander Street
Crows Nest NSW 2065
Australia
Phone: (61 2) 8425 0100
Fax: (61 2) 9906 2218
Email: info@allenandunwin.com
Web: www.allenandunwin.com

National Library of Australia
Cataloguing-in-Publication entry:

Johnston, Brian, 1966– .
  Sicilian summer: A story of honour, religion and the
  perfect cassata.

  ISBN 1 74114 735 2.

  1. Johnston, Brian, 1966- – Travel – Italy – Sicily. 2.
  Sicily (Italy) – Description and travel. I. Title.

914.58044

Typeset by Midland Typesetters, Australia
Printed by McPherson's Printing Group, Australia

10 9 8 7 6 5 4 3 2

To Tina Calascione
with affection and gratitude for a memorable Sicilian summer

CONTENTS

ACKNOWLEDGEMENTS

It was my good friend Tina Calascione who suggested I go to Sicily, and whose tales of life and food on the island first caught my imagination. Before then we'd only managed to travel together for a weekend—an unsuccessful trip in which we ended up sleeping in the car on an isolated beach in northern New South Wales. (At least, Tina slept and I sat up all night listening to the wind howl. The poor planning was all her fault—don't let her say otherwise.) It's all the more surprising, therefore, that she thought we could survive so many weeks together in Montalto. We didn't just survive but got on extremely well. I'm eternally grateful to her for giving me the opportunity to share so much of her life, and for having the courage to let me write about it in these pages.

To Giuseppe and Marcella Calascione I owe an immense debt of gratitude for housing and feeding me, lending me their car, answering my incessant questions and putting up with my presence. They accomplished it all with good grace, and never for a moment made me feel unwelcome. To them I feel an immense affection and respect. *Grazie mille*.

Anyone looking for the village of Montalto on a map of Sicily will search in vain. In deference to the people who appear in these pages, I decided to alter the name of the village and the names of its residents who, wittingly or not, provided me with so much material. To have shared a small part of their lives was an immense privilege, and I'm grateful to them all.

Back in the real world my brother Simon, who saw Sicily a decade before I did, read over an early version of the manuscript and offered supportive advice. Kelvin Li was merciless in slashing the final version, and made me see that less is sometimes all you need. He also pointed out areas for clarification, and the book is better for it. Lisa Merrifield did a marvellous editorial job, battling my semicolons, making helpful comments and correcting errors with an extraordinary gimlet eye. Thanks must also go to Allen & Unwin's senior editors Joanne Holliman and Colette Vella and commissioning editor Jo Paul for their encouragement and support.

Brian Johnston
Sydney 2005

SICILIAN SUMMER

1

FIRST COURSE

Across the water lies a beautiful and ravaged island, where saints and bandits live in the shadow of a restless volcano, and contradiction is everywhere. Pious widows hobble along streets as leering gargoyles bare their breasts. In shuttered churches Koranic verses loop in gold across the walls, while in bakeries pastries with religious names ooze erotic excess, a legacy of the brilliant cultures that once flourished here. Now death and decay are never far away. Deception too: benevolent uncles dabble in organised crime, and even the village priest turns out to be the devil in a cassock.

The island is Sicily, a fertile and sunny stepping stone in the middle of the Mediterranean, right at the crossroads of Europe and Africa. For centuries its desirable geography made it a coveted prize of the great Mediterranean powers: the canny Greeks and organised Romans, the civilised Arabs and pious, doleful Spanish. In between, the Normans settled down for a century or so and the Hohenstaufen for seven decades. The island's inhabitants were bloodied and impoverished, even battered by the Spanish Inquisition. Yet in the midst of all these horrors a dazzling artistic and cultural heritage blossomed. This is a place where breath-taking classical theatres perch over swooping coastlines, and baroque churches erupt in flamboyant frivolity. Sicily has always been an island of devastating exploitation and exquisite treasures.

Most of all, Sicily's greatest treasure is its remarkable cuisine. Every dish is a culinary clue to this island of marvels and magic, full of eroticism and fervent religion, history and culture. In Sicily there's glorious seafood, pasta glistening with tomato sauce and olives, and pastries galore. Then there's cassata, the ultimate Sicilian dessert, a baroque extravaganza of sponge cake and sweet ricotta, lavishly decorated with marzipan and candied fruit.

I went to Sicily a casual visitor, keen to hunt down cassata and learn more about cooking, and found myself seduced by the island's neglected beauty and passionate people. Against this backdrop I met the personalities of that long summer: Tina, Giuseppe, Marcella and Lucia, lost in labyrinths of familial misunderstandings and tortured relationships. The island and the people all told the same tale of a violent past overlaid with passion and nostalgia. Looking back now, I find my images of the island and its people blur together. The mummified monks of centuries ago recall the immediacy of a village funeral, and family visits to the church are seen through a swirl of baroque nymphs. I think of the island's turbulent history and am reminded of Arabs and aristocrats, a father's anger and a mother's weeping. In the background I hear once more the fizz of lemons dropped into cool drinks on a hot day. Cicadas click dementedly, and battered Fiats splutter in narrow streets: the sounds of Sicily.

This is a story of family honour, religion, tragedy, bitter history and food.

This is the story of a summer in Sicily.

All day long the train has been rattling down the length of Italy, flicking through dusty stations and fields of exhausted olive trees. I sit at the window yawning and watch railway crossings and washing lines flash past. Every now and then I page through one of my guidebooks. I've never been to Sicily before. What do I know about this overlooked corner of Europe? Not much. I'm only a curious traveller, clackety-clacking towards the island because of Tina, who is curled up in the opposite corner of the compartment and has drifted into sleep, dazzled by the sun and dust. She's surrounded by the clutter that seems to follow her everywhere, a hairbrush, a self-help book, a ghastly pink cardigan, bananas and biscuits. *She looks like a war refugee abandoned by her mother*, I think affectionately as we sway across the burnt landscape. In fact, we're going to stay with her mother and father in her hometown of Montalto in Sicily. Tina hasn't been there for years, and even her parents are outsiders; they left Sicily when Tina was eleven, taking themselves off to a better life in New York. Now, thirty years later, they've cautiously returned, drawn by cheap living, memories and sunshine.

I'm looking forward to meeting them. Rootless myself, I'm always intrigued by immigrants, by people caught between cultures and commitments. Maybe this is what attracts me to Tina: she speaks with an American accent but has a European outlook and—like me—has become an accidental Australian. Years ago we taught English together in Sydney and afterwards remained friends with a shared love of Scrabble and Thai takeaways.

And so Tina asks me to go with her to Sicily, just like that, and casually I say, 'Yes, why not?' I've always liked Tina. Now I relish the chance to get to know her better and visit the island of her origin, sensing that deep friendship may be within our grasp as the train lurches south.

Tina's reasons for heading to Sicily are pleasant ones: summer heat, fine food, a church confirmation. Long ago, the daughter of some family friends asked Tina to be her godmother. Tina accepted in an unthinking moment of delight. She'd never been asked to do anything like that before, she explained to me; at family celebrations it was always her elder sister who acted as bridesmaid or flower girl. Tina, the envious bystander, saw her chance to be involved, but the years drifted past and her godchild Claudia is now sixteen. The confirmation is something she should have done years ago, and it has now become an inescapable duty.

The temperature hardly drops as the long afternoon draws towards evening, and the air is still. Colours emerge from the landscape as the sun declines, revealing brilliant yellows and blues. Villa San Giovanni is pink from a distance, a fragile fantasy town of sugar cubes and crushed strawberry but, as the train snakes into the suburbs, ugly half-built houses with junk-filled yards crowd the train tracks. The roads are cracked and telegraph wires hang in tangles. People shout and smoke and gesticulate by the sides of the railway tracks, and I smell rust and hot train wheels. As the light fades and Tina stirs awake I feel we've reached not just the end of a continent, but the end of organisation and control. Villa San Giovanni is almost the last town in the toe of Italy, right at the crumbling end of Europe.

Then Villa San Giovanni is gone and the train shudders onto a ferry. The grimy passengers sense home and clamber off the carriages, making for the ferry's saloon counter. Dark, nervous men with lean faces buy Messina beer and fiddle with cigarettes. Up on the deck Tina and I watch as Messina itself swims out of the darkness in little pinpricks of light. Sad-looking women dressed in black crowd the railings beside me. The cranes of Messina's port look like giant grappling hooks, as if the city is making a last-ditch attempt to anchor the island to Italy. Behind the town, blue mountain ridges are steep and secretive in the purple evening light. Mafia country. As the ferry docks in the dark at Messina I suddenly feel apprehensive.

What I don't know yet is that Sicily isn't just home to godfathers but also quarrelsome saints and tormented poets. There are shabby aristocrats and naughty nuns, kings and cooks, priests and parents.

What I also don't know yet is that there's no fact or fiction, no distinction between reality and fantasy. There's only Sicily. I should have been warned. Tina should have told me to leave my common sense behind in a railway locker in far-off Rome like unnecessary baggage.

Too late now. I've crossed the water, passed beyond the boundary.

Islands are always magical places.

***

Tina steps off the ferry. Years in America and Australia have given her an adaptive respectability that often makes people overlook her sparkle and Mediterranean roots. She has an American accent, speaks more of New York than Sicily, and keeps her past to herself. Small and slight with fragile wrists and haunting eyes, she usually conceals her vivacity and attractiveness under dowdy clothes. Now she tugs the plastic clasp from her hair, shaking out her long dark curls, and shouts towards her parents in Italian. She looks suddenly different, mysterious and even dangerous. Sicily is in her blood.

A salty, oily smell comes off the water swirling around the ferry as I heave our suitcases onto the dock and watch as Tina's parents approach. Her mother Marcella is small and slight and reminds me of a sparrow, with wiry strength despite seeming fragility. Her father Giuseppe is taller and more robust. They're both in their late sixties or early seventies, perhaps, but healthy and full of energy.

'Concettina, Concettina,' her mother cries, clutching at her daughter's arm, overcome with emotion. They hug her and shake my hand warily. We clamber into a minuscule Fiat. My head is bent against the roof and the old walls of the port career by at a crazy angle as we speed along the waterfront. I can see concrete apartments and the occasional dilapidated municipal building. There's a lighthouse—no, it's a long pillar topped by a statue at whose feet a bright orange electric clock shows the time. Every now and then there are also flashing digits: 588.

'I haven't seen that clock before,' says Tina suddenly.

'No, the statue was once naked,' explains Marcella. 'Now it isn't naked because there's a clock.'

Tina giggles. It occurs to me that she doesn't usually hear her parents speaking English.

'What does 588 mean, anyway?'

'Could be the time,' says Giuseppe, peering at his watch as we hurtle along the harbour.

'Pa, it's nine o'clock!'

Horns blare and cars swerve in and out of their lanes. At the traffic lights men slouch out of their car windows, smoking and scratching, their ties unknotted. Slick teenagers on Vespas career in and out of the traffic with suicidal pleasure, then are left behind as we speed onto the motorway.

Tina's father is doing most of the talking. Marcella looks uneasy, and I remember her anxious expression on meeting us off the ferry. I study her face, dotted with liver spots and crumpled with years of . . . What? Disappointment? Regret? Beside me in the back seat Tina sounds strained and slightly querulous despite the friendly banter. It's disconcerting to hear her speak Italian; suddenly she's someone I don't really know.

'We'll be in Montalto soon,' says Tina as we leave the motorway and start swinging up a hillside.

'Yes, and just here,' says Giuseppe, waving out the window and slowing down, 'a local man was killed one night in a car accident.'

I glance out of the window and see that a low retaining wall has fallen in a heap. The man was driving too fast, Giuseppe explains, and missed the bend on the narrow road, crashing through the wall and pitching down the hillside. The leaves of the olive trees, Marcella adds in a moment of whimsy, were illuminated like beaten silver in the headlights.

The man's ghost still haunts the bend in the road, keening in the night. That's why Giuseppe's heart skipped a beat one evening when he had to drive past, and heard a groaning from the grass. His foot lurched onto the brake. Another groan. Giuseppe clambered out of the car, his palms clammy with perspiration, and found only a drunk lying in the verge looking up at the stars. The man had walked down to the harbour at four o'clock to get some fresh fish for his wife, but he'd been sidetracked by his cronies and was only now struggling home. He hadn't even managed to get the fish, explains Giuseppe indignantly.

'I just left him there, and drove away as the church bells were clanging midnight!'

Minutes later we're entering Montalto and driving past the village football field and the petrol pumps.

'Antonio used to work there, remember him, Concettina?'

'Yes, Ma.'

'Well, he ran away to Milan and started to dress in women's clothes. And here he was always in greasy overalls! I wouldn't like to mention this, but it's the truth,' Marcella adds complacently. Appropriately enough, just past the petrol pumps stands a bridal shop, painted in pink, with a sequinned dress taking pride of place in the window. Maybe this glimpse of pink silk is what set Antonio dreaming, standing down the road pumping petrol.

'Such a beautiful dress, Concettina,' says Marcella as we inch up the steep, narrow street in a cloud of exhaust fumes.

'Ma!'

Tina is forty and unmarried. She doesn't even have a

boyfriend at the moment. (If she did she wouldn't tell Marcella; the wedding date would be set in no time.) Lack of a husband and children, and residence in distant Australia: these are things that rankle about Tina in the Calascione family, she's already warned me.

'Madonna, how can you do this to me! I'm an old woman alone in the world, supposing I were to die, then you would come to my grave and feel the sorrow!'

'Ma, that's enough.'

'I'm supposing your mother isn't in my circumstance,' says Marcella, turning to me. With an apologetic grimace at Tina I have to admit that both my brother and sister have children.

'Ah, she's a grandmother! Such a wonderful thing, she must be a very happy woman, whereas I . . . Well. I ask myself what I've done to deserve such a sadness. Jesus alone can understand what I suffer.'

'Ma!' shouts Tina, before adding in a grim aside, 'Now you can see why I live in Australia.'

At that moment we burst into a tiny piazza, tyres squealing on the cobblestones. As we pull up at the Calascione house, I breathe in the oleander-scented air and smile. I'm happy to be in Montalto, a small village high above the sea, and I haven't a care in the world. When Tina casually invited me to come with her to Sicily I was delighted. The confirmation seems like a great opportunity for a fun-filled Italian festival: I imagine making merry under the grapevines and satiating my sweet tooth on some legendary cassata. Within a week Claudia will be confirmed and Tina will have fulfilled her godmotherly duty and then we can head off for some sightseeing and culinary curiosities.

I was a little naïve, of course. I smiled too soon, for this was only the beginning. How little I knew of Sicily then: the power of religion, the honour of families, the plotting and relish for disaster. This was all before the recalcitrant priest and Tina's tantrum—before the godmother, for heaven's sake, tried to renounce Jesus and then lied about her confession. This was before divine intervention in the affairs of the village, not to mention the rebellion of the organist and the arrival of a bishop.

But I'm getting ahead of myself.

This is only the beginning.

I'm staying with the Calasciones in the house of Tina's Aunt Rita. It's a huge echoing place with a lot of cool marble flooring and hardly any furniture except for a couple of sagging sofas. Gigantic old-fashioned beds, family heirlooms probably, occupy several of the upstairs rooms. On a dresser in the parlour sit some black and white photos of people in stiff dresses or black suits staring accusingly at the camera.

A few years ago Tina's parents rediscovered the pull of their roots and decided to spend more time in Sicily warming their old bones in Montalto, the village of their youth. They're thinking of buying a house here but, in the meantime, Aunt Rita's does just fine. Aunt Rita, who lives in Switzerland, rarely comes here now and the house has the slightly musty air of a place long closed up.

As we clamber up to the granny flat at the very top of the house, four floors up, Tina tells me it was meant for Aunt Rita's only daughter, killed in a mountain-climbing accident in the Alps. It's to this granny flat that I'm now banished, my own little space tucked in under the roof. I'm happy enough with this arrangement; the granny flat is bright and sunny and altogether more cheerful than the gloomy rooms below. It has a broad terrace with a superb view over the village roofs, sprouting television aerials, and a mustard-yellow church with a pink dome. Beyond, a patchwork of fields and olive trees finally disappears into mountain ridges and a milky-blue sky.

The terrace becomes my eyrie, my little floating world of sunlight and cheer perched above the sombreness of Aunt Rita's house. I haul up a rough wooden table, a hard chair and a mattress. Each morning I sit on the terrace to catch a gentle breeze and drink my coffee. After lunch I come up to write or have a siesta. The only sounds are the chirping of birds and dogs barking in the distance. Sometimes a tractor trundles down some hidden country lane. A woman's voice floats up from the street and then falls silent.

At four o'clock I wake to the sound of church bells, clanging discordantly in the village below.

Every lunchtime in Montalto I descend into the bowels of the house to haunt the kitchen. Marcella has made this room her own and it's comfortably disordered, strewn with massive pots and rustic chairs. Odd assortments of plates and coloured cups stand on shelves and olives and anchovies gleam from bottles on a sideboard. There are no stiff photos here, only recipes torn from magazines and pinned to cupboard doors for reference. Every available surface seems to be a tumble of oranges, lemons and potted plants.

More often than not I find Marcella in the kitchen making pasta, working with lightning precision. She piles flour in a heap in the centre of the table and cracks three eggs into the well she's made in the middle of it, beating them together with flicks of her fingers. She works the mixture into a paste, neither too wet nor too dry. I watch her intensity and suspect a depth of passion somewhere beneath her sensible blouses and slender gold necklaces. So far she's shown me only concerned politeness as her guest, coupled with a slight wariness. Probably she's wondering what my relationship is with her daughter and why I have such an unmanly interest in her cooking. I'm beginning to like Marcella—her endless chirpiness and good manners—and beginning to think that, like Tina, there's more to her than meets the eye.

When the dough is made up, Marcella passes it through a gleaming little metal pasta machine that she's had for forty years. It's clamped to the table and has a wooden handle to turn the mangle. It's an Imperio, she tells me proudly; probably the best brand of pasta machine. She works quickly, before the dough dries out and becomes less elastic. The sheets of dough are draped over the edge of the table where the air will help dry them.

'I used to love doing that when I was a kid,' says Tina watching me. 'Cranking and cranking that handle, and that damp pasta smell—it's one of my earliest memories of Sicily.' She narrows her eyes as if in reflection. Having just turned forty, I think it's not just for the confirmation that she's come back to Sicily. Perhaps she's taking a trip down the byways of memory, nostalgic for her childhood.

Another contraption fixed onto the machine chops

the sheets into ribbons of fresh fettuccine. It's my job to lay the fettuccine out on a clean white sheet on the dining-room table next door. The strips mustn't be touching otherwise they'll glue together, instructs Marcella. When I'm finished they're covered with the other half of the sheet and left to dry.

In the early afternoon Marcella's fettuccine are dropped into a huge pot of boiling, salted water. She's taken aback when I express surprise at the litres of water it contains. After a pause for thought she says that abundant water is vital when cooking pasta. She hovers over the pot as if my ignorance has made her nervous, determined not to turn her pasta into the overcooked, stodgy mess so beloved of foreigners. She fishes out a strand with her fork and nibbles it.

'Still a little hard, you see,' she says to me anxiously. 'So we drain it now. It'll cook a little more just from its own heat, eh?' Immediately she adds a drop of sauce to stop the strands sticking together.

Unlike Marcella, I nearly always boil my pasta for far too long out of sheer nervousness. When I mention this to Marcella she looks at me helplessly. What can she say about cooking time? It depends on the thickness and shape of the pasta, the hardness of the water. And, she adds, everyone knows making good pasta in the mountains is a challenge, because water doesn't boil as well at altitude. She couldn't possibly give me a *time*.

'We're talking about cooking, not the immutable laws of physics,' Tina smirks. 'It's an *art*.'

'Really, the only way is to taste it! Nothing scratches your hand like your own nails, eh?' says Marcella helpfully.

I nod wisely. At least when shopping I know to look for pasta made from hard durum wheat, rather than from the cheaper soft wheat, often used in foreign pasta but illegal in Italy, that tends to go soggy when cooked. It's one of the few things I *do* know about pasta. I'd be embarrassed to admit it to Marcella, but for many years I thought pasta was just brittle, yellow stuff that came out of a packet and was boiled into a sticky mess. A couple of trips to mainland Italy had quickly changed my mind: this apparently humble food actually has a bewildering variety and splendour. For a start, it isn't always yellow. There's spinach pasta, a delicate summer-green. The thin, flat nutty-flavoured buckwheat noodles (*pizzoccheri*) I saw in Lombardy are biscuit-brown. Herb pastas are flecked with green and chilli pastas hide a red bite, pasta with a touch of cocoa powder is brown, while tomato pasta is made with the addition of concentrated tomato purée that adds a beautiful blush to the dough. Saffron pasta is deep gold and delicately flavoured, ideal for seafood dishes. For more drama, there's startling black squid-ink pasta, or purple beetroot pasta that fades to an elegant rose when cooked.

'In America they don't understand pasta,' Marcella is saying. 'They use spaghetti practically all the time. Even with some chunky sauce of meat! I suppose you know that rigatoni or *conchiglie* is much better for that,' she adds, eyeing me with suspicion.

'Of course!' I answer brightly.

As a matter of fact, in my quest for culinary enlightenment, I've been secretly reading up about pasta in my little granny flat, and making notes. Still, I'll never catch up with

Marcella, who's been making pasta for fifty years or more. I've watched her do it almost without conscious thought, but at the same time with a kind of loving intensity, and I can see what Tina means when she says it's an art. I feel a little spurt of envy, a sudden desire for cooking competence. I know I'm ready to lose myself in the passion of Sicilian cuisine.

It's when I eat Marcella's homemade fettuccine that I realise again how glorious pasta can be. She serves it up at the kitchen table in a cream sauce into which onions, slowly simmered in butter, have been blended. The onions are soaked beforehand in water to remove their sharpness, leaving only subtle flavour. There are little flecks of ham in the sauce, too, although you don't even need that; simplicity is the key to all great cooking. Fresh fettuccine, onions and cream, topped with a handful of freshly-grated hard salted *ricotta* in little whorls.

Now that's pasta to perfection.

Sicily is an island of fabulous foods, and you can read its dishes the way a gypsy reads tea leaves and discover its troubled past of conquerors and curious civilisations. You can nibble on the flesh of fat olives seasoned with garlic and fennel, plump and meaty enough to be a meal, and thank the ancient Greeks for it. A simple dish of salt cod from the cold waters of the North Sea is eaten on this sun-washed island only because the Normans brought it here a thousand years ago. Drive through a landscape of orange trees, on the other hand, and you'll feel like you're in the gardens of Arabia. The food is so full of history that you can smell and taste the influences and passions of the island's heritage.

There's poetry on every plate and that's why I'm here. Food fascinates me because it's so rich in symbolic meaning: cultural, psychological, sexual, personal. In Sicily, I am reminded again that food is inextricably linked to our own sense of civilisation. The Chinese had first shown me this when I spent three years living in Sichuan Province, surrounded by fiery spices and endless literary and colloquial references to food. Then I moved to Sydney where I found outstanding variety. Before I travelled, I never noticed food much. Perhaps this is because my parents are British and not terribly interested in food, perhaps it's because I grew up mostly in Switzerland. The British and Swiss certainly don't have food cultures approaching that of the Chinese or Italians; food is just a pragmatic energy source, not the stuff of passion. My mother was a great one for making us eat our greens and drink our milk, not because it was pleasurable, but because they were supposed to be healthy. Fruit and vegetables were good, snacks were bad, and fast food was unheard of in Geneva when I was growing up. Sweets were somehow sinful. We could only take two biscuits with our coffee. At Christmas our grandmother sent a box of Quality Street chocolates from Britain, which we hoarded like jewels.

It's alarming to think how the eating habits of parents influence their children. For years as a young adult I avoided salami (despised by my mother) and pasta (my father wasn't too keen on it). My mother, who has strong culinary opinions, also banned fish and all other seafood from the house; to say something tasted or smelt 'fishy' was the ultimate condemnation. Only in Australia did I finally discover the pleasures of seafood. I've yet to pluck up the courage to abandon my biscuit allowance in Sydney, half a world away from my mother's watchful eye. Not that I regret the practicality and puritanism of my mother's cooking; it gave me sensible eating habits. But my trip to Sicily is the culmination of a journey begun in China and continued in Australia, an exploration of the joys of food. I eat pasta now, and seafood, and have acquired quite a liking for salami. There's nothing like travel for widening your horizons and your palate.

Where better than Sicily? This cuisine is a long way from the innocuous food of my youth. Sicilian food is violent and sexy. In the turquoise waters off the coast giant tuna swim to their death, bludgeoned by fishermen who chant prayers as the sea swirls red with sacrificial blood. Red, too, are the glacé cherry nipples that decorate pert little cakes known as 'virgin's breasts': a titillating treat that's actually named after a virgin saint. The islanders delight in this symbiosis of sex and religion, and there are all kinds of other pastries invented in the grim nunneries of the island's barren interior—'nun's thighs', 'pope's noses', 'chancellor's buttocks'—bursting with a temptation of cream, candied fruit, sugar and almond paste. On the feast of St Joseph you can tuck into unholy pastry balls filled with sweet ricotta, lemon zest and cinnamon, then fitted together so they look like the luscious dimpled bums of church cherubs. And then there are the island's pasta shapes that come with pious names like 'angel's hair' and 'saint's beard'. To these pious pastas the locals add a sexy sauce rich in tomato and garlic, sharp with glistening black olives and piquant chips of fiery chilli. *Alla puttanesca* they call it: prostitute's pasta. Oh yes, the island certainly has pasta dishes and pastries of confusing contradictions, delightful and excessive and oozing eroticism and cultural history.

I intend to track them down. I'll watch and learn, savour and sample. Pastas and pastries, I'll eat them all.

And if I want to eat more than two *biscotti* with my coffee—then so I will.

Every morning Tina's father, Giuseppe, rises from bed and shuffles around the kitchen, his eyes half closed, making little grunting noises. He wears tracksuit pants so worn and low at the crotch they resemble long johns. His hair sticks up on end, making him look like the mad doctor in an old Frankenstein movie. His face is brown as a walnut and he's white haired and bald on top. (Tina tells him that he's losing hair on top of his head and it's growing out his ears instead, and he chuckles as if pleased.) He never seems put out that I'm sitting at the kitchen table drinking coffee and reading; in fact he seems grateful to have someone to talk too, without ever expecting much of a response. Giuseppe talks and talks, mostly about the past and about Sicily, but I don't mind. I find it charming and inoffensive. He usually tells me he hasn't slept a wink, he heard an owl hooting, which means that someone's going to die. Or he had a bad dream. Dreams, he tells me, provide symbolic glimpses of the future. If there are white grapes in your dream they foretell many tears. Roast meat means a violent death. I tell him that, although I'm preoccupied with food, I've never dreamt of roast meat. It seems like such an odd things to dream about.

'Dreams *are* odd,' says Giuseppe. He makes *le corna*, a horned sign with the little and index fingers stabbed down, in order to ward of disaster.

Giuseppe straps his blood-pressure belt onto his arm and pumps air into it, restricting his blood flow. He takes a reading from the gauge, grimacing anxiously at the figures. Then he sits beside me at the kitchen table slicing up garlic cloves and popping the pieces into his mouth with a grimace. He never bothers with breakfast, but swigs from an enormous glass of chilled orange juice, and mumbles to himself. The odour of the garlic overpowers even the smell of my freshly ground coffee.

'Pa, that's disgusting,' Tina comments with routine distaste as she arrives in the kitchen.

'It's beautiful,' says Giuseppe. 'You know, Concettina, it's good for health. Eat garlic, you live longer, and you don't have heart disease.'

Giuseppe appears fairly robust to me, with good colour in his cheeks, and although he's quite slight he seems bigger, thanks to his energy and passion. But like many Italians he's obsessed with his health. He's forever checking his blood pressure, haunting the hospital demanding ECGs and X-rays, taking blood tests and discussing his urine samples with his cronies as if assessing the latest wine vintages. After breakfast I usually walk down to the piazza with him, weaving through higgledy-piggledy parked cars, to the village pharmacy. Here Giuseppe fingers packets of pills as if hoping to come across some miracle rejuvenation, and returns home with a supply of capsules and tonics. These are used in combination with prayers and crucifixes to preserve Giuseppe and Marcella from malign influences, since their spiritual health is also apparently under constant threat. Marcella calls on the Virgin Lady, filled with divine grace, to protect her. Giuseppe has a little red horn dangling beside a crucifix on a long necklace of plastic beads: double insurance.

One morning, to my alarm, Giuseppe blunders into the kitchen like Lady Macbeth, clutching a syringe and needle in front of him as if searching for a murder victim. He waves the needle at me and taps his finger on an ampoule of liquid.

'Perhaps you can give me my vitamin injection,' he says.

Appalled, I tell him I can't possibly do such a thing.

'Oh? I'll have to wait for my wife.'

Marcella comes back from church and her check-up with God. She jabs the needle into Giuseppe's arm as I cringe behind the coffee-pot. Italians take most of their medicine like this, she explains airily. Even their vitamins!

'We all practice on an orange when we're young.'

'I see.'

It's a phrase I'm going to use a lot in Sicily, but I don't— I don't really see. If you ask me, all this obsessing over health conceals an even stronger obsession: a worry about dying. And as it happens, I'll soon find out that I'm probably right, because there's a fear and fascination with death everywhere in Sicily. And I'm going to bump into a lot of dead people: expiring martyrs and tortured saints, assassinated judges and pickled aristocrats. And Maria, of course. Mind you, Marcella's best friend didn't simply die. Maria passed away like a saint in a halo of gold, emanating a heavenly perfume.

But that story's for later.

A few days after our arrival in Montalto, Giovanni turns up unexpectedly at the house and invites us to dinner.

Giuseppe and Marcella were in the same class at school in Montalto—they were, in fact, high-school sweethearts—and Giovanni was in their class too. They rarely see each other now. Giovanni and his wife have lived in Rome for ages, but they come back to Montalto for long weekends and summers and have built a second home in the hills just above the village. Giovanni is dapper and well spoken, with watchful eyes and a carefully trimmed beard flecked with grey. His house sits in a field of tall whispering blades of brown grass, crackling with insects. A few gnarled old olive and fig trees stand just beyond the broad terrace, and there's a sweeping view down to the sea. Behind the new house stands an abandoned old cottage that once belonged to Giovanni's grandfather. It's no more than a hut really, a tiny rectangle of rough stone with a single door and no windows. I don't know why it has been left there. Maybe Giovanni likes to be reminded of his peasant roots, or maybe it's a statement of how far he's come up in the world. Still, his elegant new house, ten times the size, is only used during Easter, in August and for a few weekends each year. It's bland and modern, with neat wooden shutters and a red roof.

We've all been invited around for a simple supper. Giovanni's wife, Carmela, is much younger than her husband, a glossy woman with discreet make-up and well-tailored clothes, smug in her good fortune. Her eyes are hospitable and lively and I take an instant liking to her. She announces that supper is ready, and we troop indoors to a dining room open at one end to a gleaming modern kitchen. We start with glossy black olives fattened in the oven with white wine and garlic, pungent and inviting. Then we have a small dish of spaghetti with olive oil, garlic and a sprinkling of tiny chips of dried chilli to give it a slight kick. More spaghetti follows, with tomato sauce. Carmela slices big, round, salted ricotta with skin so dark and crumbly it looks like plum pudding. The inside is a soft, deep yellow, and we grate it over our spaghetti in creamy, curly flakes.

'The sauce isn't very good,' Carmela apologises. 'It was given to me by someone I don't like.'

Marcella and Carmela launch into a discussion of both the sauce maker and her sauce.

'The Lady in Heaven is a witness that she was once spotted taking money *out* of the offering plate in church.' 'No wonder her sauce is too runny!' 'She used some inferior tomato with too much juice and not enough pulp.' 'Maybe she's even added water to make it go further, the stingy creature!' Marcella says she should have used plum tomatoes.

'And then added a drop of red wine,' sniffs Carmela.

I listen in amazement. I'm already discovering that everyone in Sicily endlessly discusses, praises and criticises food. Eating might be a daily routine but Sicilians have the ability to turn meals into important events; the island still shuts down for two hours over lunch. Sicilians talk about their last meal, the meal they're in the middle of eating, and the meal they'll be having later. They comment on ingredients and how dishes are cooked. They wonder aloud which is better, ricotta from Montalto or from Tripi. Which wine should you have with mixed *antipasti*, a dry white to go with the little fish, or a light red to accompany the salami? And why on earth did Sofia let the grilled swordfish dry out that day? As if she doesn't know that all she had to do was grill it quickly over the flame in a basting of olive oil and lemon juice.

Despite the watery tomato sauce everyone is happy tonight, perhaps because we're all drinking sparkling Lambrusco mixed with lemonade and wedges of lemon. The drink is sharp and cool on this hot evening, dangerously refreshing. As Carmela brings bread, pickled olives and sheep's cheese to the table Giovanni watches me and asks whether I like the food, as if assessing my true interest in Sicilian gastronomy. He offers me a bit of cheese as Carmela tut-tuts. She should remove the spaghetti plates first, she says, otherwise the foreigner will think her house is no better than a zoo.

We finish off the meal with peeled peaches and tiny mulberries. The mulberries lie heaped in a bowl, deep purple and moist. Giuseppe tells me that in wetter places they can grow as big as your thumb. Over the fruit, Giovanni asks Tina how long she'll stay in Sicily, and she explains about Claudia's confirmation. She has to set a date with Padre Perrino, the village priest who'll officiate at the event.

'You know, I think Padre Perrino has three or even more children,' says Carmela.

I swivel around to stare at Carmela, momentarily distracted from the mulberries.

'And he loves money. Oh, how he loves money!' contributes Marcella tipsily. 'When he was young, it's said his father preferred sending him to the seminary instead of investing in pigs like the other villagers. He boasted that his son was worth more than ten pigs put together!'

Marcella wipes the tears of mirth from her eyes. 'And he was right! Oh my God, the priest is worth more than ten pigs!'

'Ma, how do you know?'

'I use the same bank as the priest, Concettina. And I've seen him paying plenty of money into his personal account. Where did that come from, eh? He even saved money by sacking his assistant.'

'All the donations and collections for the church, who knows what's happening to them?' adds Carmela.

Between wine, food and a meeting of old friends the conversation has quickened. It's a good moment for Giovanni to get out his grappa, a strong alcoholic drink made from the skins of grapes. He has flavoured his grappa with lemon; the rinds lie in the bottom, curiously smooth and pale, giving the liquid a yellow-green tinge like the palest olive oil. Giovanni holds the bottle up to the light, where it shines with a pale yellow radiance, then opens it as if it's the finest vintage champagne, pouring carefully. There's a whole ceremony to drinking grappa. You don't just knock it back like other spirits, but breathe in its heady aroma and then take a tiny sip, letting the liquid sit on your tongue so the alcohol evaporates, sending the flavour through your mouth and nose.

Laughter bubbles, arms and hands semaphor, words tumble out. This is the least of Padre Perrino's alleged miser-liness, according to Giuseppe. As he swigs his grappa he tells us the Padre also owns an apartment from which he's threatened to evict the tenants, who are having difficulties over rental payments. 'He refuses to have heating in the church in winter. And you're lucky if the priest offers you anything to drink when you go around to his house of an evening.'

'I hope the Lord in His infinite mercy will forgive him,' says Marcella.

Mention of the Lord returns Carmela to sobriety. Actually, she tells us she likes Padre Perrino, and everything they say about him is nonsense. After all, although she didn't even ask him to, he came around to bless the new house shortly after they built it.

'And remember that time last March when . . .'

I can't follow the drift of the conversation any more; it's too fast and it has slipped into Sicilian dialect. I don't mind, I'm content to sit and let the conversation wash over me; and anyway I haven't yet realised the importance of the priest. I'm just enjoying the meal. I've taken a great liking to Giovanni and Carmela, whose careful courtesy and old-fashioned gentility give them an edge of glamour, like characters in a black-and-white movie. There's something very intimate about sharing food with others, even strangers: a moment of harmony and collusion. Cutlery tinkles, eyes meet across the table, goodwill flows in the satisfaction of the meal. Food is friendship, a moment of worship, and sometimes much more. Food is foreplay, a sensual caress of the senses, a prelude to seduction.

Just before midnight I walk out onto the terrace. A sultry wind purrs against my face. The outdoor lights catch the edge of the grass and the first olive trees on the hillside. The moon is almost full, and down on the coast lights are twinkling. Fireflies hover in the air. From indoors comes the muffled sound of laughter and glasses clinking on the tabletop. I close my eyes, lost in the lullaby of good food and good company.

***

Next day after lunch Marcella decides to go on a pilgrimage, perhaps to atone for the alcoholic excesses of the previous evening. It's already clear to me that somewhere in the past both Giuseppe and Marcella rediscovered Catholicism. Suffering the boredom of retirement, belonging neither to America or Sicily and (as I'll later find out) weighed down with regrets and family disappointments, they turn to the infinite compassion of Jesus and the saints. There's a sort of inevitability about their rediscovery of faith. After all, religion has sustained Sicily throughout its troubled history of infidel rule and Spanish Inquisition. On the island these days religious festivals follow one after the other, so that Sicilians stagger from feast to fast all year round, which maybe explains their visions and heavenly fainting spells. They go on pilgrimages and find the face of the Virgin Mary in the clouds. They consult their favourite saints, who in Sicily always seem to have ended up disembowelled, crucified, burnt, battered or beheaded.

Saints swoon from every corner of Aunt Rita's house. The door of Giuseppe and Marcella's bedroom sports a giant poster of the holy man Padre Pio. A crucifix hangs over the bed itself. In the kitchen there are miniature Marys and post-cards of St Anthony of Padua. Our Lady of Good Counsel offers advice from the fridge door. On the sideboard stands an icon of Jesus with his arms spread wide. A red heart blazes rays of light from his breast and his head is tilted back. A huge imperial crown slips down over his forehead. He looks like a soccer player juggling a football.

I'm not surprised, therefore, when Marcella suggests a little trip to Tíndari just along the coast, home to a miraculous statue. The sanctuary there is often visited by pilgrims arriving on foot (and occasionally lashing themselves with birch twigs) from distant corners of the island.

We pile into the car and set off. According to Giuseppe, the statue of the Madonna was being transported from Turkey in a wooden case aboard a ship when a violent storm blew up off the coast of Sicily. The ship crept into shelter at Tíndari. The next day, the crew pulled up the anchor and set sail.

'But the ship isn't going anywhere! The crew got out their oars and still the ship she doesn't move!'

The sailors took off some crates, but still the ship remained motionless. Finally they carried the wooden chest containing the Madonna onto the beach. At once the sails obeyed the wind and the ship sailed off.

'Ha! The Madonna's wishes couldn't be clearer. She wanted her statue to remain in this place, chosen by herself!'

The locals were impressed. They converted the ruins of the Greek temple on the headland into a chapel, and placed the statue reverently inside. Its fame grew, and people came from far and wide to marvel at the Madonna of Tíndari.

'One day', Giuseppe continues, 'a woman with her baby came from a faraway country to adore the Madonna at this holy place. But she saw the statue was ugly! Maybe she said some rude things. You see, this Madonna is like an Ethiopian or something. Black face. So this foreign woman, she was shocked. The Queen of Heaven shouldn't be like a savage!

'She left crossly, commenting that it was hardly worth her long and difficult journey just to see the face of a black slave.

Of course, the Madonna was listening. At once the woman's baby fell down into the empty space.'

'What?'

'The woman was admiring the view from the window. The baby fell out, down the cliff.'

The distraught mother fell to her knees in horror and, curiously enough, called to that very same vindictive Madonna, imploring her intercession.

'At that moment the sea was going away,' says Giuseppe. 'The Virgin Lady was throwing down a mattress and the baby lands safely.'

Marcella rolls her eyes. 'No, the sand was coming, it was soft *like* a mattress.'

'Oh,' says Giuseppe.

Tina starts giggling. I can't tell what she thinks of all this religious lore. We've never discussed religion; it seems an irrelevance in our lives. But, here in Sicily, it surrounds us.

'The mother was chastened,' explains Marcella. 'She would never criticise the Madonna again, only believe in her divine power. And to show this miracle, the sea never again came back to cover the place where the baby fell.'

True enough: when we arrive at the church and I lean out the window, I can see the sandbar far below, a great dazzling white hook enclosing limpid turquoise water. Inside, the statue at the centre of it all is almost overwhelmed by a gilt throne. The Madonna is plain and severe, sitting staring out with Christ on her knee. Her robes are painted in sombre medieval red and green. Her face doesn't have the standard serenity of most Virgins but is long and serious, almost scowling, yet in the middle of the crass modern decor she has an austere beauty. Her face commands me, draws me in. I stand still, captivated.

Outside, coach loads of teenagers are shouting and shoving each other on the church steps, entangled in their iPods. Rows of souvenir stalls are crowded with plastic statues of the black Madonna, silver plaques and crucifixes. Appalling holograms of Christ's face in agony, blood dripping from cruel thorns, open their eyes as I walk past. Christ-actors with long blond hair, ravaged faces and theatrical blood strike erotic poses in loincloths.

'I don't care much for this—making money out of Christian things,' says Giuseppe, although the kitchen of Aunt Rita's house is full of such religious knick-knacks which he'd told me were his, from votive tea towels and illuminated prayers to fish bones that look like crucifixes. He tells me he doesn't believe the Tíndari story actually happened. It's all just a legend, he assures me, before launching into another detailed account of the miraculous Virgin, contemptuous mother and plummeting baby.

'I believe it,' says Marcella firmly, looking me in the eye as if daring me to laugh or contradict her. When I say nothing she adds wisely, 'Well, if you believe something, it's real, no?'

She's already asked me in a corner of the church if I'm a believer. I suppose you're not, she says to me, not in an accusing way but more in disappointment. I tell her I had a Protestant upbringing and find saints a bit confusing. I went to a dull Presbyterian church every Sunday when I was young, and read the Bible, but that was a long time ago.

Marcella nods, unsurprised. Then she squeezes my arm in a show of unexpected sympathy.

'It must be hard to believe in nothing,' she says.

Impressed by this comment, I follow Marcella around the church as she genuflects and splashes holy water. She touches pictures of the Virgin Mary and then brings her thumbs to her lips, muttering prayers. *Mary, Immaculate Virgin, our Mother, Patroness of our land . . . protect us from every harm.* Tina, I've noted, hasn't crossed herself even once, and walks around staring at the frescoes with a grimace, as if eyeing graffiti in a train station.

'Everything I've asked, but one thing, the Virgin has given me,' Marcella confides. She looks old suddenly, wrinkled and confused, and her hand is flattened over her chest as if she's in pain.

I wonder what the one thing is, too polite to ask. I'm moved by this elderly woman's faith; it redeems the garish church and religious kitsch. Besides, there's something elemental and timeless about this touching of lips and bowing to gods, the miracles and wonders of a Sicily thousands of years old.

In Sicily there's no present, only a many-layered past, haunted with stories and tradition. Marcella is a Greek and an Arab and a Spaniard. Her spirit is battered and bruised, the skin under her eyes is permanently blue with exhaustion, but she has found strength. She moves around the church, muttering, and for a moment looks at peace.

Marcella's peace doesn't last long—and nor does her affection for the priest, over whose supposed failings she tittered so affectionately at Carmela's house. Cloud-wisps of crisis are looming on the horizon, and they soon build to dark thunderclouds. It's all because of the confirmation, which I thought would barely impact on my genteel research into Sicilian food. In fact, I imagined the confirmation celebrations would merely be my chance to find a real cassata and have some fun. After all, a confirmation is a relatively simple affair, isn't it? All you need is a child who studies the Scriptures and knows her catechism (Claudia), a godparent to offer spiritual guidance or at least a physical presence (Tina), and of course a priest to officiate (Padre Perrino).

This, at least, is what I naively tell myself as I walk with the Calasciones through the village to pay a courtesy call on Claudia's family. We pass a small square with a water pump and Tina points out the house where her mother grew up: a tiny place, now forsaken and sealed up. The windows are shuttered and thick with dust, and the brickwork is chipped.

'When I was a kid I used to stand at the front door while my grandmother brushed and braided my hair. I picked at the masonry, you can see it right here,' Tina says, pointing to where the old sandstone has crumbled off to reveal orange brickwork. 'My mother used to yell at me. "You're pulling our house down!" But it was never our house—my grandmother always rented it. Right, Ma?'

'Right, Concettina. Rented. *Dio*, can you believe that seven of us used to live in there?'

'God, I'd love to get inside,' mutters Tina.

Claudia's house, in contrast, boasts one of the finest outlooks in town, with sweeping views down across the hills and out to sea. There's no chance to admire the scenery, though, for Claudia's mother is out in the street clucking at us. Her name is Elisabetta, almost comically elegant when attached to this huge woman encased in rolls of fat. Her hair is done up tightly in a bun and she wears sturdy peasant shoes. She envelops Tina in cries and kisses and urges us inside with pantomime good humour.

Inside, the hallway smells of furniture polish and tomatoes. We're ushered through to the sitting room, where an ancient television squats in one corner among Formica furniture. At that moment Claudia comes in. She's sixteen now. Tina hasn't seen her for five years and at first doesn't recognise her, much to her embarrassment. She's a well-built girl with big breasts under a tight top that ends at the navel; an expanse of skin follows, then blue jeans. Her hair is extremely short and sticks up in little spikes, and she wears a smear of bright pink lipstick. Claudia doesn't seem overjoyed to meet Tina again. In fact, she's tongue-tied and sullen. As we settle in around the supper table the conversation limps along with embarrassing politeness.

'Sixteen now, huh?' Tina says. 'My, how you've grown, last time I saw you . . .'

'Time flies!' Claudia manages.

'All ready for the confirmation now though!'

We sip our wine and nibble on bread crusts. I tune out of the dreary conversation, thinking to myself: *the confirmation isn't as simple as it seems*. Claudia has waited so long for the godmother to turn up that she's now sixteen, sulky and with a mind of her own—or, at the very least, a mind on other things. Claudia is far more interested in her new Vespa and hanging out at the village football field with the local boys, than she is in the grace of the Holy Spirit. As for the godmother, I know Tina can no more recite the catechism than the Magna Carta. Soon, I sense, she will regret being involved in religious duties for someone she barely knows.

Elisabetta brings out a light salad of lettuce and artichoke hearts mixed with pine nuts, capers and shavings of Parmesan cheese. We tear at crunchy hunks of bread dotted with sesame seeds. The atmosphere relaxes and even Claudia breaks into a smile.

It's then that her mother drops the bombshell. Padre Perrino has decided he won't carry out the confirmation. Claudia went to see him this morning and he said he was too old to carry out the task, explains Elisabetta vaguely. Besides, he claimed Claudia isn't ready to be confirmed.

Immediately the Calasciones are in an uproar.

'All her friends have been confirmed for years!' shrieks Marcella, wringing her hands as if longing for her rosary beads.

'Impossible!' shouts Tina. 'We can find another priest!'

But apparently we can't. Padre Perrino is the only Montalto priest and the undisputed authority in the village. It's out of the question in the hotbed of Sicilian village politics to invite a stranger to perform the ritual.

'Dear God, I might've known to watch out for the appearing mushroom,' Marcella adds obscurely.

Giuseppe has been sitting at the table while surreptitiously reading the stockmarket page in the newspaper folded on his lap. Now he suddenly looks up. 'We can't do nothing! We can't do nothing!' he shouts in English. And then in Italian: 'He's the Montalto priest and Claudia belongs to Montalto. This priest is a *Mafioso*! He's no good! We can't do a thing!'

He looks at me as if I've brought a malign influence into the village. I'm somewhat bemused by the outcry, and it's only later that I realise the importance of a Catholic confirmation in Sicily. Refusal of confirmation is considered by many to be a mortal sin, and it's the strict duty of parents to ensure their children are confirmed. On a practical level, it's a requirement for future ceremonies such as marriage. Moreover, the rite can't be conducted without the participation of a sponsor or godparent, and who knows when Tina will be back in Sicily.

'Maybe we can go to Messina and see the bishop,' Elisabetta moans, aghast at the drama she's unleashed. She sits fanning herself with a paper napkin and clutching at her breast.

I'm thrilled, going to see a bishop seems so medieval and fantastic.

'You think we can go to Messina and visit the bishop? You don't even know the bishop!' Giuseppe yells this accusingly, but I can tell he doesn't know the bishop either.

'We can make an appointment. Montalto is part of the Messina diocese.' Marcella brightens visibly. 'The Bishop of Messina is a good man.'

I cautiously sip my coffee and take a bite of an almond biscuit. Giuseppe says nothing, only looks weary. It's clear he hasn't much faith in the Bishop of Messina.

'We'll just have to wait another couple of years and do it then.'

Tina has been relatively quiet up to now, but this is her cue. She would be offended by any comparison to her father, but I can see the resemblance: she too is prone to sudden rages and illogical tirades.

'No, Pa. I'm not coming back again. Coming back! Do you know how much this has cost me, the time I've taken off?' And then, in a breathtaking moment of rudeness, 'Why does Claudia want me, anyway? I don't even know her. Why can't she choose someone else?'

Claudia looks down at her varnished fingernails and says nothing, but from her expression she couldn't care less about her godmother, or even if she's confirmed at all.

'It's too late now,' says Marcella, wisely steering the conversation into English. 'Maybe at the start, if you'd said no—*maybe*, because you live overseas. But now . . .' She shrugs in resignation.

'No, there's no *maybe*,' interrupts Giuseppe. 'Claudia's parents asked me, I accepted for you. Maybe I don't want. Maybe. But I can't refuse. Is tradition, the Sicilian way. Impossible!' he shouts, banging the table and making the cutlery jump.

I'm impressed and a little nervous at Giuseppe's sudden energy. His face is contorted, his eyes glare. Of course it's all a matter of honour for Giuseppe. As head of the household he's the source of family honour and must do the right thing; to slight Claudia's family would perhaps be cause for retaliation, something that in Sicily escalates easily to a full-blown vendetta. I perceive the confirmation isn't just important as a religious issue but also as a personal one.

'If you refuse, is not just your trouble,' Giuseppe is yelling. 'Is your mother and me, your whole family and their whole family! We become enemy, we no longer speak in the street. I am hate and they are hate! Claudia's father see me in the road, he must spit on my shoe! Impossible you refuse.'

'Oh, Christ,' says Tina.

There's a heavy silence. Marcella is blinking back tears, gazing into the dregs of her coffee cup. Elisabetta is staring, her mouth a round *O* of surprise, not able to follow the English. As for myself, I'm startled at the way the reason for Tina's trip has suddenly collapsed on a whim—the whim of an old and uncooperative priest I haven't even met.

Giuseppe sends his chair flying back against the fridge, then bangs out the front door, slamming it behind him. Tina smoulders in the corner. She left Sicily when she was eleven, and less than a decade later had already left her parents' home. She might want the nostalgic Sicilian memories, but I don't think she wants to know about the traditions that once weighed her down.

'Jesus Christ, Jesus Christ,' she hisses.

Marcella is calling on Jesus Christ too, though in an entirely different tone of voice.

'Let's get out of here,' Tina says abruptly.

Flushed with embarrassment I thank Claudia's mother for the meal and edge out the door. Tina storms down the street in a fury; I follow and almost immediately we're out of the village and in the fields. Gradually Tina's rage subsides as we're enveloped in the evening air, cool and purple.

'Jesus, this is exactly why I invited you here . . .'

'What?'

'This is why I invited you here! Don't you see, it's started already?'

'*What* has?'

And then it all comes out: Tina has secretly invited me to Sicily so she'll have some kind of buffer in her tempestuous and sometimes violent family relationships. With me around, Tina reckons her mother might just give up on her constant nagging about Tina's immoral lifestyle, and her father might try and moderate his shouting and ranting.

'He's mellowed a little in the past ten years. But last time I saw them in America I started to argue with my Dad about what time we should leave for the airport. It all ended in a screaming match and my Dad picked up a chair and smashed a mirror with it. That's why I haven't seen them for so long! You just don't know where you are with him.'

I stare back at Tina, aghast. I don't think I'm at all fit for the role of protector. I've rarely heard my father shouting, and I get on very well with everyone in my family. I'm also disturbed that I was invited to Sicily for reasons I knew nothing about.

But I say nothing of this. I want to get to know Tina better and now I have; she's opening up her darkest secrets to me as we wander on across the fields. Tina, it seems, broods endlessly on her past, utterly rejects it but can never truly let go—in this I'll later realise she's a true Sicilian. It all started when they lived in New York, she tells me, and her father became domineering and abusive. Perhaps it was the fact that her mother had become successful running a driving school and was financially independent.

'My mother could have left, she had the money. She did leave a couple of times, and took my sister and me with her. But she always went back! She always went back . . .'

Tina harbours an immense anger at her father and resents her mother's weakness. She hasn't forgiven either of them, because neither of them has admitted to the sins of the past.

Instead, they lament the lack of bonds in the family, are always harping on about marriage and grandchildren.

'Don't you see? They can't make the connection between what they did and the present. Why do all my relationships end in disaster? Why is my sister already on her third husband and not even *talking* to my parents any more? She hasn't seen them for over ten years!'

Tina isn't like her sister. I admire Tina's courage, her attempts to face the truth of her past. She wishes she could walk away and abandon her family forever; she also longs for apology, for love and reconciliation. She has come back to Sicily to face her history, to understand herself and her parents. And her agreement to act as Claudia's godmother, I see, is another way of clutching at normal family ties.

Tina falls quiet now, and we walk on through the evening. Pink geraniums cascade down the walls and white clusters of giant daisies crowd gardens. We take a dirt track, brushing past long grasses: the stems crackle and snap, but the dry leafy fronds are soft as feathers. The fields are covered with yellow blooms and purple flowers grow in the hedgerows. On the hillside behind us the village itself is a great mass of tumbling cubes in white, orange and brown.

'You never told me you came from such a beautiful place,' I say at last.

'I know. I guess I don't want it to be so beautiful.'

Oh yes, because with beauty always comes anguish. Part of Tina would rather forget Sicily; it's too close to home. It *is* home in a way, but home to Tina is a hurtful place, full of sadness and violence. She's a lovely, lonely woman whose sense of fun and laughter conceals a painful heart.

'It's like all those damn photos!' cries Tina out of the blue. 'The ones at Aunt Rita's, staring and accusing and following you with their eyes, like the chorus in a Greek tragedy. You can never get away from it all!'

A dog barks somewhere, the only sound but for the rhythm of our feet. Grave lights flicker in the cemetery above the village. In the distance, beyond terraces of olive trees, lies a dark blue sea, smooth and motionless as glass. Swallows tumble overhead in a purple sky.

Tina doesn't say anything. There are tears in her eyes as night falls over Montalto.

2

PASSION PLAYS

The smouldering bulk of Strómboli rises out of the sea, dark against the horizon. Up close it's even more intimidating, a massive pile of tumbled black rock rearing nearly a kilometre into the air, wreathed in clouds and volcanic ash. Between fire and water there isn't much room for people. The village on the crumbling flanks of the volcano clings uneasily to a tiny strip of flat land between lava and waves. Many of the islanders fled to Australia and the Americas in the 1930s and 1960s after major eruptions, seaquakes and tidal waves, but a few hardy souls remain, lulled into a false sense of prosperity by the tourist industry. They whitewash their houses and plant geranium bushes along the rambling lanes, but the prettiness can't hide the danger of their predicament. Strómboli is the youngest of the volcanoes of the Aeolian Islands off Sicily's northern coast and the most active, with frequent highly incandescent showers of lava. A recent, particularly powerful blast hurled lava down the mountain and set fire to the vegetation on the upper slopes of the

volcano, while ash fell over the village. At various times pyro-
clastic flows or chunks of falling rock have killed tourists
here. One day the mountain will gather its energy and
explode, and the island will be engulfed.

Visitors to Strómboli are slightly manic, caught between
wonder and nervousness. They sunbathe on black sand,
admire the lava fields, and listen to the rumblings of the
earth's belly. At night the sky above the village glows orange
not with street lamps but with fire. *Stop! Vulcano con attivita
esplosiva!* warn signs as the village peters out. No one stays
long. Only a handful of locals linger year round, battered by
winter storms as the mountain moans under their feet. They
have the same soulful eyes as the saints in their church, and
a very un-Italian equanimity. Nobody shouts and gesticulates
on Strómboli for fear of attracting the attention of the fates.
There's passion enough from the volcano.

We're here at Tina's suggestion, so she can get a few days'
respite from her parents. The confirmation affair has rumbled
on over the last week. Reproachful sighs emerge from
Marcella over the dinner table, while Giuseppe mutters
constantly about family duties. Can they get the priest to
change his mind? How will Claudia's family react if Tina
storms off without acting as godmother? All we can really do
is wait and see if the priest can be persuaded to carry out the
confirmation and better to wait away from the taut emotions
of Montalto.

Now Tina is urging me to make a night climb of the
volcano to view the glowing lava, while at the same time
highlighting the sheer lunacy of doing so. For a start, it's an
extremely arduous route across steep slopes of loose lava and

rock. It will be freezing cold on the summit. If poisonous gases don't overcome us we might be hit by flying pieces of molten rock. Not long ago lava bombs fell on the tourist path several hundred metres below the crater, causing authorities to temporarily suspend access to the summit. Not that she's trying to put me off, but am I really sure I'm up to it? And those miserable little sneakers I have, couldn't I have brought a pair of sturdy hiking boots?

I begin to get a little alarmed. I fret that my shoes are too flimsy, my sweater too thin and my waistline too fat. We'll get lost in the dark and fall into an abyss. Shouldn't we use a guide?

'Of course we're going with a guide,' says Tina. 'We'd be mad not to. But remember you can always ask him to turn back if you can't make it.'

I look at Tina suspiciously. It suddenly dawns on me that she isn't worried about my fitness at all, but about her own. I begin to feel a bit smug.

'We'll go this afternoon,' I decide.

Our guide is a handsome Frenchman called Henri. He issues us with miners' helmets and torches. He has a sexy accent, a square jaw and brown eyes, and I can see Tina perking up as we start out of the village along a cobbled lane. As we climb upwards the sun sinks slowly behind layers of pink cloud, and an hour later we're high above the sea. There's no other land in sight, just expanses of purple water and sky, as if we're peering out of an aircraft window.

The change is sudden and shocking. We reach the edge of a massive scree, tumbled from summit to sea like a great black slag heap. As we stand gazing in awe-struck silence at this river of cold blistered lava and twisted rock, the crater way above us erupts with a bang. A shower of orange lava tears from the mountain and spits high into the air, falling back in flaming drizzle.

Henri is raiding his enormous pack. He chews on a chocolate bar and dresses himself in a thick sweater and heavy anorak, even though I'm sweating in a T-shirt from the hard walk. His equipment and organisation make me nervous. As we climb higher, following the edge of the scree, Tina falls silent too, almost fearful. The little white houses far below and the brightly-painted fishing boats bobbing at their moorings in the tiny harbour suddenly seem inconsequential, little scraps of civilisation on a vast mountain of primeval violence and power.

The sun is a red fireball on a pink sea. Suddenly it's cold, and the wind howls across the bare slopes. There's no vegetation now, only rust-red rock and black, ankle-twisting rubble that crunches underfoot like broken glass. In the twilight we skirt the crater at a distance, climbing behind and above it into a monstrous landscape from the dawn of time. On our left black smoky ridges of sand and lava fall away into the sea somewhere. On our right smoke billows in orange clouds and the crater booms and coughs. A sulphurous stench chokes the air.

It's now pitch black and bitterly cold. We're the only people left in the universe, squatting on a ridge thrown up from the crater below. Our plastic miners' helmets seem hopelessly inadequate against ejecta that can reach a thousand degrees in temperature. 'Their impact with the human body might prove catastrophic', comments my Strómboli brochure gaily.

But Henri says it isn't often that lava gets thrown this high. If it does, we should stand our ground and watch the molten missiles arching towards us, because it's easier to dodge them than to run out of range. Despite this advice I notice Henri hunkers down on the far side of the ridge, out of reach of hurtling rock.

At that moment there's a growl, followed by a mighty explosion. Showers of burning pumice and huge lumps of molten lava light up the sky in a firework display of power and heat. The orange rock hangs suspended in the air, then falls back to earth. It's dark and silent once more, smoke and steam drifting towards us in pale clouds. This is how the world began, how Strómboli and Sicily were born, in splendid symphonies of light and formless heaps of darkness.

We wait and watch, marvelling.

The moon is almost full, adding a silvery glimmer to the landscape. Our torches stab the darkness as we stumble down the volcano by a different route, across huge slopes of volcanic sand and ash. We walk almost on each other's heels; stepping off the path could mean falling over a cliff. It's nearly midnight now. My legs are aching. I'm choking on dust, parched with thirst. Tina stumbles behind me in silence.

Finally long grasses appear, and we follow a tunnel of dust through tall canes that leads us to the village. Despite shuttered houses and shadowy streets, we're surprised to find the café on the piazza is still open in a welcoming glow of flickering candlelight. We thank Henri and wave him off, and Tina sinks onto a rough wooden chair at a table that looks down over houses and the sea. Her eyes are smudged and her face has sagged. She looks exhausted, and suddenly I can see her resemblance to her weary mother.

'We did it!'

It seems cause for celebration. We order a bottle of Corco Lanco di Casteldaccia, a wine as magnificent as its name, which glows yellow in the light of the candles.

'We need something to eat with this,' I say idly.

'Snails,' says Tina, glancing at the menu. 'I love snails.'

She stares at me coolly as if to say, *You came to Sicily to find out about food, well, here's your chance*. I suspect she's trying to challenge my British sensibilities, since the British, of course, traditionally sneer at snails, as do most Australians. Serious gourmets like the French and Chinese know better. So do the Sicilians. According to a Sicilian proverb, sucking snails out of their shells, like kissing a woman, is something of which you'll never tire. Snails have been enjoyed in Sicily at least since the time of the ancient Romans, when they were fattened in flour and milk for added taste. In his *Historia Naturalis* Pliny the Elder enthuses about the many varieties available from a snail breeder called Fulvius Lippinus, and he particularly recommends the snails of Sicily, which are supposedly a marvellous cure for hangovers. There are still buckets piled high with *babbaluci* snails in the local markets—cultivated ones, as the use of pesticides has done away with most of the wild ones—as well as bigger varieties imported from North Africa.

I tell Tina that I'm quite happy to have snails. Perhaps she doesn't know it, but I'm an adventurous eater. 'You forget that I grew up in Switzerland. And I actually ate my first snails when I was seventeen.'

I remember the drawn-out preparation process all too well. First, you have to place the creatures in a box for a day, wash them thoroughly in cold water, and then leave them for at least another week. Clean out the box regularly otherwise it will start to stink—sprinkling the snails with salt or bread crumbs will help speed the purge. On the day you want to eat them, soak the snails in salted water and vinegar for several hours to wash away the last of the slime. Some of the snails might have starved to death—cooking isn't a pastime for the squeamish—so pop them into hot water and see if they poke their horns out. The ones that do are still alive and can now be cooked. Sauté some mushrooms, garlic and onion in a frying pan, then add your snails. Season with salt and pepper and a good dash of white wine. After the wine has reduced, add some butter and, if you want to be indulgent, a splash of Cognac.

I have to say that snails themselves don't really have a lot of taste. The taste is in the preparation, and that can be as simple as squeezing lemon juice over them, just like oysters, or gently frying them in pesto. Garlic goes very well with snails, too. In Fellini's film *Roma* there's a rather grotesque scene in which patrons sitting in a neighbourhood eatery suck steamed snails from their shells, accompanied by whole garlic cloves—something Tina's father would enjoy, I'm sure. For a bit more refinement, pack the shells with garlic butter and bake them. During the Festival of St Rosalia in Sicily, snails are dipped in garlic and parsley sauce and eaten as a street snack.

The café in Strómboli village can't be bothered with such refinements. The *babbaluci*, when they arrive at our table, have simply been roasted. That works well with little snails; all you need is a slight rubbing of butter in the bottom of the pan. Disconcertingly, the snails make a popping noise rather like popcorn, and the smell is reminiscent of burnt popcorn, too.

I grin at Tina. I take a snail from the rough pottery plate. It's a beautiful thing, the shell dark green with black spirals, yellow at the edge. I pick off the hardened membrane at the mouth of the shell with a fork, then prong out the body and dip it in salt, and wash it down with a sip of mellow wine.

Perfect.

On the neighbouring island of Vulcano the red rock is clawed apart as if by an infuriated giant, exposing hardened layers of black sand, lava and volcanic gravel. The path to the summit of the crater follows a deeply eroded gash of contorted pink rock: twisting pinnacles born of heat and power. The crater burps up a foul stench, grumbling to itself, its sheer walls streaked with splattered saffron and orange minerals that leach out of the earth and are smeared across the landscape by rainstorms. Wisps of steam hiss from fumaroles under the warm rocks. *Do not sit down. Do not lie down. Dangerous gases at soil level!* reads an ominous sign at the summit. Fifty metres below us, the bottom of the crater is covered in a lid of mud. The release of gas creates dangerous underground voids, causing cave-ins without warning: sharp sighing implosions that might suck you into the belly of the earth.

Vulcano used to be a highly active volcano and is still smouldering along nicely, giving the island permanently primeval and outlandish scenery. And yet it's a beautiful landscape too, I reckon as I make my way back down the volcano. The red rock has turned to evening pink. The sea is like Murano glass against the palest of pink horizons, scratched by the silvery wake of a solitary yacht. There are volcanoes strung along the skyline (Strómboli capped by a mushroom cloud of ash and smoke) and a cluster of flat-roofed white houses down below me, huddled between the crater and the tumbled pinnacles and cliffs of the coast. Gulls career overhead, crying against a flushed sky. Towards the base of the volcano the slopes are covered in shrubs: wild geraniums, yellow broom heavy with perfume, pretty pink cistus. Pink and cream oleanders grow in profusion in the village.

You can't escape reminders of the awesome power of the earth on Vulcano. Things are hardly normal: there are outcrops of rock stained red and orange, a beach of black sand, a sea that bubbles warmly and is said to cure skin diseases. Household showers make use of hot water from subterranean springs, and the sulphur smell is pervasive—it takes me weeks of effort to rid my clothes of the vile volcanic stink. In the middle of the village fat old men sit encased in mud, holding their noses against the nauseating fumes as they attempt to alleviate their rheumatism. The muddy water is almost scalding, poisonous enough to tarnish rings and necklaces, and so radioactive it isn't recommended for pregnant women or children.

'I wouldn't stay in too long,' warns our host Tanino, half-serious. 'By the time you get out you'll have three legs.'

Tanino has opinions on almost everything, and isn't afraid to share them. I'm glad he has; I was keen to come to the

Aeolian Islands when I heard he knows a lot about local history and is a lover of fine food. He's some sort of distant cousin of the Calasciones.

'I'm not sure exactly how, everyone is your cousin in Sicily,' remarks Marcella. 'He owes us a favour,' she adds, when she phones him to ask if we can stay.

We track down Tanino at the foot of the volcano in a flat-roofed, Spanish-style house surrounded by a garden of cactus, bougainvillaea and rows of scented geraniums. Thick walls keep out the heat, and the whitewash is picked out around the window and door frames with a bright red and green trim. A wide, shaded verandah is hung with old wooden farming implements and racks of drying chillies and tomatoes. Tanino sits on the verandah in his underpants, a wrinkled, sunburnt lizard of a man. He drinks coffee and gives me witty little lectures on everything from Italian literature to preserving green chilli peppers. And what do I think of Italo Calvino's novels?

Tanino thinks I'm a meddlesome foreigner, and tells me so in an amiable way. How absurd to think I can write a book on Sicily after staying for just a few months! Why, he's been living here all his life and he couldn't do it. Don't I know that Sicily has seven thousand years of history? He has a friend who's spent ten years researching nothing more than vascular Attic pots from the late sixth century BC, found on the island of Lípari.

Luckily I'm not writing about vascular Attic pots, I say. (I'm not even sure what vascular means.) And I'm far too much of a dilettante to be bothered about studying anything for ten years. I've no desire to explain Sicily, I say, merely to savour it—quite literally, as a matter of fact. Mostly I want to write about food.

'Food?' says Tanino.

I shrug. 'Like cassata, for example.'

'Cassata! It's only for special celebrations!'

Okay, okay. Although the thought of finding a real cassata was one of my motivations for coming to Sicily, I'm already realising that only some truly remarkable event would justify a confectionery that combines sponge, fresh almond paste, ricotta, diamonds of homemade candied fruit, and a decoration of intricate baroque splendour. Wherever I find such a lavish concoction, I guess it won't be in the austere landscape of the Aeolian Islands. The islanders have to import just about all their foodstuffs from the mainland, and cassata isn't high on their list of priorities.

Tanino doesn't think much of cassata but he's happy to tell me about Aeolian cuisine which, despite its limited ingredients, is inventive. There's seafood, of course, and local herbs, olives, figs and wild fennel, supplemented by currants, pine nuts and almonds. Sun-loving capers are also grown in the rich volcanic soil, and used in fish and pasta sauces as well as salads. Capers pop up all over the place on the Sicilian mainland too, their distinctive flavour ideal for the quick and casual nature of the cooking.

Hanging from the rafters of Tanino's house, still on the vine, are bunches of tiny orange-coloured local tomatoes, no bigger than walnuts, with skins so thin and inconsequential they burst into juicy richness as I bite into them. The skins dry in the open air and then separate from the pulp, leaving the insides fresh and moist. The tomatoes will hang on the racks for the entire winter and feed Tanino for months. The locals eat them raw in salads dressed with hot pepper and olive oil, or cook them for only the briefest of moments, slicing them on top of pasta dishes. For a spaghetti typical of the islands, the tomatoes are halved and fried with a generous addition of garlic, paprika and oregano, until they've almost dried out. Then they're served with fresh pasta and chopped basil.

'But for other sauces, now, they aren't so good,' says Tanino. 'They're a little bit watery. For a sauce, you need the long plum tomato from the mainland. The flesh is better, there aren't as many seeds.'

We sit under the hanging tomatoes and while away an entire evening muttering about food and literature. Tina scribbles in her diary, dusk settles over the verandah and the scent of sulphur and lemons wafts around us. Tanino detects in me an Italianate passion for food, and approves. Knowing about literature is quite all right, he confides, but you have to enjoy the basic things in life as well. Now, Plato thought that cooking was a decadent distraction from the spiritual life, but he was a miserable fool.

'All brain,' says Tanino, tapping his near-bald head.

I suddenly realise that Tanino is getting a bit drunk. He's lying back in his wicker chair munching on olives and drinking his vile homemade grappa, and occasionally leering at Tina's tanned legs. I'm probably a bit drunk myself, because I start laughing when he mentions Plato. You can't think of the brain all the time, I agree. What about the stomach? Don't underestimate the stomach.

'People say the brain and heart inspire our actions and

thoughts—or the genitals! But the stomach! Right from the beginning we're controlled by our stomachs!'

'Yes,' I say thoughtfully. 'We're slaves to the food we're brought up on, and you can never appreciate foreign food in quite the same way . . .'

'The good old stomach!' says Tanino in a bout of maudlin Sicilian passion. 'It's about the only part of us that remains faithful to what it loves . . .'

'You guys . . .' says Tina, rolling her eyes.

But we ignore her. Oh, yes. Food is mood. Don't eat at all and you become aggressive with hunger or lose your concentration and feel sorry for yourself. (Parents threaten to send their children to bed without supper, a threat that strikes us with primal fear.) Eat a bad meal and you feel revolted and uneasy. But have some good food and you'll never feel a more satisfied afterglow. Chocolate makes us feel amorous, champagne joyful, gin pleasantly tearful. Walk into a bakery and even the smell relaxes us. My mother's chicken pies and apple crumbles can still make me feel nostalgic for my childhood. For Tanino, it's his mother's cannelloni browned in the oven with butter and cheese, and the peach preserve he hasn't tasted in twenty years. Is there any emotion that isn't felt by that most underrated of organs, the stomach?

Of course, we don't say it quite like that. Tanino and I actually ramble on for hours, talking about stomachs and commiserating with each other on the sad fate of the modern culinary world. The level in the grappa bottle drifts dangerously low, and Tina has already taken herself off to bed, rolling her eyes skywards. Tanino and I linger on in tipsy camaraderie. Then at midnight he scratches and yawns and says we should go and find something to eat. He has an urge to share sea urchins with me.

The moon is hanging full above the volcano as we walk down to the coast. We hunt among the rocks, stumbling in the silvery light. There were plenty of urchins years ago, mutters Tanino, but now only the locals know where to find them. He skips across the rocks like an ageing Pan, laughing to himself as he prises the prickly creatures off the rocks with a knife. He pours olive oil, from a little stoppered bottle he's brought with him, into a cleft in the rock, as if offering a libation to the gods.

'This is life! This is living!'

We dip hunks of bread into the luscious oil, its fruitiness offset slightly by the flavour of sea salt it absorbs from the rocks. The crusty morsels are perfect with the tender subtlety of the urchins—salty, slightly bitter, meaty as mushrooms. The moon droops overhead, casting glittering shadows across a silvery sea, and above us the volcano belches and grumbles.

There are several sea urchin dishes in Roman cookery books, but the first people to populate Sicily and the Aeolian Islands enjoyed such simple fare long before Roman times. The most ancient settlements on the Aeolian Islands were those founded on Lípari and Salina some time at the end of the fifth millennium BC. The inhabitants were soon exploiting and working obsidian, a natural black glass that erupts from volcanoes and which was highly prized for making tools and weapons. By the third millennium BC, Lípari supported a settlement larger than today's, probably the largest settlement in the entire western Mediterranean. It was a wealthy island that steadily grew in refinement and produced pottery and art of impressive quality and elegance.

This ancient island seems a good place to start investigating the historical beginnings of cooking in Sicily. I imagine the sophisticated early people of Lípari must have eaten well. Certainly they pulled shrimp and lobster from the sea, for in the fourth century BC Archestratus said of the lobster that 'they are most numerous and best of all for quality in the Aeolian Islands'. There was squid, too. These days local calamari is served stuffed with bread crumbs, cheese and garlic and sautéed in syrupy Malvasia wine with caramelised onion. Another kind of squid, the fat *totani*, is often stewed in white wine with chopped onion and laurel leaf. Then there's local fish such as rudderfish, scorpion fish, sea bass and amberjack. They were probably cooked in the same simple ways in ancient times as they are now: grilled on coals or poached *all'acqua pazza* (in sea water).

There were anchovies as well. Sicilians are still very fond of anchovies, and many take the trouble to prepare their own fillets. Whole, fresh anchovies are bought in the marketplace out of huge drums packed with salt. A canny shopper will look for meaty fish and will only buy from the top of the drum where the fish are fresher, less salty, and full of flavour.

'Even then you have to rinse them to get all the salt away,' Tanino tells me as we convene in the kitchen the next day. His kitchen has the same contrived but appealing rusticity as the rest of the house: cheerful Mexican tiles on the walls, baskets of herbs, obsolete wooden farming tools fixed to the walls.

I watch Tanino scrape away the anchovy skin with a knife, chipping off the fins and splitting the fish open on a massive chopping board. It smells rich and fishy. Tanino lifts out the bitter entrails. Having given his demonstration he hands over the knife and I scrape and chop at the little fish: not a bad attempt, but much slower. Then we place the fillets in a glass jar, drowning them in olive oil, where they'll keep perfectly well for two or three weeks. They're superb just as they are as an antipasto, especially with a lump of crusty, fresh bread and a light cheese. Anchovies also crop up in a variety of Sicilian dishes, generally unseen. Many pasta sauces call for a few anchovy fillets to be diced into small pieces and then fried in olive oil on a low flame until they almost dissolve, giving a full-bodied richness and depth to tomato sauces. In ancient times there were no tomatoes, but the use of anchovies in this way echoes the ancient Roman passion for using garum. Garum was a sauce made from the rotting intestines of small fish such as anchovies and mackerel, mixed with vinegar, garlic, poppy seeds and various other herbs. The result was a pungent condiment used in small quantities to flavour vegetable, fish and meat dishes, similar perhaps to Asian fish sauce.

Tanino, ever one for erudite and slightly raunchy anecdotes, tells me as we fill the jars that the Roman writer Apuleius actually turned garum into a drink that he swore was an aphrodisiac. He gave some to a wealthy widow and ended up marrying her. Her relatives took him to court for corrupting her with a magic potion, but Apuleius won the case.

'He argued that the widow was delighted with her new-found vigour and happier than she'd been in her life!'

I'm fairly sure that the first people to settle the Aeolian

Islands and Sicily ate anchovies and other seafood, but what else did they eat? I'm finding the question difficult to answer, because evidence of food and cooking habits in prehistoric societies is hard to come by. Archaeologists have to rely on coprolites (fossilised faeces) and refuse from middens, scattered animal bones, various cooking vessels, the wear on human teeth and an analysis of trace elements in human bones to deduce what prehistoric people ate. Written evidence begins to appear only in early classical times, and cookery books as we recognise them today didn't really emerge until the fourteenth century. The other problem is that the few cookery books that were produced before the Renaissance describe the dishes of the upper classes, with barely a word on how ordinary people might have eaten.

I'm curious about the ancient diet, but I have to accept that most of its secrets have been lost to history. Still, Tanino isn't going to let that stop him from sharing the pleasures of the modern table. It could be, he claims, that the early islanders ate baked fish, and as it happens the best restaurant on Vulcano serves it. In the interests of research, he adds with a gleam in his eye, I should probably take him there.

'Good idea,' says Tina. 'You can take me too.'

Tina is an inattentive eater back in Sydney, often skipping meals and seemingly indifferent to what she eats; there are only two things she abhors, mustard and beetroot. She's the kind of person I describe as a 'nibbler and picker' and such disinterest has always seemed to me highly suspicious. But since arriving in Sicily she's been wolfing down her mother's home cooking like a trooper on leave, and becoming as enthusiastic as I am to find out more about Sicilian cuisine.

The restaurant is housed in an old farm building sagging with ivy and climbing flowers, but the tables are formally laid out with stiff white cloths and gleaming cutlery. We sit at a table in the courtyard, under the stars, and have an antipasto of sun-dried tomatoes, salami and cheese, accompanied by wholemeal bread. It's followed, on Tanino's recommendation, by *spaghetti all'Eoliana*, full of garlic, olives and fat capers. I've only just realised that capers are actually the unopened flower buds of beautiful pinkish flowers with long purple stamens, which makes them seem delightfully elegant.

'We cure them in barrels of sea salt here in the Aeolians,' says Tanino. 'They keep for a couple of years, and taste much better than the ones pickled in vinegar.'

Tanino grows eloquent once more on the subject of food, and Tina and I are happy to sit back and listen. Vinegar affects the flavour of capers, says Tanino, making them sharp and acidic. Not so good for cooking, because they end up dominating the sauce. But you have to make an effort with salted capers; they have to be rinsed really well, which can be tricky to do without the buds falling apart.

'Salted Sicilian and Sardinian capers are the best in the world,' he says boastfully.

We fall silent as the waiter removes our dishes. We've ordered a whole baked fish stuffed with fragrant leaves of basil, fennel and parsley and covered in a mound of sea salt. After a while, the waiter brings it out and cracks open its carapace of hardened salt, spilling salt crystals across the tablecloth. Then he expertly slices off pieces of flesh, flicking away the bones with a fork before laying it on our plates. It doesn't taste as salty as I anticipated. The flesh is delicate and fine and full of flavour.

'That was the best!' crows Tina, collapsing back in her seat.

For dessert there's *semifreddo alla mandorla*, an ice cream mixed with meringue and a praline of sugar and toasted nuts. The waiter brings a glass of orange Malvasia with the dessert, a wine produced on the neighbouring island of Salina. Once called 'Malmsey' in English, it makes a fine finish to any meal, particularly when accompanied by *biscotti pizzicati*, little pastries filled with figs, honey and almonds.

This is just the sort of meal I've come to Sicily for. Tina, too, is satiated and dreamy-eyed. She came to the Aeolian Islands to regain her composure and so she has. (She doesn't yet realise that calamity is gathering over Montalto like sulphurous fumes on the mountaintop.) Tanino licks Malvasia off his lips, and even he falls silent at the exquisite pleasure of the meal. Oleander blossoms flutter to the ground to the accompaniment of clinking glasses. Stars stud the sky, except where the massive bulk of the volcano sits smouldering black against the horizon. As for our stomachs—well, our stomachs! Our stomachs know that all is right with the world.

And that, says Tanino, is the way it ought to be.

I leave the Aeolian Islands with a sense of loss; it has been a magical kingdom, bizarre and beautiful. Tina and I say our farewells to Tanino, a merry philosopher-king reclining in his underwear, munching on sun-dried tomatoes, imparting wit and wisdom.

Marcella is in the kitchen when we return to Montalto,

about to prepare a meal for Claudia and her mother, who are coming over with a confirmation update. Tina scowls in annoyance when she hears this and takes off to her room. Marcella seems surprised when I volunteer to stay and help chop garlic. It isn't much of a sacrifice; I like this subterranean kitchen with its aquarium light filtering down through high narrow windows, through which you can glimpse the sturdy black-stockinged legs of passing village widows. It's the most cheerful room in the house, the only one active and lived-in. Besides, I find chopping garlic quite a sensuous culinary task. I pull off a clove from a young, fresh bulb. Then I take my knife blade and, with a sharp smack of the palm, squash the clove against the cutting board. My favourite moment: the satisfying crunch and sudden stinging aroma. After that it's easy to peel off the skin like old parchment, admiring its ribbed purple veins, as delicate as any illuminated manuscript.

As I peel and prepare I ask Marcella about her early life. She seems pleased by my interest. In fact, she says, when she was young she was energetic and dreamed of travelling the world. She taught herself French. She attended college in Messina and worked as a travel agent in the city. Then she went to Geneva and London to spend time as an au pair. She worked for a rich family in London which lived in a beautiful house near Wimbledon. But after a while, Marcella discovered the father was an alcoholic who beat his wife.

'Naturally, I couldn't stay there.'

'I can see that,' I say encouragingly, as I dice up the pungent, soft juicy flesh of the garlic. The knife is the length of my arm: Marcella has choppers and knives of frightening size and sharpness, plunged into wooden blocks beside the stove. The garlic leaves a sticky residue on my fingers, where pieces of garlic skin get stuck.

Marcella returned to Italy, to Milan, where she met and became engaged to a young man from Bergamo. Alberto was in his late twenties, very handsome and intelligent. He spoke five languages and worked as an interpreter. He seemed ideally matched to Marcella; a better catch than Giuseppe, her high-school sweetheart. Only one thing disturbed her about Alberto: whenever they went out, instead of ordering coffee, Alberto would have a half-litre flask of wine. He'd drink it all which was unusual in those days, especially, adds Marcella, when courting. The experience in London with the alcoholic father preyed on her mind. She realised Alberto was drinking a lot, and sometimes he was drunk in the middle of the afternoon. Even his own sister warned her about his habits. Marcella broke off her engagement. Then Giuseppe turned up in Milan, trying to win her back.

So Marcella married Giuseppe.

Garlic sizzles as Marcella throws it into a pan of oil, frying it to a pale gold. As I stand chopping and stirring it seems to me that Marcella must have loved Alberto. But I suspect her regret comes not from turning him down but from marrying Giuseppe. Marcella would be horrified if I knew—she hasn't so much as hinted at it—that her husband is a man with a violent temper who used to beat his wife and children. Giuseppe has neither a brilliant mind nor a good education, and I've already worked out that Marcella is longing for intellectual stimulation. She speaks to me in French, she discusses philosophy and travel. Giuseppe isn't interested in these things. The only thing he reads, Marcella confides in me one day, is the financial columns in the newspaper. He talks only about his health, football and his life in America, with all the self absorption of a true tyrant.

'Well, there you are,' says Marcella at last. 'That was the end of my travels, when I married Giuseppe. Though of course in the end I went to America.' She adds some chopped fresh tomatoes, some oregano and basil to the garlic in her pan, and a bit of chilli, raising the heat so the sauce starts to bubble and the garlic releases its pervasive flavour. Marcella is teary-eyed, whether at her story or the garlic fumes I can't be sure.

'When I was growing up, I don't remember my mother ever using garlic,' I say to Marcella to ease the tension. She stares in disbelief.

But it's true. I suppose it was part of the irrational fear of garlicky odours so entrenched in British culture. The poet Shelley, though an Italophile, was nevertheless amazed that even the gentle classes 'eat—you will never guess what—*garlick!*' a habit which he found 'degraded, disgusting and odious'. Maybe the Swiss thought the same, although when the fashion for Mediterranean and, later, Asian cuisines arrived, great piles of garlic started appearing in the super-market and, more timidly, even in my mother's kitchen, although I was an adult by then. Still, I was swiftly converted, my liking reinforced by three years in China, where I ate garlic in every dish. Like any convert, I wonder now how I ever did without it.

'I use garlic in nearly all my cooking these days,' I confide to Marcella, hoping for approval.

'Thank God! I tell you something Brian, rub some garlic on a chicken before you roast it, you'll find the flavour is so delicate, so . . . ah!' Marcella breaks off, giving an eloquent Italian moue.

'I'll try it,' I say, making a note in the little book I've been carrying everywhere.

When it comes to Italian cooking, there's no point in being timid with garlic; use it like Marcella does, with considered abandon. Garlic is fundamental to pasta sauces, and spaghetti needs no more than a dash of olive oil and some chopped garlic to make a delightfully refreshing dish. Garlic is a must for seafood, especially clams. Rub your frying pan and salad bowl with a garlic clove, and the inside of your fondue pot—a little Swiss secret that achieves perfection. Garlic insinuates itself into hot buttered bread and enlivens a tomato salad. As a French writer once put it: 'What garlic is to salad, insanity is to art.' Garlic may look shabby, but there's not much it can't achieve. In the hurly-burly jostle of Sicilian ingredients, surely it's garlic that takes the grand prize.

Marcella likes talking about food; her tears seem left behind and she becomes animated. Marcella likes talking about lots of things, and after I while I realise she has few people to talk to; maybe that's why she shares so much with me. She likes speaking to me in French, especially when Giuseppe's around, because he can't understand it. She can talk to me about books; she's always read a lot. Marcella is an intelligent and cultured woman who doesn't really belong to this village anymore. And she likes me, I think, although she reacts to me with both horror and delight. She's concerned I have no real home, no wife, no children, no proper job; I'm a bit of a circus freak in Sicily. But she likes the idea that I'm a writer and traveller. Sometimes I see her looking at me with a wistful envy. Perhaps I'm Marcella's alter ego, doing the things she'd like to have done.

Well, Marcella will never do those things now, but in the kitchen she can let her artistic inspiration flourish. We're having *pasta alla Norma* tonight, a typical Catanian dish, named after a character in an opera by Bellini; the composer was born in Catania on Sicily's east coast. The recipe is simple—nothing else remains except to toss in some browned cubes of aubergine and dust the pasta with grated ricotta—and without the garlic it would be uninspiring. Garlic adds flavour, lets the other ingredients soar. Long after the meal is finished, the lingering smell of garlic in the kitchen reminds me of the meal and the magic of the bulb.

The very smell of garlic gives me a lust for life, and somewhere in the past Marcella was lusty too. Now she's merely beset with problems. We all settle around the dining table— a silent Tina, a sullen Claudia, her anxious-looking mother Elisabetta, Giuseppe, Marcella and myself—and the gloom of the room seems reflected in everyone's face. Thanks to the guests, we're eating in the dining room tonight. It's an ill-lit, echoing space with only a few sticks of furniture: a dark varnished sideboard, a massive table and, oddly enough, an empty hatstand. There are more dusty photographs here, sitting in ugly frames along the sideboard: village ancestors looking stiff and awkward in suits and corsets. Rows of spider plants grow in rough ceramic pots along one wall; the soil is cracked and dry but the plants are flourishing, the only bright note in a cold room. Our voices bounce off the floor tiles and the sound of our cutlery echoes loudly around the empty walls.

Elisabetta announces over the *antipasti* that no progress has been made in the unfortunate confirmation saga. Padre Perrino has stuck to his decision to delay it until such time as he feels up to the task.

Which will be never, according to a downcast Tina.

Marcella hasn't given up yet, but her opinion of the priest seems to have sunk to new depths. She sits eating hunks of bread dipped in olive oil and letting us know just what she thinks of him. Elisabetta nods in agreement.

'The truth is, he's completely senile,' she adds helpfully.

'He's not a man, he's an animal,' says Giuseppe angrily, waving away the grated ricotta. He's red-faced and one day will probably die of a heart attack.

'But I'm not going to do anything this time, because if I go and see him, I'll end up burning his house down! We'll have to wait for another few years and see what happens. Hopefully by then the old bastard will be dead. I swear I'll go and spit on his grave!'

'Now, now, Giuseppe,' says Elisabetta placidly. She's a big comfortable woman who seems to let troubles wash over her, unlike Marcella. I can imagine Elisabetta bringing up a whole household of kids, managing a volatile husband, starching collars and bottling olives and grappa all at the same time, magnificently unflappable. She's sitting now spearing mouthfuls of pasta and aubergine as if it's taking up all her attention.

Claudia is pushing food around her plate and hasn't said a thing.

'And do you know,' says Marcella, 'I was in the bank once, and the priest was paying in an awful lot of money . . .'

'. . . and they do say he has *children*, though the divine Lord strike me dumb if I repeat such gossip,' says Elisabetta.

Tina is becoming increasingly impatient. A side of her relishes village gossip—it's part of the quaintness of her happy fairytale memories of Sicily, before she moved to America and things fell apart—but not when it's something that affects her. She huffs impatiently and clicks her rings against the stem of her wineglass. Marcella is looking harried by the confirmation disaster. But Claudia and her mother, I can't help suspecting, are actually enjoying the whole disagreement. They're much more Sicilian than the Calasciones; they've been in Montalto all their lives, and there's nothing the Sicilians like better than convoluted tales of pesky priests.

Maybe it's the garlic and chilli we've just consumed, but now the whole Calascione family is shouting and gesticulating and banging wine bottles on the wooden tabletop. Giuseppe leaps up and paces around the room with his hands thrust into his pockets, shouting about spitting on graves and priestly embezzlement, expecting us all to be shocked.

The women aren't impressed. They're too busy shrieking about mistresses and altar boys, and possibly even satanic cults in the vestry.

It's perfectly clear to me that the confirmation isn't going to be taking place any time soon.

I'm beginning to wonder if it will actually happen at all.

***

Lucia, one of Marcella's oldest and dearest friends, lives in a house on the corner of a tiny piazza, not far from the church. Her home is permanently shuttered and still. Lucia lives alone, and she only ever goes out to mass; even her shopping is delivered to the door. She's seventy-four, and although her father died two decades ago, Lucia still hears his voice telling her to stay inside because the world is a dangerous place.

This information in itself is enough to make me want to meet Lucia, but Marcella also comments that she still does everything the old-fashioned way, particularly in the kitchen. Marcella describes her heavy old iron stove with a kind of wonderment, and admires the way she bottles olives and makes jam and dries her own salami. She's lonely and would like the company; I'm looking for culinary anecdotes and can find out how things were done in the good old days before people started buying olives in jars and salami at the Montalto supermarket.

I imagine Lucia as a suspicious-minded Miss Havisham figure, wrinkled and forgetful, living in a forlorn, dusty wing of a crumbling palazzo that has the same doleful feel as Aunt Rita's house. But one evening, when I walk over with Tina, I see Lucia's house is small and modern, with pale blue shutters and a glass-panelled door. Light spills out into the square as Lucia opens the door, and she's warm and welcoming; not at all what I expected. Chatty and jovial, she wears tight clothes that show off her rolls of fat. On a chain around her neck hang a crucifix and a cluster of saints' medallions that clank and jangle cheerfully every time she moves. Her hair is only slightly grey at the temples, her face pale and smooth. She doesn't look a day over fifty.

We step from the door straight into an L-shaped room. In one corner an old-fashioned television stands surrounded by shoe boxes and piles of magazines. There's not much other furniture: a cheap Formica table, an old sofa covered in a sheet decorated with fluffy cats among bunches of violets. But the room is packed with religious icons and statuettes. They crowd the top of the television, dresser and table: plastic Virgins, a Jesus with spread arms, crucifixes, a snowdome of Bethlehem, various statues of saints. There are several large, plastic, baby Jesus dolls dressed in frilly white clothes, lying in glass boxes. Sitting on top of the television is a silver aeroplane piloted by a yellow plastic duck. I recognise a statue of St Anthony because it's similar to the one in Montalto's church. There are vases of plastic flowers everywhere.

I mustn't look very thrilled by the decor, for Lucia wants to know if I'm a Catholic. Tina tells her I'm Protestant. But they believe almost the same thing as Catholics, she adds diplomatically, except that the saints aren't quite as important.

'But Protestants believe in God?'

'Oh, yes.'

'Of course, of course,' Lucia reassures herself. 'Yes, the Pope says as long as we believe in God, then it doesn't matter, Catholic or Protestant.'

'Right.' I'm amazed the Pope has said such a thing.

'But do Protestants believe in the Holy Spirit?'

'Err . . . yes,' I say, not wanting to admit I've never really understood what the Holy Spirit is.

'And the Virgin Lady?'

'Well . . .'

Every inch of Lucia's walls is covered in pictures of saints and miracles. Pride of place is given to an eerie hologram that changes from Christ to Mary as I walk around the room. From where I sit on the sofa Mary seems to have sprouted a beard and has three arms and glaring eyes.

'So that's why you're not married yet, eh?' Lucia is saying knowingly. 'Religious problems.'

'No, we're just friends.'

'Oh, engaged.'

'No, we're not even engaged. Just friends.'

'How long have you known each other?'

'About ten years.'

Lucia pauses. 'Oh, well, there's time yet.' And when Tina gets up to put on the coffee-pot, Lucia smirks at me and pats my knee.

'One blond and one dark-haired, eh? Beautiful *bambini*,' she whispers.

Although Lucia never leaves the house these days, I discover to my surprise that she once lived in New York. She emigrated there with her father after the war, and worked in a factory run by Italians. She didn't learn much English and led an isolated existence, returning straight home after work and always subject to the strict rules of her father. Anyway, she was afraid of New York. You can imagine her terror when one day she was walking down a Bronx street and a car pulled up at the kerb. The driver shouted at her to get in. Lucia walked on, saying nothing, and the man called to her again. Lucia shouted at him to go away. He climbed out of the car. She thought she was going to be raped. At this moment of her greatest peril she called on the help of the Beautiful Mother of God.

'Suddenly I realised the man was actually my cousin's son! Imagine that I didn't recognise him!'

Well, this is what New York does to you, of course; you end up terrified of everyone. Frankly, it was the last straw. Lucia took a ship and came back to Montalto, followed by her father. She hasn't been anywhere since then, not even to Messina, where she has a beautifully furnished flat. Her father forbade her to go out at all, even around the village, except with a few select friends. On his deathbed he implored her to uphold his rules.

'Well,' concludes Lucia comfortably. 'I never went out when my father was alive. So why should I go out now that he's dead?'

Mention of death reminds Lucia that her brother passed away just six months ago. In fact, she says, it was only last week that she had her hair done for the first time since the funeral, so our visit has come at the right time. Her brother died from a heart attack. It was the fault of his daughter, Lucia's niece. She got divorced, which was bad enough. And then she remarried, to another divorcé with two children!

'She killed her father,' says Lucia emotionally, rattling her coffee cup on her saucer. 'He died of a broken heart! I don't speak to her any more. She phoned from New York the other day, wanting to come to Montalto for a visit. I told her she couldn't stay in this house. Not unless I'm dead! Of course her sister can come, and her children. I don't mind seeing *them*.'

Tina is nonplussed. Six months have passed, she says. Maybe it's time for reconciliation. She sounds wistful and uncertain. But Lucia has no patience with such talk.

Reconciliation! Even the heart of Jesus would find it hard to smile upon her niece. After all, she killed her own father. That's not something you can forgive in a year, or even a lifetime.

She gives me another roguish smile. Would I like another pastry?

We munch in companionable silence. Then Lucia says she's heard I'm writing a book about Sicily. She's a little worried about what I might be writing about *her*, and about Montalto. I'm sincere in my protestations that I find Montalto a marvellous village. I'm already growing absurdly fond of the place and the people who live here.

'And what about me?' asks Lucia anxiously. 'Do you think I'm a crazy woman with my saints?'

I think Lucia is a delightful woman with a wary heart. I'm determined in the next few weeks to find out more about her, and soon I'll be hearing tales of a mad mother, a cruelly eccentric father, and Lucia's tragic love affair with the village schoolteacher. Lucia is a woman with a passionate past, although I don't know it yet.

For now, I tell her that I'm glad she lives here, among her paradise of icons.

Lucia is pleased with this answer. She gulps at her coffee cheerfully. What I should really write about, says Lucia, is her nephew who lives in a flat she owns in Messina. The poor soul, he hasn't been able to find a job for thirty years, may the Virgin protect him. It's the government's fault, of course. Italy has so much money these days, but the government is useless. In the old days there wasn't any money, but plenty of jobs, and everything was good. Imagine if Mussolini commanded the money that the Italian government has these days, what he could have achieved! Instead, it's not even safe to go out on the streets! In Mussolini's day, people could go out and sit in the piazza at two in the morning and nobody bothered them.

'*Non c'è più religione.*'

Lucia sighs and nibbles on a biscuit. Crumbs and icing-sugar from the pastries drop over her bosom. Medallions jangle. *There's no more religion.* She means it literally, no doubt, but also in its figurative Italian sense: 'the world has gone to hell'. She doesn't say it with any regret or accusation in her voice; it's just a fact. Lucia seems to have a boundless capacity to accept things just the way they are: her nephew, her father, her own life. Maybe this is the secret of her youthful face and cheery personality, or maybe it's her faith that keeps her going. Her face is almost as smooth and serene as one of her many Madonnas.

Lucia comes to the door to say goodnight. I feel like hugging her, though being hugged would surely startle and embarrass her. The yellow light from her room swings across the flagstones of the piazza and she waves as we walk away, a jovial smile on her dimpled face.

The next day I head with the Calasciones out of Montalto along a narrow, corkscrewing road up into the mountains. To the left, the edge of the road plunges away into a deep, water-less valley filled with stones. The remains of German pill-boxes guard this narrow access to the coast. Further away stand the ruins of a castle, little more than fangs against the sky on top of a pyramidal peak.

Tina is screaming at her father to slow down. Across the valley, the village of Tripi straggles along a ridge of rock, as spectacular as a drawing in a book of fairytales: a thin ribbon of brown houses and the spire of a church teetering between heaven and earth.

'You want to drive? You want to drive?'

'No, Pa. I want you to go more slowly.'

'She doesn't trust her father!' says Giuseppe, twisting round in his seat to look at me as the car slews off the side of the road, spraying up gravel.

We slow down when we arrive at Novara di Sicilia, a town of battered honey-coloured houses with sagging wrought-iron balconies decorated with washing. We stop to buy a huge loaf of crusty bread, still slightly warm, which fills the car with a rich smell. Then we drive onwards towards San Basilio through hazelnut and walnut trees. It's June, the walnut season, when the green fruit is picked for the feast of San Giovanni and made into *nocino*. The nuts are pickled in alcohol along with sugar, cloves, lemon zest and cinnamon. The alcohol is then strained off and bottled until November, when it's traditionally cracked open on All Saints' Day.

'There's a nice crunchy pasta you can use them in, too,' comments Tina. '*Conchiglie alla noci*, with a sauce of cream, butter, pepper and walnuts.'

'And marjoram, *bella*, don't forget the marjoram,' adds Marcella.

We're not here for the walnuts, though. This is a picnic organised by Marcella who, despite the confirmation fiasco, is in high spirits today. She's come up here in search of cheese. The whole family seems to be joining me in my growing obsession with everything culinary. No one seems to think it strange that we should drive for over an hour into the wild interior of the island in search of a piece of cheese. In fact, Giuseppe is filled with restless anticipation, leaning forward eagerly to peer out the windscreen as the car swings ever upwards. Marcella huddles in the back seat, sweater held up against her neck, fearing draughts. When Tina isn't remonstrating with her father she's arguing with her mother about having all the windows wound up.

At San Basilio the streets get steeper and more narrow. Great geranium bushes and magnificent roses tumble over garden fences. Marcella says the soil is so wonderful, you could stick a table leg in it and grow an oak tree.

'Ma, I have to put the window down. I'm going to ask for directions.' Tina has spotted an old woman loitering outside her house. The woman speaks in a slurred, incomprehensible dialect that baffles even Giuseppe. We drive on out of the top end of the village, until the road finally peters away into a dirt track.

Finally, a man in a battered green Fiat drives by. He knows a place where someone makes cheese—his cousin, in fact. He can show us the way.

Then the green Fiat is careering down a dirt track towards the valley bottom, and Giuseppe is hurtling after it. Branches whip past the windows. Marcella calls on the Blessed and Glorious Lady and several saints.

At a fork in the track the man in the Fiat stops and gets out. He explains that he's going down to the left to plant tomatoes. We only have to continue down the right-hand track to get to the hut of his cheese-producing cousin. We can't miss it.

Twenty minutes later we're still lurching down the dirt road. We come to another fork with two fences made of wire and sticks hauled across it. There's no sign of habitation, no turning back, pinned as we are between trees and the plunging valley. Anyway, there's no question of giving up, for Giuseppe is determined to find some cheese. We pick the lower route, and he waves his hand dismissively every time the small car bangs and shudders on a rut.

'Loving Mother help and defend us,' moans Marcella.

It's a beautiful drive along the dirt lane, with hedgerows full of grasses and wild flowers: golden broom and butter-cups, tiny wild geraniums, purple orchids. Butterflies flutter across the windscreen. And then suddenly there's a barking dog and a small hut made of rough stones with a flat-tiled roof built into the hillside. Beside it stands a lean-to of sticks housing a couple of calves that snuffle and snort as we climb out of the car. A man comes out of the hut and greets us: young, wearing black jeans and a trendy, tight white top. His black boots are caked with mud. His name's Antonio, he tells us, and he comes here from San Basilio during the season just to make cheese.

If Antonio is surprised to see us turn up here in the wilder-ness he doesn't show it; he's affable and seems pleased to have a distraction. He's a handsome fellow with stiff black stubble and a hooked nose. He ushers us into the hut with all the politeness of a butler showing the way into a gentleman's club. My eyes momentarily water: the hut is smoky and has no windows, and it's a moment before I become accustomed to the dark. A smouldering pile of wood ashes lies in one corner, and a huge cauldron hangs over it.

'Milk and rennet,' says Antonio, as I peer in at the thick-ening slop, reeling at the smell. As the contents become soft and rubbery Antonio separates it into curds and whey, sloshing water in from a battered pail. His movements are slow and considered, almost meditative. The curds are white and grainy, and Antonio slices bits off and offers them around on the edge of his knife. Marcella enthuses politely, but I find it almost tasteless.

Later Antonio will mould the thickened curds into pear-shaped cheeses. The cheeses will float in brine for some hours before being tied together in pairs with twine and hung out to dry. The remaining whey is made into ricotta by boiling it; ricotta simply means 'recooked'. The creamy residue comes to the surface and is strained off to produce this very soft, granular cheese. It doesn't have a strong flavour, making it ideal for use in desserts (when sweetened with sugar) or as a filling, combined with spinach or chard, for vegetarian ravioli or gnocchi. Add salt, however, and the cheese will last longer, enabling it to dry out and become hard and sharp tasting, suitable for grating over pasta.

I buy a hunk of ricotta off Antonio, as fresh as it can possibly be, still slightly warm and very moist. I invite him to join us for lunch; Marcella has already spread a rug out on the grass among the camomile and clover. The smell of wild mustard is heavy in the hot air. There's our crusty bread, just bought in Novara, made with semolina flour, dense and yellow, and thin slices of pink Mortadella ham encasing tiny jewelled nuggets of fat and little green flecks of pistachio. We crunch up spicy green olives and chew on salami. Marcella picks some wild fennel from the meadow. Sicilians love fennel, especially in salads such as the dramatic, pungent salad of fennel with sliced orange, black olives and fresh thyme leaves. I can't stand it; I abhor the aniseed taste.

Antonio, inspired by the simple perfection of the meal, gets out a battered little frying pan. With ease born of long practice he dices up a garlic clove, sprinkling it on top of some slices of cheese. Then he thrusts the pan into the ashes of his fire inside the hut, watching with intent passion as it curls and melts, stirring it with the sharp point of his knife. He carries it back to the picnic with an air of triumph. Soon we're scooping up stringy dollops of melted cheese with our bread, revelling in the richness.

Afterwards there are sweet-scented strawberries from the Madonie Mountains. I lie back in the grass and pop them slowly into my mouth, where they dissolve into an essence of summer. The sky is brilliant behind the flickering golden leaves of the trees, and I understand perfectly why Sicilians drive for miles in search of a piece of cheese.

3

THE BOLD AND THE BEAUTIFUL

Balmy picnic days flare into hot summer, catching us unawares. As I drive west with Tina, the green hillsides and oak trees are left behind and the landscape becomes drier and hotter, a patchwork of brown fields, dead thistles and sticky tar. We follow a dried-up river valley beneath white and yellow hills scattered with straggling olive trees and abandoned farmhouses. Shepherds have lit fires on the hill-sides to encourage new growth. The hazy air wavers above the flames and smoke hangs heavy by the roadside, drifting in sullen clouds close to a ground of blackened stalks and charred stones. Dust drifts through the windows and swirls around the car.

Tina slows down to a crawl as the dust flies around us. Normally she drives too fast and a bit recklessly. In towns she shunts through red lights and forces her way past other cars with the same impatient disregard as other Sicilian drivers. Tina has spent so little of her life in Sicily, but sometimes you wouldn't realise it. She seems to become more Sicilian as the days pass. Her skin has darkened in the sun, her hands flutter as she talks, her Italian becomes less hesitant. She's had another tiff with her father this morning at breakfast and now she hunches over the steering wheel, glaring out through the windscreen.

We're on our way to some of Sicily's most famous historical sites. Tina is happy with my sightseeing plans because there are several places she's never been to in Sicily, and as for the rest, she barely remembers them. Over the next few weeks we plan to go to them all, Palermo and Siracusa and more, in short bursts that will give us a break from Montalto. Short, too, because we've borrowed Giuseppe's car and don't want to inconvenience him for more than a few days at a time. Besides, always at the back of Tina's mind is the confirmation: you never know when there might be a breakthrough.

By five o'clock the sun is less cruel as it edges down towards the west. When we finally arrive at Selinunte I barely pause for breath as I down a litre-bottle of mineral water, cold from a fridge. The bottle is cool with condensation and I gulp, almost sob, in satisfaction. Feeling better, we set off to the ruins of Selinunte, an early Greek colony sacked by Hannibal in 409 BC and later devastated in an earthquake; it sank into the sand dunes and coastal marshes and very nearly vanished forever.

The hot dusty journey, I decide immediately, has been worth it. Selinunte is a glorious place: history as it happened. No one has been along to tidy it up, never mind reconstruct any of its buildings. There's nothing here except a great tumble of collapsed walls and temple columns lying where they fell two thousand years ago, knocked down by the earthquake. The stubby bases of pillars stick up from the ground like worn-down teeth from a skull; vast columns lie in the same staggered sequences as vertebrae in a dinosaur museum, bleached to dazzling white in the sun. In the disarray I trace the shadowy imprints of streets and foundations as lizards dart across fallen cornices.

I scramble with Tina across the hillside, picking over the brilliant bones of this lost city in delight. Hot rock bears the ghostly marks of ancient chisels and invocations to the gods. Wild celery (*selinon*), the ancient city's emblem and source of its name, grows along the edges of the pathways. Much of the ruins are overgrown and jasmine bushes drop delicate stellar blossoms onto the ancient masonry, floral offerings to a fallen civilisation.

Only part of a single temple remains standing: 'Temple E' the archaeologists simply call it, as if their imagination has been left stunned by the magnificent desolation. A party of schoolchildren screams and dodges around the columns, the only things alive in this city of dead stones. Despite their noise I can't help enjoying their energy and fun. The children set me thinking about Selinunte. Trapped forever in vanquished ruins and museum displays, Greek civilisation can sometimes seem overwhelmingly static and dead; there's not much left to testify to Greek vigour and inventiveness. But these ruins, after all, are only the physical remains left behind, the way a butterfly abandons its cocoon. Greek civilisation never died, really; it never faltered for a moment in its ability to influence people's minds. Selinunte lives on in these Sicilian students, in the way they're educated, in their frames of reference, in the society that defines them—not to mention in the food they eat.

I'm glad, for once, that I'm surrounded by screaming kids in this evocative place, because they remind me that we're all Greeks, one way or another.

In the eighth century BC the Greeks began to find Greece too cramped for their liking, and set sail to find more agricultural elbowroom elsewhere. They settled along the west coast of the Italian peninsula, and in order to protect their shipping routes through the Straits of Messina founded their first Sicilian colony at Naxos in 735 BC. Soon Greek colonies were popping up along the southern and eastern coasts of Sicily. The settlements proved highly successful and Magna Graecia, the collective name for all the Italian colonies, became richer and more powerful than Greece itself. Jealousy set in, and there were bitter disputes between the new world and the old, not to mention between rival cities within Magna Graecia itself. The history of the times is a confusion of shifting alliances, destructive rivalry and frequent warfare, the most famous example being the disastrous attempt on Siracusa by an Athenian fleet in 415 BC.

The Greeks have acquired a reputation for being civilised, but in their time they fought constantly among themselves. No doubt they knew a lot about philosophy and literature, but the art of compromise seems to have passed them by. It was Sicilian Greeks who invented the catapult, the most effective military weapon of its day. In the third century BC, the great Archimedes spent much of his time dreaming up horrendous war machines for Siracusa, including giant iron pincers that were fixed to the harbour walls and could pluck attacking ships from the sea. 'A ship was frequently lifted up to a great height in the air, a dreadful thing to behold,' explains Plutarch of the pincers in his *Parallel Lives*. 'It was rolled to and fro, and kept swinging, until the mariners were all thrown out, when at length it was dashed against the rocks, or let fall.' When the Romans finally overran Siracusa, people were horrified to learn that a soldier had killed Archimedes with his sword, apparently while the great mathematician was working out a problem in the sand. If you ask me, the inventor was asking for it.

There's waste and destruction aplenty at Selinunte, but inter-Greek rivalry didn't stop at wrecking just one city. It happened all over again at Segesta in the northwest corner of the island when, in 307 BC, Agathocles, tyrant of Siracusa, swept into town and imaginatively massacred those Segestans he didn't enslave. Some had their arms and legs torn off on wheels, some were placed in catapults and hurled over the city walls, and others were strapped to a bronze bed and grilled until they burst into flames. Fortunately, Agathocles was eventually assassinated, though not until the age of seventy-two after a reign of cruelty exceptional even by the standards of his day. As for Segesta, the devastated city struggled on for quite some time, but its days of glory were well and truly numbered.

It's a bit perverse that tourists now visit Segesta to admire Greek civilisation rather than to ponder Greek cruelty and spite. Still, this is another dazzling ruin in another inspired setting. What little remains of Segesta lies scattered on a windswept hill, covered by rank stands of wild fennel and purple thistles. Down below, the landscape falls away into gorges and hills, reaching to the bright blue of the distant sea; the Greeks had an uncanny knack of turning the practical considerations of location into pure poetry. Yet despite the magnificent views it's a melancholy place, the only sound the sighing of the wind and the screeching of birds tumbling high in the sky. Most of the once-powerful city has vanished underground, or sits in great mounds of jumbled stones, hot in the sun and alive only with fragile white butterflies. A magnificent theatre, hewn from the hillside, and a solitary temple are the only things that have escaped the passing of the centuries.

The temple is utterly brilliant; people turn up in this quiet valley to stand and gape at its beauty. The thirty-six honey-coloured columns of the temple stand like stone exclamation marks after the rest of the city's text has vanished, leaving you to wonder at its significance and marvel at the poetry.

'The survival of civilisation over destruction,' says Tina, who has been wandering about humming to herself and running her fingers over bits of old stone.

Segesta is a very Sicilian ruin, a place of defeat, abandoned forlornly on a hillside. Yet it's also a triumphant memorial to the artistic brilliance of those who built it, and testament to the resilience of the Sicilians, who still turn up to admire its glory.

Back in Montalto, Giuseppe never seems to be at ease in the house. In the mornings he pauses only long enough to drink orange juice and swallow a mouthful of pills and garlic slices, and then he's hurrying off to get dressed so he can make his escape. He often wears a purple paisley tie tucked into his belt, and a clashing green-chequered shirt. His trousers are hitched far too high. When he's ready he sets off for what he affectionately calls his office, the bar in the piazza. It's an ordinary little place, more like a worker's club than a proper café, with rickety metal tables and a television that seems to be permanently howling out race results. But Giuseppe sits outside in the piazza, gazing over parked cars and the distant Aeolian Islands, keeping a watch on people passing by. Often he plays card games like *scopa* and *briscola*.

'I haven't played poker since 1983,' he comments one day.

Giuseppe often says things that I find slightly odd, and I wonder why he stopped playing poker, and how he can remember exactly when he made the decision. I don't have time to ask, though, because moments later he's onto some completely new topic. Like the time in New York when he went to visit a psychiatrist at a place called the Newton Institute.

'You know Newton, eh? He's a famous scientist, maybe the best, so psychiatrists in this institute must be good. So I think, I go there! This shrink, he show me his office, make me lie down on the couch like in the movies. I talk to him, this and that. Suddenly I realise he's sleeping! Yes, really! So I think, this Newton Institute is no good. I get up from couch. Shrink, he not even waking up! So I just leave, just walk out his damn office, and never go back to any psychiatrist.'

Tina isn't surprised the psychiatrist fell asleep; she finds her father's monologues boring and repetitive. The bar is a man's territory, anyway, and she doesn't bother to come here often, except maybe for an evening ice cream. Giuseppe's talk can be a little tedious but I find him rather charming and occasionally fascinating. Despite what I know about his past I reluctantly find myself liking him. It's quite pleasant whiling away a morning sitting out in the street in the sunshine, drumming my fingers on the metal table top, drinking coffee, chatting, eating olives.

Ah yes, good old olives. I like sitting in the sun and contemplating the olive which, although a fruit, is certainly the ugly stepsister of the family. Consider fruit for a moment, and you'll see that it's generally a cheerful food. Fruit is fun: the soft-skinned sensual peach, the crunchy freshness of an apple, the sassy colour of an orange. Strawberries are sexy and bananas are amusing. What, then, about repugnant, wrinkled black olives? They're salty and sour, as if permanently discontented. Straight from the tree they're particularly awful, but eaten in any form olives are distasteful and an acquired taste. For years I picked olives off my pizzas, convinced from an early age that they were an abomination—another legacy from my mother, who viewed olives with contempt.

Yes, the olive is an ugly, difficult fruit. It says a lot about human inventiveness and perversity that it's been the glory of Mediterranean civilisation for thousands of years. The ancient Greeks were into olives in a big way: felling olive trees was punishable by death and, because they were sacred, only virgins were allowed to cultivate olive groves. (Extra-virgin olive oil indeed!) The Romans spread them further along the Mediterranean coast, improving curing techniques and inventing the screw press, which made the production of olive oil simpler. The olive was important enough to get lengthy treatment in Cato's book *On Agriculture*, written in the third century BC. Cato gives detailed advice on how the trees should be cultivated, and how to cure the fruit by crushing it and soaking it in a mixture of vinegar, olive oil, salt and fennel. He thoughtfully gives a few recipes too, such as a spread made from chopped olives with olive oil, vinegar, mint, rue, fennel, cumin and coriander.

And so I sit in the piazza in Montalto and pop a bit of classical civilisation into my mouth and crunch it up, squinting. I'm still not convinced I really like olives, but I've been sucked into the romance and tradition of this funny fruit. Giuseppe eats them by the bucketful. He's sitting with me now munching his way through a dish of speckled green ones, stuffed with slivers of bright red chilli. Hard, sharp and sassy, with a piquant kick as you bite into the middle, it's no wonder the Sicilians call them *olive infocate*, 'inflamed olives'. Giuseppe will be here all day, munching and crunching and relaxing.

'You see that guy over there with the white hair?' asks Giuseppe.

'Yes, what about him?'

'I don't know, he's nobody.'

I take another olive, so sour I wrinkle my face in doubtful appreciation. Maybe this is why the oil produced from olives has always been more important than the fruit itself. You could cook with olive oil, and also use it as fuel for lamps, as a base for cosmetics or as a medicine. Olive oil is constantly referred to in ancient medical treatises as an astringent and laxative, and was thought to provide relief for toothaches, fevers and malaria. (It does; we now know it contains salicylic acid, the active ingredient in aspirin.) The Greeks and

Romans needed little excuse to pour olive oil over each other at every opportunity: while exercising, after bathing, during meals, when receiving honoured guests, when departing and arriving from long journeys. Olive oil was rubbed on the skin and then scraped off with a *strigil*, a curved wooden blade. The oil was thought to penetrate the skin and promote vitality and long life, not to mention maintain supple muscles, soft skin and shiny hair. Honey on the inside, olive oil on the outside was, according to Democritus, the healthy way to live. The more hedonistic Romans preferred wine on the inside, but still thought oil on the outside a good idea. Young Romans did nothing but lounge about dripping in olive oil and enjoying luxuriously oily massages, driving Martial to complain about the youth of his day never doing any hard work.

Out in the piazza the old men are still muttering about degenerate youngsters. Most of the time, though, they run out of things to say to each other, because they're out here at the tables all day. They sit in their suits and ties, their hands clasped in their laps or around the top of walking sticks, watching people and cars pass by with vacant reptilian intensity.

We crunch up more olives, black ones this time, a pleasant accompaniment to our glasses of white wine. This type of olive is called *greche* (Greek) in Italian, but it has nothing to do with the purplish *kalamata* olive most often used in Greek cooking, with its strong, salty flavour. Black olives are merely riper green olives; they're big, fat, glistening and oily. I've shared long hours with the olives, I know their every contour and colour. Violet black, some tending to a suggestion of dull red like an old wine, flecked with brown. Sometimes I think time in Montalto is counted in olive pits, piled on the edge of the plate.

Giuseppe eats another olive, chewing slowly and methodically.

'You want to know about my youth? I tell you about my youth,' he says, spitting out the pit.

And he does, starting off just after the war, when he was nineteen and moved to Milan in search of work. He found a job with the police; there wasn't much training required in those days, and he worked on everything from robberies to murder. Because of his youth—so young he couldn't even grow a beard—no one ever realised he was a policeman. He hung out in bars, played pool and listened to the talk. He travelled all over northern Italy. It was an enjoyable life for a young man, says Giuseppe: free as a monkey in the jungle, money, nice hotels, a touch of glamour.

One month Giuseppe was working on the case of Giovanni Mondello, a notorious criminal who was wanted on thirty-two counts that included breaking-and-entering, assault with a deadly weapon and attempted murder. Eventually he tracked the man down and followed him to a hotel room. He kicked the door open and threw Mondello on the bed before he had time to react—luckily for Giuseppe, since there was a gun concealed under his pillow. Mondello was arrested. Giuseppe gave evidence at the trial and had him jailed.

Time passed and Giuseppe became involved in other cases. One day he was mooching around a crowded piazza during a festival, keeping an eye on the crowd and warning the petty criminals he knew to steer clear of his patch. Suddenly he felt a tap on his shoulder. He turned around and found himself eye-to-eye with his old foe.

'I've been released, thanks to the new president.' Mondello produced his papers and showed them to Giuseppe; as was the custom in those days, he'd been freed in an amnesty after recent elections.

'Jesus Christ!'

Giuseppe was dismayed. He toyed with the idea of picking a fight with the man, at which point he might be able to arrest him on the spot for assaulting a police officer. Instead, he invited Mondello for an espresso in a local bar, then made an excuse to leave the table and phoned his commander. The commander could hardly believe such a hardened criminal was already out of prison.

'Well, as the Virgin is my witness he is,' replied Giuseppe. 'I'm sitting here in the Caffè Faraglione having an espresso with him.'

The commander was horrified. He was even more horrified at Giuseppe's plan to pick a fight. Giuseppe had no choice but to finish off his coffee and let the criminal walk away.

'And I never saw him again. But two months later there happened a triple murder. A car slowed down on a mountain bend, and my old friend shot the driver and his passengers, killing them all. The police knew it was him all right. But never he was tracked down.'

Giuseppe leans back in his chair. There are a few black olives left. They sit in the dish, skins wrinkled, pungent and desirable. *Profumate*—'perfumed'—they're called elegantly in

Italian; they've been soaked in crushed garlic, bay leaves and orange peel. Giuseppe rips off a crust of bread and folds an olive into it. There aren't many left, so I know the story must be drawing to its close.

After ten years of working in such a volatile job, Giuseppe began to fear he'd become a target for criminals and, newly married to Marcella, retired from his post and went back to Sicily. He found a job with a major Messinese importer, and by the time his two daughters were born he had risen to the position of Head of Administration. With a thousand clients and dozens of different supplies, this was no mean task. Giuseppe worked extremely hard to keep up with the job. He went home at four o'clock with the other workers, but after having his meal he returned to the office, usually until midnight. He worked Saturdays. Even in August, when the whole city virtually shut down and everyone went off on holiday, he worked. The streets were empty, the restaurants and tobacco shops all shuttered up. Even the buses, which came only every two hours, were almost deserted.

'I could walk naked in the street, nobody would notice! I work and work. And I decide to go to America.'

And off Giuseppe went, with his wife and two daughters.

I'm in Marcella's kitchen and feeling a bit like Apicius, a famous Roman gastronome who taught himself the art of cooking and then arranged sumptuous banquets for his cronies. He must have become a good cook in the end, but I can imagine him just starting out, wondering if his guests were about to arrive as he rushed in a panic between stove and notebook. Somehow he managed to produce the greatest cookery book of Roman times, known to posterity as *De Re Coquinaria*, but you can tell it was rather hastily scribbled and sometimes just urgently cobbled together from other sources. Ingredients are often listed without any direction to quantity, or how to prepare and mix them, as if Apicius was too busy frying fish or simmering sauces to be bothered with such niceties. Times are equally vague, naturally enough—it was to be many centuries indeed before anyone got around to inventing accurate clocks, never mind using them in the kitchen. Apicius probably just cooked things for as long as he could, until his friends banged on the door.

And what a genius Apicius turned out to be! Most of Western cuisine is entirely indebted to his rambling opus. Unfortunately we don't know much about the man himself, except that he was renowned in his day as a glutton. The facts about his life are somewhat confusing, especially as there were several gastronomes named Apicius wandering about Rome. The author was surely Marcus Gabius Apicius, a wealthy gentleman born in 25 BC who lived under the reigns of Augustus and Tiberius. It's said he sought out the finest ingredients for his meals, bidding ridiculous sums in the market place for choice fish, and on one occasion even setting sail for Libya because he'd heard the shrimps there were especially large. (They weren't, and he sailed home empty handed.) He was particularly interested in aphrodisiacs; truffles from Libya were highly rated in the sexual stakes. Not surprisingly, Apicius eventually ran out of money and committed suicide. As Seneca explains in his *Dialogues*: 'Apicius, oppressed by debtors, was forced to review his accounts, and when he discovered that he had only a few hundred *sesterces* left, he poisoned himself for fear of dying of hunger.' Here was a man who lived life and enjoyed food to the extreme.

I'm feeling like Apicius because Marcella doesn't seem to have much of a clue about cooking times and quantities either. She's been in this business so long that it comes naturally to her, and my anxious need to know how much of everything she's flinging into the cooking baffles her. She has just dropped handfuls of chopped bacon and ham into a bowl, together with some sliced mushrooms—but how many? I'm a little uncertain what the best balance is for all these ingredients, yet Marcella doesn't seem to care. She shrugs and says *Pfut pfut pfut!* and flings in some juniper berries without even counting them. I'm sure she thinks I'm a tedious Swiss.

Marcella mixes all these ingredients with the livers of some little birds she's bought in the market. I don't know what they are. Italians eat just about anything that flies (and also birds that don't): thrushes, blackbirds, finches, pigeons, quails, even robins. Once they're plucked they all look the same to me and have confusing, lilting names: *palombacci, piccioni, beccafichi, allodole, uccelletti*. Whatever they are, they're being stuffed with the mixture Marcella has just thrown together. Then they're wrapped in bacon and put into the oven.

Later it's time to make the sweet-and-sour sauce (*agrodolce*) that frequently goes with game in Sicily and throughout the peninsula: the juices from the birds, a bit of chopped mint, some caramelised sugar, vinegar. I'm trying to watch what Marcella is doing and at the same time running back to the table and scribbling wild guesses in my notebook. About two tablespoons of mint. The same of sugar. Vinegar—I'm not sure, a good splash. Then just stir it all up. My recipe is becoming almost as incomprehensible as those in Apicius' cookbook. The ingredients are there, but by the time I get home I'll have no idea how they're combined, or how much of everything I'll need. Some pine nuts go in when I'm not looking.

The sauce is Roman, too. Apicius has a recipe for *agrodolce* that includes pepper, mint, carrots, sultanas and pine nuts mixed in vinegar, wine and musk. Honey takes the place of sugar. He's just as distracted as I am when it comes to exact amounts. Maybe he just made it up as he went along. But little birds in sweet-and-sour sauce are only one of the many similarities between Roman and modern Italian (and indeed European) cooking. The fact is that the foundations of Western cooking and eating, like so much of everything else, were laid down by the Greeks and later reinforced by the Romans, and we haven't done anything about it since.

Apicius and his cookery book get a lot of the credit, but the Greeks were there before him, and they started it all. When they weren't at war they had the wealth and time to indulge in the pleasures of the table—and write about them. One of the most important books on cooking that has survived, at least in fragments, is *The Life of Luxury*. It provides the first major clue in Sicilian and European culinary history and was written in verse by the Sicilian Greek poet Archestratus in the fourth century BC. It might be described as a cookery book, but was probably intended to entertain people at banquets rather than for use in the kitchen. From it we can glean that a Greek meal at the time of Archestratus consisted of three parts. The first course was made up of various strongly flavoured dishes such as small birds, pickled sow's womb, eggs, bitter greens, soup or pickles. A second, more lightly flavoured course of fish or meat came next. Archestratus concentrates almost exclusively on fish, usually cooked in the simplest manner: boiled, roasted or grilled with the addition of oil or herbs. Vegetables accompanied the fish—onions, legumes, cabbage, squash, artichokes and cardoons were all available. The meal was rounded off with small dishes of nuts and fresh fruit, sometimes in sweetened combinations such as mashed figs with nuts and honey. Various kinds of pastries sweetened with honey were also common.

See what I mean about the similarities to modern cuisine? Pickled sow's womb mightn't be to your taste, but a meal described by Archestratus isn't terribly unusual. Echoes in Sicilian cuisine are particularly strong. A traditional Sicilian meal still opens with a luxury of choice among numerous strongly flavoured dishes that make up the *antipasti* and *primi*; this is where the chef's imagination blossoms. Many of these are the same sorts of food mentioned by Archestratus: cheese, olives, cold vegetables and maybe soup. Pasta is a major *primo* these days; the Greeks ate bread or barley stew instead. In contrast, the *secondo* is austere, usually grilled fish or roasted meat accompanied by vegetables. Finally the dinner closes, as it did for the ancient Greeks, with fresh fruit and nuts, and occasionally something sweet too, such as a small pastry.

We're doing without *antipasti* tonight, and we're having pasta for our *primo*. For a foreigner like me pasta seems a whole meal in itself, but Marcella finds the idea ridiculous. Pasta, she says, should be eaten in small amounts and is only half of any decent dinner. You have to pause before passing on to the next course in order to drink wine, nibble on bread crusts and thank God for his benedictions. Of course, adds Marcella, getting into her stride, the *primo* and *secondo* are totally different, but you have to think about their relation to each other. You'd never eat *spaghetti alla bolognese* before roast beef in wine sauce, for example. That would be far too rich and meaty, wouldn't it? No, you'd be better off following with a pleasant roast chicken, or maybe a piece of grilled fish with a simple lemon and olive oil dressing. But if your *primo* is something light like a broth or vegetable gnocchi, then there's no problem with a serious meat *secondo*.

Am I following?

Yes, I'm following, I say as I scribble away in my notebook. We're having roast birds for *secondo*, so that's pretty light isn't it? So no wonder our *primo* is *rigatoni alla boscaiola*, because that's quite rich.

I'm relieved when Marcella nods happily. She's just fried big thick slices of aubergine in the pan until they've browned, and now she's chopping them up into cubes and leaving them to one side. She's back at the pan sautéeing garlic cloves and fresh basil, and as the smell invades the kitchen I'm scribbling away in my notebook like a mad thing. *Basil— five leaves*.

'Do not burn garlic. Remove garlic,' dictates Marcella helpfully in my direction, seeing my panic. 'Add chopped tomatoes.'

'How many?'

'*Madonna*, just add the tomatoes, eh?'

Salt is thrown in. Freshly ground pepper. Then it's all left to bubble away for a while before the garlic cloves and basil are fished out. The pasta is already done. The tomato sauce is mixed in with it, together with the aubergine cubes and some sliced mushrooms. Phew!

Marcella's expertise in the kitchen also comes from a long tradition, because Sicilian cooks were once renowned. If the Greeks created the traditions of Western cuisine, then the influence of Sicily can't be overlooked. A cookery school opened its doors in Siracusa in the third century BC, the first in recorded history. There was also an academy devoted to the art of hospitality, run by a fellow named Terpsione, who instructed his students in laying tables, serving guests and choosing appropriate wines. In *The Republic* Socrates praises 'the refinements of Sicilian cookery'; many Sicilian dishes were well known throughout the classical world. Sicily became so closely associated with fine food that the comic writer Antiphanes called cooking 'the Sicilian art' and Diogenes teased Plato about travelling to Siracusa for the sake of its luxurious dishes and famous chefs.

An apprenticeship in the kitchen lasted two years and was followed by rigourous examinations, and chefs were held in such high esteem that seven famous cooks were even compared to the seven sages of ancient Greece. (Sicilian chefs remained all the rage well into Roman times, as much a status symbol as French chefs now.) These top chefs earned their reputation by inventing brilliant new dishes which were patented so that the inventor had exclusive rights to them for a year. It was a profitable business. According to Athenaeus, a chef named Moschion was so successful that he owned three large houses in a salubrious part of Siracusa, to the irritation of his snobbish neighbours. Although chefs were much sought after, they were hardly patrician. Indeed, when Sicilian chefs pop up in classical comedies they're often uncouth, fat and foolish. Aristophanes has several Sicilian cooks as main characters in his plays and they're often thieves and drunkards.

Marcella is neither fat nor foolish but she is a good cook. The *rigatoni* is wonderful, studded with diced aubergine heavy with olive oil and chewy morsels of mushroom that have barely wilted in the heat of the sauce. We have a couple of twists of pasta in our shallow bowls, sprinkled with freshly-grated cheese; just enough to appreciate the flavour and take the edge off our appetites.

Understand the philosophy of food and you have the key to an entire culture. I'm learning a lot of things I never knew about Sicilian cuisine, and what I've gathered so far is that simplicity and harmony lie at its heart. The Greeks were big on the theory of balance, and the Greeks set the ground rules. After the pasta, the little roast fowl are perfectly satisfying, light and tender, accompanied by sugary green peas and a couple of tiny potatoes—a triumph of taste and tradition.

For once we all eat in silence, mesmerised by the fine meal.

I still haven't met Padre Perrino, and I'm willing to take much of what's said about him as little more than village gossip. But when I hear that the priest has managed to reduce Lucia to tears, I find myself irrevocably on the villagers' side. Anyone who upsets such a gentle and pious woman, I tell myself, must indeed be the very devil.

It was only a couple of days ago, says Marcella, as we settle down to our grilled fish. Tuesday morning, in fact, and Lucia was preparing herself to slip across the square to attend mass. She put on her dark navy dress and best gold crucifix, and above her bosom she pinned a medallion of St Anthony. She darted across the open space and entered the church, settling herself in a pew and looking forward to an hour of communicating with God. Then the priest came sweeping in. To Lucia's horror he wasn't wearing his vestments—not even a plain black cassock. He was, in fact, dressed in a suit with a natty red tie. Abruptly, he told the small group of elderly women huddled in the pews that he didn't have time for mass that day.

'Oh, sweet Mary Mother of Jesus, someone has died!' exclaimed Lucia, clutching her handbag to her chest.

'No one has died,' snapped the priest.

'But Father, it's your duty. We're all waiting to hear mass.'

Lucia was hovering on the verge of tears. Now she pleaded with the priest. How could she get through the day without the spiritual comfort of Holy Communion?

But Padre Perrino, apparently, didn't care. He wheeled around and stormed off down the aisle, out of the church, and off to Messina. Lucia was left behind, weeping in her seat and calling for the intercession of the Virgin of Virgins.

'And,' adds Marcella dramatically, 'she had to be carried home! That poor woman, alone in her house with all her icons! Isn't the daily mass her only joy and comfort? And still in mourning these twenty years for her father as well! Of course it's all the priest's fault. The Heart of Jesus should inspire him, instead of which . . .'

I'm indignant as I clear away the lunch dishes and start the washing up. I have a soft spot for Lucia. She may be obsessed with saints and feud with her family, but she's a cheerful soul. I like her bizarre living room with its collection of grotesque iconography, and I admire her steadfast refusal to step out the door. Could Marcella perhaps tell me more about her?

'Of course! Lucia was very beautiful when she was young, with blond hair and blue eyes. You know why? Her mother was from Trieste originally, and came from a background that was half northern Italian and half Austrian. Not like we Sicilians, eh?' says Marcella in an after-lunch glow, nibbling on her endless supply of pastries.

Lucia's mother, it seemed, didn't adapt easily to life in the closed society of pre-war Montalto. She was scorned for drinking coffee for breakfast, because in those days most Sicilians made do with a glass of rough wine and a few olives. She never did anything right, it seemed, and she wasn't helped by her domineering mother-in-law. Slowly the 'Woman from Trieste', as everyone called her, withdrew from village life. She began drinking. First it was a couple of glasses of wine with her midday meal, then nips of Campari in the afternoon and shots of strawberry grappa after dark. Her mother-in-law turned the children against her, and eventually the Woman from Trieste was thrown out of the house. It was only much later, when her mother was dying in hospital, that Lucia realised all she'd been through. There was a tearful deathbed reunion.

Now, it wasn't long after that, Lucia fell in love with the

village schoolteacher, who was at the time studying to become a doctor.

'The teacher returned her feelings, and why not! Lucia was intelligent too,' said Marcella. 'She had many accomplishments: she could sing like a lark, recite poetry, and knew a lot about mathematics and history. And beautiful!'

Lucia's cheeks were fresh and smooth, her lips scarlet as rubies, her figure beyond compare, continued Marcella, getting into her stride. It seemed the perfect match. Everyone could see it was only this man she loved and no one else. But one day Lucia was walking through the village when she heard some startling gossip. The schoolteacher had just become engaged to the niece of a general in the Italian army! Naturally, she couldn't believe her ears. She jumped on a bus and went all the way to the girl's house in a neighbouring town to confront the family.

'Well, the family was equally shocked by the discovery that the schoolteacher already had a girlfriend from the village! But of course, they immediately saw how beautiful and intelligent Lucia was, and how honest, and they realised they'd all been made to look like fools. The engagement was broken off!'

The schoolteacher was shunned and ran off to Turin. It was not until many years later that he returned to Montalto for a visit. He'd married in Turin and had two children, but the marriage had never been happy. Now he was separated from his wife. It was said that he still loved Lucia and regretted all his past mistakes.

'But Lucia had gone to New York, and no one thought to tell her of her former lover's visit!'

Marcella falls silent. We both stare up out of one of the kitchen windows, where a collection of boots are tramping past in the street, black and severe and covered with dust. Farmers' voices float on the air and then are gone. Our coffee cups clink companionably against our saucers as we think about Lucia. Her schoolteacher lover could have rescued her from an unhappy home, but instead she was left abandoned to a father whose tyranny grew with the passing days.

It was all too late for Lucia, says Marcella finally. She'd ruined her reputation. Her father became ever more controlling and she never married. It seems she never really stopped loving the schoolteacher, or got over his betrayal.

Marcella dabs the corner of her eyes.

That's Lucia's story.

I drive down towards Piazza Armerina for a day on my own. The temperature has soared. I crinkle my eyes against the glare and suck greedily at my water bottle. I'm more prepared than I was at Selinunte, but the water is tepid and tastes of plastic. At lunchtime I stop off in Agrigento to see its famous Greek temples, then wander into the modern streets. The shabby provincial town, full of dust and concrete, is one of the poorest in all of Italy, but the main Via Atenea is lined with classy clothes shops and jewellery stores. The outskirts are an astonishing tangle of highways and flyovers, and speculative building projects dwarf the town. Agrigento doesn't need any of these things; they're simply a reminder that this is a Mafia stronghold and probably the European centre of cocaine trafficking from South America. One of the Mafia's most notorious bosses, Giovanni Brusca, was arrested in Agrigento in 1996. Agrigento is a place where everyone lives behind secretive shutters, and in the blaze of the mid-afternoon sun all the streets are deserted. The flagstones of the pavement are blinding. Behind shop windows hot to the touch I can see designer dresses and heavy gold bracelets. A solitary police car rolls along the street, tyres hissing. The officer inside doesn't look at me as he drives past. I suppose he must have a lot of experience averting his eyes in Agrigento.

It's a relief to slip into a dark, cool trattoria. Near the door an old man in a baseball cap is sitting in front of a gigantic plate of spaghetti, sucking up great coiled forkfuls of the stuff—slurp, twist, slurp. He's the only customer and doesn't even look up as I sidle past. I order a dish of small pickled olives, pale green with brown splotches like tiny mottled eggs, sharp, crunchy and surprisingly sweet, followed by a chicken lasagne. When the waiter brings them I notice he's wearing no socks. As I eat my modest meal, I thumb through my reference books and discover Agrigento was well known in its heyday for culinary luxury and especially its seafood. It was famous for sea urchins, eels and tuna fish. Under the Romans, Agrigento's eels were much sought after, and red mullet commanded staggering sums at auction in the market.

An exaggerated passion for food was common among wealthy Romans. According to Athenaeus it was Lucullus, the second-century general and consul, who was the 'first teacher of luxury' and encouraged excess at the table. His dining room was converted into an aviary so his guests could munch on roast thrush while other birds flew hysterically overhead and Lucullus lounged on a couch, rolling his eyes and stuffing himself silly. Italians still use the expression 'fit for Lucullus' to describe an especially hearty dinner. They might equally say 'fit for Heliogabalus', since that emperor died of gluttony in 222 AD; his favourite was a sausage of his own invention made with oysters, crab and lobster. Emperor Septimus Severus died of the same complaint just a decade later, after eating a rich meal in a fit of pique when his physician cautioned him about the need for restraint. A notable exception to all the excess was Augustus, who nibbled only on bread, cheese, fish and fruit. He died in 14 AD at the ripe old age of seventy-seven, one of the few Roman emperors to expire in his bed.

The rich indulged in meals of staggering excess. Everyone was getting so carried away with this overindulgence that legislation was introduced to try and control it. At first, shellfish and imported birds were prohibited. Then the price of luxury wines was fixed, and limits were put on the number of guests at a banquet and the overall expenditure on the food served. The first century biographer Suetonius mentions that prohibited dainties were seized in the market place, and soldiers conducted house-to-house raids during meal times to check that the laws were being followed. In order to prevent corruption, magistrates were forbidden to attend banquets for fear they'd be swayed by the delicacies on offer.

There were plenty of temptations: sow's womb with crackling; lion's dung baked in pastry; cock's combs; small roast testicles stuffed with nuts and fennel seeds. Everyone enjoyed small birds fattened on sweet figs, millet and wheat flour. Big birds were all right too; ostrich brains were served at imperial banquets—six hundred of them at one particular sitting—while the rest of the bird, considered too tough, was ostentatiously discarded. Mark Antony was very fond of a paste made from flamingo brains. The flamingos' tongues came in useful as well. First century poet Martial wrote in an epigram: 'My pink feathers gave me my name / But my tongue among gourmands gives me my fame / What would the tongue say if it could speak?'

What indeed! The bird didn't stand much of a chance, because unlike the ostrich its flesh was considered rather nice, too. Thumbing through my books on ancient Rome makes me feel exceedingly austere as I finish off my lasagne and a glass of wine. Outside the sun is still beating down as I head off to Piazza Armerina. As I drive along I wipe my brow and listen to an endless incantation of Italian on the radio. Olive trees shiver like tinsel in the heat. Outside Barrafranca I nearly run over a sheepdog. The haze off the road batters my eyeballs, and the landscape is ugly and monotonous, full of pine plantations and wretched towns.

There's nothing wretched about the Roman villa at Piazza Armerina. The only thing left of the place is the floor mosaics, but their exceptional quality makes this one of the most important Roman sites anywhere and a fine statement of the luxury enjoyed by the wealthy of the day. The remote villa, set among wooded hills, once belonged to the Emperor Maximian, who came to power in 287 AD. To guess from the subjects depicted in the mosaics, it was probably a hunting lodge. The floor of one of the smaller rooms shows hunters making sacrifices to Diana; there's a small fire lit at the base of the statue of the goddess, and two men hold their horses' bridles as they offer prayers. Servants restrain barking dogs on leashes and other members of the party take a refreshing drink in the woods. Meanwhile, a man spears a rabbit, a boar hunt is under way, and mounted hunters herd deer into a net strung up between the trees.

Another vast hunting scene occupies the full length of a sixty-metre corridor. At one end there are numerous animals being chased and captured alive; in the middle they're depicted being loaded and then unloaded from a galley. Africa and Arabia are shown as the source of animals such as sable antelope and rhinoceros. A man wrestles with a flamingo (which is about to lose its tongue, I assume), another carries a boar slung on shoulder poles. An incredible amount of care and detail has gone into the pictures. The poor flamingo's feathers are lovingly picked out in shimmering shades of pink flecked with gold under the wings. Various servants are identified by different uniforms, soldiers and hunters all have individual features and hairstyles, and every background landscape is populated with trees and wild animals.

I become quite entranced by the mosaics. I wander slowly on with my eyes cast down like a monk in meditation. There's hardly anyone else here and I suddenly feel absurdly happy. I grin like a madman at the best known series of mosaics, which show sporting girls in bikinis, a winner accepting a laurel wreath, competitors taking part in a race, and gymnasts doing exercises with balls and dumbbells. Other mosaics are surreal, with cupids floating in boats surrounded by dancing dolphins and an enormous duck pulling a man seated in a chariot. By the time I reach the dormitory room I'm practically cackling out loud as I peer down at a couple kissing, on the verge of making love. The woman's cloak has slipped aside revealing a pink bottom, and suddenly I realise she must already be completely naked. The man paws at her, leering like a Roman Benny Hill.

I look up to find one of the villa's staff looking at me oddly, so I straighten my face and, deciding the heat has addled my brain, head off for a drink. I slurp at a Coke so cold it makes me wince. I've enjoyed the mosaics; they're beautiful and quite fascinating, but surely it's a bit indulgent to create works of art just to walk over. And I'm a bit uncomfortable with this Roman taste for exotic animals and the almost voyeuristic nature of the naked cupids, bikini girls and dormitory bums.

Bare bums are a recurring theme in Sicilian art. The Romans learned all about them from the Greeks, but the Romans couldn't help being crass. Greek nudity is natural and admirable; it isn't provocative and I've never giggled at it. In Roman art and Roman eating habits I detect a meaningless titillation and pointless excess that was to come back again with the Spanish baroque a millennium later. It's interesting that both empires came to Sicily not to settle and integrate like the Greeks, but to exploit the island for their own benefit. The mosaic work is rife with social implications, and so, nearly always, is contemporary writing about Roman food. Art and eating are political and moral metaphors. The Romans were greedy folk. I can see it on their floors, just as I'll soon see it on Spanish ceilings. Most of all, I notice it in their opulent meals.

I suck up my Coke and put on my sunglasses, and getting into the car drive back to Montalto, leaving the Romans behind.

We're having lunch the next day when the telephone rings. Marcella answers; it's Padre Perrino, she mouths. Suddenly she stands very still. Her voice becomes respectful, and all we can hear is *Si, Monsignor* at occasional intervals. She hangs up and turns to us with eyes shining. Oh, clement Virgin Mary, a breakthrough! Marcella announces. The priest has agreed that the confirmation should go ahead! It's to take place next Saturday. Tina and Claudia have to meet Padre Perrino next week, after mass, to prepare for the event. Marcella laughs delightedly. She's practically prancing around the table.

No one's quite sure why the priest has capitulated so suddenly. He says he received a call from the Sacred Heart School in New York, where Tina herself was confirmed— maybe this is why. Tina, in her usual disorganised fashion, hadn't realised she needed her own confirmation certificate to be godmother. Over the last couple of weeks she's been phoning the Sacred Heart in New York trying to get it faxed through to the priest, who's the only one in the village with a fax machine. Although the priest doesn't speak English we speculate that the phone call perhaps reassured him that Tina was indeed confirmed.

'Or they were probably just shouting at him to press the receive button on the fax machine!' says Tina, too stunned to be delighted.

Giuseppe grunts. Marcella is overjoyed. I haven't seen her looking so happy since my arrival in Sicily. Now she's claiming she knew the priest would do the right thing in the end. After all, Sicilians are always willing to help each other. Everybody knows they're much more friendly and charitable than other Italians, she says, turning to me as if she wants me to write it down immediately in my little black notebook.

'Right, that's why everyone in Montalto is feuding with everyone else,' sniffs Tina. 'And especially with Padre Perrino.'

But, according to Marcella, carried away by this moment of joy, the disagreements have been no more than idle gossip. There's nothing malicious in it. Why, Our Lady of Heaven knows that she, Marcella, might say something bad about him, but she'd do anything for him when it came to the crunch. Yes, she says, tugging at her blouse, she would even give her clothes and go naked for him.

Tina rolls her eyes at the idea of the priest wearing her mother's blouse, and I think she's about to question Our Lady of Heaven's judgement, but Marcella doesn't notice.

'Sicilians are so trustworthy!' she says, warming up to her theme. 'For example, I have two friends who kept promising to come and visit me in New York. But whenever I pressed them about coming, they had one excuse after another!'

There's a short silence after this.

'But that's not being trustworthy,' I say, puzzled.

'I know!' says Marcella triumphantly. 'You see, they're from Calabria! No Sicilian would say one thing, yet do another.'

She giggles into her coffee.

'Everything's going our way! Concettina can be a godmother. We can all celebrate! Brian, maybe you'll even get to eat your cassata . . .'

It's clear that, as far as Marcella is concerned, all is now right with the world. I should have taken this as a sign that our confirmation troubles were far from over, because Marcella is a woman who attracts disappointment the way a wilting plant sucks up rain. Poor Marcella! Death is coming soon to Montalto, and the confirmation isn't going to happen next Saturday because both priest and church will be needed for a funeral.

Marcella doesn't know this. No one does, except perhaps the Blessed Virgin. We pour out more coffee and break open another box of marzipan pastries, celebrating our good fortune.

4

SWEET DREAMS

Sirocco weather has come to the island, and the world is a white-hot explosion. The road is a mirage of dancing air above sticky tarmac. Dust blows through the car and into our eyes, where it stings like pepper. Bleached, flat-roofed houses melt under a cloudless sky. There are no more trees or wild flowers, only rocky soil, rows of stick plants in vineyards, lizard walls and a sea of steel. Along the edge of the water a couple of old windmills stand out against a glare of salt pans in chequered squares and piles of salt glitter unbearably against an indigo sea. This is almost a Saharan world: dusty foreshores, whitewashed houses, monkey-puzzle trees tortured against a brilliant sky.

With minds at rest about the confirmation and a few days in hand before Tina has to meet Padre Perrino, we're heading along Sicily's western coastline. By the time we crawl into Mazara our eyes are reddened and faces taut from the hot wind. We pull up at the waterfront and park the car on a blistering pavement. Mazara is one of Italy's most important fishing ports, and rusting boats and scrubbed fishing smacks bob in the harbour, moored by a tangle of ropes. The reek of oil, heavy in the sultry air, almost masks the smell of fish and sea water. Everything is hot and silent; even the fishermen have abandoned the streets to the heat. Perhaps they're loitering behind shuttered windows, or maybe they've all gone off to the rich fishing banks towards North Africa. With the fishermen absent, the town seems leached of energy, shimmering in a provincial torpor.

Mazara wasn't always like this. It started life as a Greek colony, but really prospered after 827, when it became the first town in Sicily to be conquered by the Arabs. Vast numbers of Arab settlers poured into the island throughout the ninth and tenth centuries and Mazara became the seat of an emir and the capital of one of the three administrative districts into which Arab Sicily was divided. It was one of the most glorious periods in Sicilian history, coinciding with the height of Arab power in the Mediterranean, and Mazara must have been a dazzling town. Ibn Hamdis, a great poet of the day from Siracusa, wrote lyrical verses describing the good life in Arab Sicily: midnight revelries, sumptuous festivals, entertainments by dancers and musicians. Houses of the rich were decorated with glass from Tyre, silken hangings, precious carpets from Persia, breathtaking silverware. Sicilian Arab cities were renowned for their magnificent architecture, artistic life and scholarship, and Arab culture and science was channelled through the island into Europe: algebra, the concept of zero, paper, the lute, translations of many of the Greek texts long lost to the West. After six hundred years of nasty Romans, followed by Vandals, Ostrogoths and bumbling Byzantines, it must have been a positively pleasant moment in history for Sicily. It's not hard to see why this island of fervent Christians is still proud of its Arab past.

In the end the Arabs were ousted by 1073; Mazara was the last place to hold out against the Normans. The town is therefore the alpha and omega of the Moslem era, although the opulence of Arab times has long vanished. Yet, appropriately enough, Mazara's modern Tunisian immigrants still lend it a distinctly North African atmosphere. As Tina and I wander around the Pilazza quarter we find cafés full of wrinkled men sitting puffing at hookahs and drinking coffee against the mesmeric click of dice and backgammon pieces. They smoke reeking cigarettes, twirl their worry beads and nibble endlessly on deep-fried fritters made from chickpeas. This is practically the only place in Italy where chickpeas are used in cooking—certainly an Arab legacy. Later, in every snack shop along Sicily's west coast, I notice other Arab influences: aubergine slices in batter; stomach-stoppers (*ammarra-panza*) filled with honeyed raisins, nuts and dried figs; crusty pyramids of deep-fried saffron rice combined with meat and green peas or cheese. I develop a craze for deep-fried *zippula*, a sort of doughnut that's crunchy on the outside and soft on the inside, dipped in honey or topped off with sweet ricotta.

Right now I'm too hot for deep-fried snacks, and the thought of going anywhere near a vat of boiling oil is enough to make me wilt. Tina has a better idea; in her newly cheerful frame of mind she suggests an ice cream. It's a happy snack, and the latest phone call from Padre Perrino has certainly put Tina in a happy mood. She swings her sunglasses in her hand

and hitches her skirt to cool her thighs like a little girl let out of school for the day.

I spot an ice cream stall further around the harbour and we trail towards it through the heat, watched by a man propped against the counter. He's wearing a baggy grey suit, has a white moustache and is holding a cone that he munches on while reading his newspaper.

'You should have a granita!' he urges as we stagger up. 'Franco makes the best granita in town! Come down here in the evening, even at one in the morning, and you'll find fifty people waiting here for granita. Eh, Franco?'

Franco is a big, fat, beaming man. He smiles and makes a vague gesture as if to say that it's quite true, although he's not a man to boast about it. He leans on a fridge full of coloured ice cream that looks cold and inviting. There certainly aren't fifty people clamouring for ice creams now, but then it's the middle of the afternoon, and only mad dogs and travel writers are abroad in the heat.

I think an ice cream could be a good idea, and ask what flavours there are.

The man with the newspaper spreads his arms wide. Everything, he says. Chocolate, melon, hazelnut—even pizza flavour, probably. He chuckles at his own joke. But as for granita, there are only two kinds, mint and lemon.

Granita is grainy and slushy and made with ice, and right now seems more seductive than ice cream. Tina has mint, a flavour I've never cared for much. I opt for lemon. When Franco passes it over to me the plastic container is cold in my hot hand. The granita is smooth and sharp and melts instantly in my mouth, then trickles coolly down my throat.

The newspaper man winks at my pleasure. 'Thanks to Franco and Marco Polo!' he says. Franco laughs modestly and wipes down the bench with a blue cloth.

I grin back at the newspaper man before sauntering off, too hot to argue. I know it wasn't Marco Polo who brought ice cream or granita to Italy from China, as legend has it. Marco Polo doesn't write about anything like ice cream or even anything frozen in his *Travels*. Perhaps he didn't feel the need to, since the Italians already had chilled food and drinks themselves. In Romans times, natural ice was used for this purpose. Emperor Nero, when he wasn't fiddling and murdering his relatives, enjoyed eating fruit salad mixed with honey, rosewater and snow.

It isn't Marco Polo we have to thank for ice cream—it's the Arabs. Ice cream probably started off in the form of a sherbet, a water-based drink that contains either fruit juice or an infusion such as mint, jasmine or tea. In the past, natural snow chilled the drink nicely and gave it a granular texture. I've already seen several sherbet sellers trundling around Mazara with their little street carts painted with Moorish warriors and Norman knights against a background of castles and fluttering pennants. A massive block of ice sits on top of the cart, and the sherbet seller creates artificial snow by shaving it with a steel blade. The shaved ice is popped into a glass from the row along the front of the cart, along with syrups whose flavours still evoke the elegance of the Arab court at Mazara in days gone by: mint, anise, lime, almond.

These street carts can hardly have changed since medieval times. In those days in Sicily ice could be harvested from Mt Etna. Granita, which is clearly a variation on sherbet, originated either in Sicily or somewhere else in southern Italy. In its simplest form it was probably just flavoured snow, giving the dessert the characteristic graininess after which it's named. Like Franco's granita they're usually served in cups and eaten with a spoon, or sometimes scooped onto a cone. Tina tells me that in expensive cafés a refreshing dollop of lemon granita might be added to a tall glass of iced tea. Like those of sherbets, the most popular flavours—in fact almost the only flavours—reinforce granita's Arab origins: lemon, coffee, mint, almond milk. Another typically Arab ingredient, cinnamon, was once popular but has now fallen out of favour.

Granita is a funny thing, not quite solid and not quite a drink either. You have to eat it with a spoon, but the minute it touches your tongue it dissolves into a cold trickle of liquid. Sometimes you can crunch it, if you're quick, but crunchy granita is a sign that the temperature has dropped too low during freezing. Franco hasn't made that mistake. My lemon granita is cold and seductive, the sharp sting of the lemon juice an ideal combination with the grains of ice. It's the perfect antidote to the hot breath of the sirocco that stirs around street corners and dries out my skin as we wander the streets.

We soon get lost in a maze of crumbling back alleys, a confusing tangle that owes more to Arab than European town planning. With a lemony moistness on my lips and a chilly trickle on my tongue I don't mind. We pass a couscous shop, a Turkish bath, a mosque. The empty churches that stand on almost every corner have Islamic-style cupolas; many of them were built under the Normans during the eleventh century by pilgrims stopping off on the way home from the Holy Land. We find what little is left of Roger the Norman's castle, standing almost unnoticed in the corner of a piazza choked with cars, just a bit of wall and an arched window. Then we blunder into the nearby cathedral, where I walk over pompous bishops' graves set in the flagstones before I even notice that they're there. There are casual reminders of the transience of power and glory everywhere in Mazara.

Mazara's glory has trickled away like granita in the sun, and the only thing that survives from Arab days is a brooding melancholy and oriental fatalism. On Sicily's west coast I don't see much of the operatic energy for which Italians are supposedly famous, and no one is living the *dolce vita*. The people here are fierce and reserved, and sometimes their reserve explodes into a desperate violence. You can't blame them really; Sicilians have nearly always been under the thumb of outsiders and disconnected cultures. In Mazara I get a feel for how tired the island is, with its cruel heat and worn-down abandoned monuments. The foreign powers came and went, and although they left behind the gift of ice cream it was poor compensation for centuries of imposition. The Sicilians had no choice but to stay on, becoming ever more secretive and insular.

Tina sometimes dismisses Sicily as backward, but it isn't that exactly. It's simply battered and bruised, so mired in its past it can no longer look forward. And while Tina might be cheerful today, her sense of relief at being away from Montalto says it all. It's just the same with her: at forty she's the product of a violent past that prevents her from truly enjoying her present. Just like Sicily, the personal history of the Calasciones is a matter for quiet desperation and helpless fatalism. In Mazara I see clearly that history is a nightmare from which both Sicily and Tina are trying to awake.

We slip out of Mazara in dancing clouds of heat and exhaust smoke. Tina guns the car as if the infidel is in pursuit, and soon we're jumping red lights on the outskirts of Marsala. This is another harbour town, and was once the principal trading port of Arab Sicily; its name means 'Port of Allah'. Marsala is hotter yet than Mazara, and even the sea has fallen into a threatening stillness, bringing no breeze as a respite. By eight in the evening it's still over thirty degrees, and the air is draped motionless over the narrow streets. A few clouds hang in a jaundiced sky. In the piazza in front of the cathedral old men gossip with each other, shirts sticking to their backs.

There isn't anything left in Marsala from Arab days, at least not that I can find. In Marsala, just as elsewhere in Sicily, most Arab monuments have long since disappeared. Disappointed, I cheer myself up by heading for the market, where I inspect the wooden crates of seafood sitting out on trestle tables under awnings, and plucked quails lying in rows with their legs in the air. I watch housewives stack their shopping bags with sweet young courgettes with the blossoms still attached, proof of their freshness and a treat in themselves when fried. I puzzle over summer squashes (*zucchina*) that I've never seen before: some are shaped like fuzzy pale green pears, others are as long and skinny as bits of garden hose, still others are striped green and white, or mottled green and brown. Further on, beans, marbled in pink and red, burst out of their pods; they'll turn dark red when cooked and will be full of a wonderful chestnut flavour. Barrels of olives marinated in rosemary and lavender are pungent with herbs and oil.

Tina buys a slice of watermelon as scarlet as a post box; I've heard that vendors surreptitiously rub them with tomato to heighten their colour. Next door there's a stall selling freshly-squeezed lemon juice with water, sugar and ice. I drink greedily. The pile of discarded lemon peel at my feet momentarily blocks the whiff of seafood and sewers, and the air is scented like an Arabian palace. It's that passing thought that makes me realise, all of a sudden, that I can find Sicily's Arab legacy right here in the market, because the Arabs helped define Sicilian (and indeed European) culinary culture. The little sacks of sesame seeds, the pyramids of cinnamon sticks, and jars of precious saffron, the glorious piles of oranges and lemons—all these the Arabs left behind. I watch women weighing artichoke hearts thoughtfully in their hands and squeezing them for freshness; the Arabs introduced artichokes, too. And spinach, the squashes I've been puzzling over, the melon Tina has just devoured. Asparagus, which was eaten by the Romans but had disappeared from cultivation, also returned to Sicily during the Arab occupation.

And so I always circle back to Sicilian cuisine, that vast repository of history and culture. Take a look at the island's food and you'll find the most lasting legacy of Sicily's Islamic interlude. This is thanks to the enormous impact the Arabs had on agriculture. The Arabs broke up the vast estates that remained from Roman times and developed an unparalleled irrigation system, so successful that market gardens flourished and many of the fruits and vegetables now so common were introduced. Only winemaking suffered under Islam, although the conquerors did bring with them the juicy Zibibbo grape, still reckoned to be the best table grape in Sicily.

Tina hauls me out of the market with difficulty; I'm pleased that I've discovered a lively corner of Marsala and fascinated by the colour and history of the produce being sold. Tina is a little perplexed by my fascination for food. She enjoys eating too, and is a decent cook, but she's a little too austere in the kitchen for my liking. Food is a necessity and it might even be enjoyable, but it will never be a passion for Tina, and a market full of goodies just has her glancing at her watch and sighing in my ear. But Tina is very happy later that evening when we find a cheap trattoria down a side street from the cathedral. (Cheapness is a quality to be admired in restaurants, according to Tina.) No sign advertises the restaurant; that, no doubt, would only attract the attention of Marsala's tax collectors. But we know it's there because the owner is hovering outside. For eight euros, he tells us, there's a full set menu on offer, including mineral water and local Marsala wine.

'Sure, and I'm a vestal virgin,' says Tina to me out of the corner of her mouth; eating out in Sicily doesn't come cheap.

'There's no service charge either,' says the owner persuasively. He's a thin little man with a neat moustache and a relaxed manner who looks as if he doesn't mind too much, one way or the other, whether we eat in his restaurant or not.

This clinches it for Tina. She shrugs off my hesitation at what we might have to eat for that price, pointing out that the restaurant is full of local men. As we go inside I see that she's right: there are lots of customers, sitting with their jackets off and ties loosened, reading the pink sports pages and bantering with each other. My hopes begin to rise.

The restaurant walls are panelled in pine and there are rows of rough wooden trestles covered in cheerful chequered tablecloths. The place smells of wood and wine, and reminds me of Switzerland. I've eaten in plenty of places in the Alps just like this, after a morning's skiing—great warming plates of schnitzel and chips, or big pots of steaming fondue to fortify me against the snow. No such fare here, thank goodness, where it would induce a heart attack in the heat. Instead, we're offered a small plate of *antipasti*: fat olives, good salami, a delicious dry *grana* cheese. The olives are the enormous southern Italian Bella di Cerignola variety, cured in ash and a magnificent blue-green, sweet and crunchy on the palate. The cheese is hard and yellow, with a strong taste I find reminiscent of Gruyère; it goes well with the flat loaf of semolina bread, which is just as yellow.

'This bread is the best made in town,' says the restaurant owner to us in unexpected English when I ask for some more.

He pours us both a glassful of amber-dark Marsala, carefully twisting the neck when he's finished so none of it drips. The best Marsala is generally dry, and this is a bit sweet, but it has a nice nutty and slightly sulphurous flavour. Anyway, I have a penchant for sweet wines, and it *is* Marsala—it seems appropriate to drink Marsala in Marsala.

After we've polished off the last olive we're served spaghetti with a strong, rich tomato sauce flecked with tiny curled pink shrimps the size of a fingernail, no doubt hauled out of the sea that morning. The *secondo* that follows is superb: lightly fried squid in batter with a dribble of lemon juice over it, so tender it dissolves in my mouth.

'See?' says Tina smugly. 'Who says cheap food isn't good?'

'In my experience, good food is hardly ever cheap,' I answer ungraciously. And then as a concession: 'Mind you, a lot of expensive food is pretty bad, too.'

But I'm very happy with my meal, and I'm even happier when the owner comes back with dessert, a little mini-cassata decorated with marzipan, icing, a sprinkling of silver balls, quarters of preserved fruit and a single glacé cherry. It's not the ultimate extravagance I'm looking for, but at least it's a start. And appropriate, because cassata might well be Arab inspired. The deep bowl used as a mould in its preparation is called a *qas'at* or *qas'ah* in Arabic, from which the word 'cassata' is possibly derived. Some people claim the name comes from the Italian *incassate* (encased) because the cake is sealed in marzipan.

The cassata is delicious, although Tina finds it overly sweet.

'Dante thought sugar a danger to the soul,' she comments, eyeing the way I scrape the plate with my finger. 'Gluttons for dessert were packed off to one of the levels of Hell.'

'Well, I feel like I'm in heaven.'

I relish this sweetness which, above all else, must surely be the most significant impact of Arab tastes on Western palates. Sugarcane was the most important of all the crops the Arabs introduced to Sicily. The Arabs supplied the whole of Europe with sugar for several centuries, and it proved a revolutionary ingredient, much better than honey because it could be produced on a vast scale and didn't impart a strong flavour of its own. In the end, Arab sugar made the whole of European confectionary possible. Not surprisingly, the word 'sugar' comes from the Arabic *al zukar*, and 'candy' and 'caramel' are other words the English language has borrowed from Arabic.

'The ladies of the harem originally used caramel to remove hair from their legs,' I tell Tina.

'Yeah, that must've been a compensation.'

'For what?'

'For being locked up with nothing to do all day,' she says sarcastically.

Our cassata is all scraped up, our coffee finished.

'Utterly brilliant!'

'And only eight euros,' Tina reminds me smugly.

Thoroughly satisfied with our bargain-price meal, Tina and I wander back through the still-hot streets towards the cathedral square. The gelateria is doing good business. The locals buy ice cream that melts and trickles as soon as it's out of the freezer, sticky in warm fingers. We sit on a hot bench, swinging our legs, and watch dusty pigeons pecking at the paving stones. Teenagers ride by on scooters. People walk up and down slowly, sucked dry of energy. A hot moon sulks overhead.

The sirocco doesn't abate in the next few days. I write in my shuttered hotel room, my pen moving with zombie-like reluctance, or sit gasping in local bars. I drink chilled wine mixed with lemonade in tall glasses that slide with condensation, cool on my fingertips. Waiters wilt in the shade. ('I always think of Italy and see the waiters flopping among the flies,' wrote Henry James.) Green paint, brittle in the heat, flakes from rough wooden tabletops. Sunlight glints off chipped glasses and metal ice-cream bowls. Tina swings her sunglasses from a limp hand, and again lifts her skirt up to her thighs, hoping for a current of air.

In the afternoons I walk through the streets of this low-key town, past horse butchers and tobacconists and barber's shops. I can feel the flagstones burning through the soles of my shoes, and the sun bounces off the honey-coloured build-ings in dazzling sheets of light. I sneak into empty churches and press my forehead against cool marble as if supplicating the Virgin. I leave stonework impressed with damp marks as I feel my way around altar railings, blinded by the dark.

In one church I come across a Madonna surrounded by flowers and bowls of fruit. The railings are almost cold to the touch, making me shiver in ecstasy.

We head north, hoping to find respite from the heat at Érice. The village crowns a hilltop high above the coastal plain of western Sicily, where it catches sea breezes and often dissolves into the cloud and mist. Its origins are ancient and lost in legend; in the days of the Greeks it was already famous for its massive temple to Aphrodite, goddess of fertility. The temple has long gone, and part of the rubble was used to build the impressive Norman castle, completed in the Middle Ages with the addition of sixteen towers and six gates. No sooner was this labour of centuries complete than Érice began to fade away, overtaken by the town of Trápani below, which had once been no more than Érice's port and doorway to the world.

The ruins of the Norman castle are an empty shell covered in weeds. Tina and I clamber about the ramparts, taking photos of each other. Then we watch the sun set: the rocks turn purple, the sea pink, the cubed buildings of Trápani golden, reminding me of the lurid backgrounds of paradise on the saintly posters that decorate Lucia's walls in Montalto. Yet despite the expansive views in every direction, Érice is an aloof, inbred town that has been shut off from the outside world for centuries. Winding cobbled streets, tiny, enclosed squares and secretive, high-walled courtyards reinforce the grim appearance of the town. There are no cars, no markets, no outdoor cafés; everything is silent. Even the children have disappeared, perhaps devoured by a wicked witch. *Cleanliness and silence are signs of civilisation*, reads an inscription on the town gate, like something you'd see in Singapore rather than Sicily. The locals don't seem to linger in the chilly streets, but scurry from doorway to doorway.

Érice is eerie, but as far as I'm concerned its inhabitants can do whatever they like as long as they continue to make the sugary delights for which the town is famous. Érice is another step forward in my search for cassata, since it's the source of several of its components. Candied and preserved fruit and marzipan have been made here for a long time, probably since the days of the Arabs. The Greeks and Romans already had methods for preserving fruit and flowers in honey, but the sugar of the Arabs allowed the process to become far more sophisticated. They candied all kinds of things, including lemons, oranges, citrons, quinces and even varieties of squash.

In Érice today old ladies still follow the same tried and tested methods. They blanch the fruit—the peel doesn't need to be removed—until the flesh softens, and then the fruit is immersed in sugar solutions for two weeks. After this it's diced and ready for use in Sicilian pastries.

As for marzipan, sugar and almonds were quite a common combination in the courtly dishes of Arabia and Persia, often in paste form. Marzipan delicacies were also served at the end of banquets, sometimes varied with the addition of ground pistachios, honey or rosewater. Sicilians embraced this *pasta reale* (royal paste) with delight. One of the earliest printed recipes for marzipan in Europe appears in the mid-fifteenth century in *Libro de Arte Coquinaria* by renowned chef to the king of Naples Martino da Como, in which the almonds, moistened in rosewater, are pounded with sugar. Under the Arabs, Sicily became a major producer of marzipan, as well as of candied fruit, rose-petal preserve and comfits, or sugar-coated nuts and seeds. Laws were passed under the Normans to regulate the growing trade. During the Middle Ages and the Renaissance these treats became an exotic favourite of the nobility across Europe, who liked to nibble on them between meals. Candied flowers and other preserves also decorated the tables. Even in distant England no banquet in the Elizabethan period was complete without marchpane, a large wheel of marzipan decorated with icing sugar and often gilded in gold leaf.

Sicily is still famous, among connoisseurs, for marzipan, and Érice has some of the best on the island. Passionate about marzipan, I'm in a state of culinary delight in Sicily, for almonds or marzipan are included in a huge array of pastries, desserts, ice cream and even drinks. Fresh Sicilian marzipan bears little resemblance to the jaundiced manu-factured variety in Australian supermarkets, because it's usually made with freshly ground almonds. High-quality marzipan is pale and gritty and has a high proportion of almonds to sugar, about sixty-five percent almonds if you really want the best results. Quality is important on an island where cakes are frequently sealed in marzipan or decorated with all kinds of marzipan flourishes, ribbons and rosebuds. Best known of all marzipan creations is Sicily's marzipan fruit. There are plenty piled in the windows of Érice's shops. Lush scarlet tomatoes turn to green around the stems, peaches are rubbed with cotton and cornstarch to give them an authentic-looking fuzzy skin. Dark colouring is pressed on with a paintbrush to create blemished skin. The imitations are truly extraordinary, and even Tina seems impressed despite her lack of sweet tooth.

'Now I know why we call window shopping "window licking" in Italian!' says Tina. She taps her finger on the pane of a confectionary shop, directing my attention towards some marzipan artichokes with spiky, close-fitting leaves.

According to tradition, Sicily's marzipan fruit was invented at the convent of Martorana in Palermo, which is why it's often called *frutta di Martorana*. One Easter, the story goes, the Mother Superior of the convent decided on an amusing prank after the archbishop announced his intention to visit her convent. She had the nuns make lifelike apples and pears out of marzipan, and then hung them out on the cloister's bare trees. Legend doesn't record if the archbishop was fooled or amused by the out-of-season blossoming; but being a man, he mightn't even have noticed the Mother Superior's efforts. Whatever happened, a Sicilian favourite was created that day. In keeping with their religious origins, at first marzipan fruit made an appearance at Easter and on All Souls Day. On All Souls Day marzipan fruit, as well as nuts and historical figures made of melted sugar (*pupi di cena*), appear in baskets at the foot of children's beds—a gift from dead ancestors. (The next day the entire family will head off to the cemetery and tuck into a picnic spread out on the ancestral graves.) At Easter the fruit often accompanies marzipan lambs on the top of cakes; the lamb supports a red flag or red flower to symbolise the Resurrection.

'You wouldn't believe the decoration on those things, it's even more amazing than your cassata,' says Tina. 'I used to love the little lamb from the top of the cake when I was a kid, it had little pink eyes and a fluffy marzipan fleece. And little chocolate hooves—I always ate those first.'

Érice produces the best marzipan fruit in Sicily, and people drive here from miles away at Easter to buy marzipan lambs and Paschal cakes. In contrast to the grim exterior of the grey village, the window displays of Érice's confectionery shops are opulent and gaudy, piled with marzipan figs, bananas, oranges and limes. One window is resplendent with a model of the temple at Selinunte made out of macaroons. Inside, Tina and I are confronted with a counter stuffed with an Aladdin's cave of goodies. Rich almond pastries glisten with chocolate and raisins, almond bites are sprinkled with sugar, 'mother-in-law's tongues' ooze a sharp marmalade of candied lemon peel, and fig biscuits curl in imaginative baroque shapes. The names are as rich as the pastries themselves: *dolcetti al liquore, cuscinetti, bocconcini, lingue di suocera.*

Tina doesn't like marzipan much. I hesitate for a long time over the temptations, then decide on a simple marzipan strawberry. It has a bright red glaze on top, fading towards the bottom to palest pink, almost white. My teeth crunch through the crusty outside to the grainy, sugary-soft centre. I can see why Tina doesn't like marzipan; it's incredibly sweet. You have to be a bit of a marzipan fanatic to appreciate the paste by itself. The sweetness is all the more startling considering the austerity of the village where these marzipans and pastries are made. Silence and cleanliness, indeed. Temptation and excess, more like.

The people of Érice might be silent and grim, but their culinary imagination is dazzling.

We drive down to Trápani, where we find a *pensione* occupying part of an eighteenth-century building right in the heart of the old town. A giant arched door of studded wood leads from the street into an arcaded courtyard covered in flagstones the size of double beds. The courtyard is cluttered with old bicycles and rubbish bins. A dilapidated rocking chair and an old tin bathtub lurk in one corner. When I pass across the courtyard in the evening I can see through the lighted window of the ground-floor apartment, where a family sits around a wooden table eating their supper, frozen into a Caravaggio tableau of wine bottles and red fruit. After they've finished eating, the courtyard echoes with the sounds of children playing. Their voices float all the way to the upper floors of the silent *pensione.*

A steep flight of grand steps leads upwards from the courtyard to the first floor of the building. From here the stairs become narrow, creaking and rickety. Pots of plastic flowers sit on alternate treads, and pictures of the Virgin Mary hang in the stairwell. On the top landing there's a heavy wooden door and a buzzer. The owner's voice crackles over the intercom. 'The visitor from Australia, room ten', Tina always says over the next few days, announcing herself like a spy. Then the buzzer snaps silent, and the lock clicks open.

I haven't seen the *pensione* owner since we checked in, but sometimes I hear her creaking down the stairs from her lair on the top floor, and I hear her tinny, crackling voice on the intercom. When we're out she slips into our room; we come back to find white sheets tucked in and smoothed with hospital competence and the pillows plumped. The smooth white sheets are the only luxury, apart from the size of the room, which has the dimensions of a grand suite and ceilings as high as a fireman's ladder. The bathroom is gigantic as well; the pipes gurgle and moan in the night, and water spurts out of the tap fitfully. Otherwise the room is a Spartan place, virtually empty. A wobbly table sits between the two beds, and there's a scrap of rug over by the door.

I find the emptiness restful. Besides, the room has one feature to die for, a balcony jutting out like a swallow's nest over the main street of the old town, where the facades of handsome palazzi, broken only by the bulk of the cathedral and the Jesuit Novitiate, erupt in a baroque madness of twisting columns and statuesque women. The town hall faces the top end of the street in a glory of pink marble. I like it here, watching people pass by underneath: two men ambling along with ice creams, a woman hauling her daughter by the arm, gossiping neighbours. Trápani is a Mafia town; I keep an eye out for mysterious assignations, maybe a quick murder.

Later in the afternoon we venture out to explore the churches much to Tina's disapproval, since they remind her of the confirmation. We find them full of the dusty finger bones of holy men, gruesomely dying Christs and naked swooning saints. In the Sanctuary of the Annunciation a renowned Madonna works overtime answering the prayers of endless visitors, surrounded by the reek of candles and sweat. Weather-beaten old men and women in black head-scarves crowd the statue, muttering to themselves and making endless Signs of the Cross. They shuffle forward in stout shoes, and coins clink as they drop offerings into the collection boxes. Nearby, St Joseph holds a fat *bambino* in one hand and a basket in the other, as a gaggle of *putti* look on with amused smiles on their faces. Possibly they're amused at the thought of a man in Sicily taking an interest in child rearing and shopping.

By six o'clock we're back on our balcony, resting up after our desultory sightseeing as we watch the light shift across the Corso's baroque facades. As evening approaches, the marble of the town hall blushes, and long shadows lie across the cobbles. Soon it's time for some food at one of the restaurants lining Trápani's waterfront. Some Gaeta olives first, perhaps, smooth, plump and purple, with an eye-squinting sour taste but magnificently tender flesh that melts in the mouth. Then I look forward to *spaghetti alla trápanese* with a cold sauce of pesto and raw tomato, perfect for this sirocco weather. The spaghetti is tossed with crunchy little cubes of deep-fried potato and unexpected chips of hot chilli.

Later I'll finish up with an ice cream as I stroll idly along the sea front with Tina. Locals sit on the low harbour wall or one of the benches, gossiping and exchanging news while their kids scream and run about. Everyone is nicely dressed: hair ribbons, pressed skirts, crisp blouses, freshly washed hair. ('It's said that the women here are the most beautiful on the island—may Allah make them the captives of the Muslims!' gloated tenth-century Arab writer Ibn Jabair.) Mafia types in dark suits and slicked-back hair show off their gold chains and mobile phones as they sit at roadside tables with red tablecloths, drinking coffees and licking ice creams. The evening smells of perfume, car exhausts and fresh Arabica. Boats lie lopsided on the shingle, and a ferry chugs in from the Égadi Islands and ties up at the wharf. An old man in a three-piece suit props himself against a chunk of abandoned masonry, waiting for someone to disembark.

Across the salt pans the sun sets, making the sea sizzle in red and violet.

There's nothing I enjoy more in Trápani than wandering down to the fish market in the early morning, where trestle tables groan with seafood: rust-red squid, glittering mackerel, mullet pink as marble. Eels twist around on themselves to bite their tails, mussels with hairy shells are piled high in baskets, slippery green fish shimmer with phosphorescence. A shouting man pushes a pram along the street, loaded with dusky pink shrimps straight from the ocean. Vendors flick water over the fish until the scales shimmer in the sun.

Beheaded swordfish ooze thick, crimson blood across wooden chopping boards. A man with a knife the length of his arm cuts slabs of marble flesh off the corpse. Fresh seafood is one of the great blessings of life in Sicily. Even in inland Montalto the fish seller drives through town every morning in a battered red van with a loudspeaker on the roof. He shouts through his microphone, distorted and crackling: *'Ngive! Tonno! Pesce spada!* In the back of the van there's a stained wooden board with a great hunk of tuna on it, red and fresh, with the white knuckle of the backbone showing through the middle, and you know this magnificent animal has only died that morning.

At lunchtime I stop at the Trápani market for baby octopus fished straight from a bucket and thrown onto a grill. I eat them with a twist of lemon, standing there on flagstones wet and slippery with water and entrails as fish slide and drop scales like glittering tears onto the cobbles. Later in the day the market is packed up, leaving only a lingering smell of fish. Tina and I retreat to our balcony to share a bottle of chilled white wine. Then it's again time for the evening meal—some fresh tuna. Tuna may be grotesque on the market slab, but on the plate it's quite superb. Fine steaks cut from the neck, as well as from the rather fatty but delicious underbelly, are highly prized in Sicily. Larger cuts are rubbed with garlic and herbs and roasted in the oven like joints of meat. In Trápani, thin slices of the fish are fried and covered in a sweet-and-sour onion sauce and mint leaves. The dish is left to stand a while, then served at room temperature. It's not just the flesh of the tuna that's valued: Tina tells me that the roe is delicious when dried and grated over spaghetti.

I'm content to eat tuna steaks, or tuna simmered in rich tomato or wine sauces, mopped up with bread. I sit out at a street table with Tina and we make up stories about the people passing by as we eat. We're very aware that Trápani is a Mafia town, that the west has always been the stronghold of the Cosa Nostra. So we sit over our tuna and speculate. A harried-looking grandmother scuttles away around a corner with a basket of washing. Tina says she probably has a machine gun concealed beneath the top sheets. A grey-haired man squats in a doorway across the road from the restaurant, watching us. Slick men in suits and sunglasses (at this time of the evening!) amble past in the street. At the next table, a family is eating violent red spaghetti, reminding me of the scene from *The Godfather* where Peter Clemenza, Don Corleone's right-hand man, slides meatballs into the pasta sauce like so many corpses. We make jokes about violin cases and horse's heads.

After a while our jokes make us nervous, and we fall silent.

A family comes in for dinner. It's obvious from their muffled conversation with the waiter that we've taken their regular table. The man waves his hand dismissively, and sits with his wife and daughter at the table behind us. The woman is as thin and dried up as a stick of cinnamon, her daughter is plump and dimpled. Her husband is wearing dark glasses and has white, balding hair and an expression of smug satisfaction. He looks like the sort of person who's used to getting his own way, and he barely speaks to his family. When the waiter brings out their food they eat quickly. As soon as they're done the wife and daughter scurry off, disappearing down the street. The man sits for a while on his own, smoking a cigarette. Then he gets up and leaves, too.

Tina watches him go, and notices he hasn't paid the waiter. She's sitting with her back to the street, and wants to know what kind of car he's got. By this time we're on to our dessert, a slice of tiramisu dusted with chocolate powder and—amazingly enough in a country of espresso—a *caffè americano* just the way I like it: piping hot, black and not too strong. I glance over Tina's shoulder. A Mercedes, I tell her as the man approaches a sleek grey vehicle parked near the cathedral.

We exchange significant glances.

And then the man walks past the Mercedes and squeezes himself into a battered white Fiat bubble car. The engine roars and splutters like a lawn mower as he drives off, so loud that everyone in the restaurant looks up from their plates. Tina turns around too.

The Mafia man makes his getaway.

Tina and I look at each other and start to giggle.

Back in Montalto Marcella never seems to go out of the house unless she's scurrying off to church or the shops. Despite her many years in America and her success as a businesswoman there Marcella retains many of the habits of a traditional Sicilian woman, or has maybe reverted to them now that she has nothing else to do. If the bar in the *piazza* is Giuseppe's domain, then the house is certainly Marcella's. She haunts the kitchen, rubbing at worn but immaculate bench tops with a cloth, loiters in the sitting room straightening the curtains, stares out the window, sits on the balcony with her worries. Like the women of Trápani, Marcella's balcony is the main vantage-point from which she views the world. At the moment, one of her worries is the small apartment block next door, in which the ground floor was supposed to have been a garage for residents' cars. Marcella had managed to work out an arrangement whereby she would own a space for herself. Yet when the apartment block was completed, relates Marcella to me in outrage, the builder-owner rented out the space as a fitness centre and martial arts club. He hasn't budged an inch on the issue, despite repeated threats from the residents. Now they're taking him to court, but Marcella is gloomy about the outcome. Knowing Sicilian courts, she says, it will take another ten years to resolve. The owner has already been summoned once; he failed to appear, and the case was deferred for a year. A year! And now, well, everyone must find parking in the street as best they can.

'What can you do? You just have to walk in your slippers until you can find your shoes,' concludes Marcella philosophically.

There are always people coming and going downstairs: young women in leotards, for heaven's sake, and cocky teenage boys showing off with their dumbbells. Claudia hangs around making eyes at a handsome fellow in a singlet called Carlo. Loud music blares. I can see how this makes Marcella fretful, poised on her balcony overhead, tut-tutting and helpless. She hangs halfway between the serenity of her organised house and the hurly-burly of life outside, which is ripe with unpredictable events. She wasn't always like this, though: I know about the Marcella who was young and full of life, who almost married Alberto and wandered about Europe. Even after marrying Giuseppe and moving to America she was full of energy and ambition. After all, she'd opened a driving school in the Bronx and soon had six cars operating from it.

'I was president and chief instructor!'

Then she opened a branch in Little Italy right on Knickerbocker Avenue, the heart of Mafia country. Not that she ever needed to pay protection money; she was instructing Mafia kids how to drive. When her sister-in-law's Thunderbird was stolen, she just phoned the Mafia and got it back.

But one day Marcella decided she'd had enough of this shady world, good business or not. That was the day she found a black man dead of a drug overdose on the roof of her car. She phoned the police, they took the body away, there was a lot of trouble. And so she decided to take her children out of the Bronx to upstate New York. She started a driving school in Siracuse, but it was much smaller.

'The roads! So icy! And Giuseppe opened a pizza parlour in a converted gas station. Later he gave up and returned to New York, but I stayed on for a while. I bought a big house, as a matter of fact. You know, I thought one of my daughters would come back from college and move in with me . . .'

But they didn't. Tina's sister barely spoke to her parents for years, Tina went overseas, there were no grandchildren in the big empty house. There are no grandchildren in *this* big empty house either.

Marcella is a sad old woman, and impulsively I lean forward and kiss her on the cheek. Her face is lacquered like a geisha's, sticky against my lips, her skin feathery with age.

'It's not you who controls life,' says Marcella wistfully. 'It's life that controls you.'

And somewhere, somehow, I think to myself, she just gave up. Now her religion is her only comfort as she descends into old age and her family falls apart around her. And there is her balcony, of course. The balcony is her last remaining window on the world, and Marcella sits there, enveloped in memories and mistakes, not realising another tragedy is just around the corner.

We've returned to Montalto for Tina's appointment with Padre Perrino. It's part of the spiritual preparations necessary for her role in Claudia's confirmation, which is to take place on Saturday. The thought of the coming ordeal has caused Tina's new-found cheerfulness to melt away like granita, and she has sunk into a glum silence. On the morning of her appointment I see it still hasn't dissipated. Yet while Tina is dragging her heels, I can hardly wait for the day's events. I'm bursting with curiosity, because I haven't even *seen* the infamous priest yet, let alone met him. I'm up and breakfasting early—Giuseppe has been dreaming of white cats but isn't quite sure what this means—and then I'm hurrying off down the road with Tina, Marcella, Claudia and her mother. We shall attend mass and then meet the priest. We all crush into the one pew, and then I look around the church in eager anticipation.

The priest is nowhere to be seen yet, so I gaze around. The church has a lot of heavily scented candles, vases of wilting gladioli, pink walls and a madness of gilt moulding. Above the altar, glass lampshades dangle on long chains; two of the bulbs aren't working, and some of the shades are broken. A great triangular piece of glass hangs dangerously askew, waiting to decapitate an unsuspecting penitent. Between the windows hang the Stations of the Cross, stamped out of heavy-duty plastic. This is only Montalto's second most important church, and it doesn't appear to have much money. The air is heavy with dust and the cloying smell of old candle wax.

Life-sized plastic statues of various saints line the walls; one swarthy fellow is brandishing a bunch of roses as if he's about to smite someone. At the front, above the altar, stands Lucia's old friend St Anthony, the patron saint of Montalto, not to mention of all Italy. I've learned to recognise him by the typical features of his iconography: a baby Jesus sitting on an open book in one arm, and a lily grasped in his other hand. This particular St Anthony is also wearing a black robe and has a halo of stars like party sparklers shooting from his scalp.

At that moment Padre Perrino appears. He's a small, rotund man with white hair and red cheeks, and not much evidence of cloven hooves. He launches into the service, and I try to follow, bewildered and uncertain. I don't think I've ever been to a Catholic Mass before, let alone one in Italian. As the priest intones the liturgy all I can make out is the word *Cristo* repeated again and again like a secret password. *Cristo, Cristo*. The sibilant hisses around the church in an almost sinister fashion. The congregation stands and sits down, stands and sits down, and I do the same, always a fraction too late. The old woman in black in front of me grips the back of the pew, hands knotted with veins, and lowers herself shakily and painfully as she follows the rest of the congregation onto her knees. Two other grey-haired women at the back of the church are having a loud conversation with each other. The church doors are wide open and occasionally a passing car drowns out the priest's words. Some kids are bouncing a ball out in the street. The rhythm makes me sleepy. Bounce, bounce, *Cristo*, bounce.

Suddenly the service is over. The vases of lilies, silver platters and communion goblets are whisked away into a cupboard like a magician's props into a spangled hat. We head up the aisle towards the vestry, and I spot Lucia sitting near the altar. I shake her hand and wish her good morning. She waves her finger waggishly at Tina. *Ha, bringing the boyfriend to church now, are we?* she seems to be suggesting. *And to think you only claimed to be friends!*

The priest has been wearing a stiff white cope with a raised collar and an image of St Anthony embroidered in gold thread on the back, making him look like a gnomic Elvis Presley. Now he has changed into a plain black cassock with a long row of buttons down the front. He has a short barrel figure, glasses, and a bald head with hair neatly clipped around his ears. He seems a little out of sorts. Without bothering to greet us, he tells Marcella to be at his house in ten minutes.

Then he hobbles out of the vestry and off down the street.

We shadow him through the village at a respectful distance. We mustn't crowd him, says Marcella nervously. We must give him some time. She says that she feels happy now, and has forgotten all the trouble the priest has caused.

Inside the priest's house, there's no evidence of his supposed riches. We're in a small, cluttered room containing a large fridge, several bookcases and some hard chairs. Rows of Christian volumes and several very substantial dictionaries (Italian-French, Italian-Greek and Italian-German) line the bookcases. The table is heaped with a pile of mail and some issues of *Gesù* and *Famiglia Cristiana*, still in their cellophane wrappings. The walls are covered with pictures: a decorative plate with a scene of Jerusalem, a photo of Padre Pio, a plastic table mat of the birds of Australia, and a bronze relief of an Aboriginal man throwing a boomerang. (I later discover Padre Perrino has a sister who lives in Adelaide.) Behind the door is a rack containing more correspondence; at the front I can see a postcard from the Philippines.

This isn't at all what I expected of the priest's house. I can't tell much from one room, but it seems to me he's a well-educated man with a hankering for distant shores. Maybe the village is just too small for him, and he's taken out a lifetime of frustration in little acts of spite and unhelpfulness. Maybe, as the focus of village gossip, his eccentricity and surliness are his only means of protection. I begin to feel a slight sympathy for the infamous priest, who is now enthroned in a high-backed chair. Mind you, he hasn't offered us any refreshments, surely a calculated insult in Sicily, where food is everything.

Now he's waving an envelope covered in American stamps at Tina. If this letter was posted in Chicago on the sixth and has already arrived, he asks, why hasn't Tina's confirmation certificate come from the Sacred Heart in New York yet?

Marcella shakes her head and tut-tuts. You never know, she says mournfully, where you are with the Italian post office.

Padre Perrino grunts, and this seems to exhaust the conversational niceties. He slots a video into his machine and sits in silence as we watch it. Claudia looks bored and Tina annoyed. Marcella, ever the peacemaker, is attentive as shots of the galaxy, the night stars, jumping gazelles, a reef of fish and the Great Ocean Road come up on the screen. The theme, apparently, is the wonders of the world as created by the Almighty. It has barely come to an end when Padre Perrino jabs the video out of the machine and shoves another one into it. I glean a bit about the guidance of the Holy Spirit, which is about to imbue Claudia with wisdom, right judgement and reverence.

There's a silence as the video comes to an end an hour later. Then Padre Perrino suggests Claudia and Tina should come back tomorrow for more videos. Claudia is sullen; she's supposed to be going shopping in Messina the next day. Marcella quells her with a look. Tina's face is stony and she doesn't say whether she'll be there tomorrow or not. No doubt the priest's lazy way of preparing for the confirmation is irritating her. These videos seem more suited to Sunday school children than adults.

'Thank you *Monsignor*, the videos were beautiful,' says Marcella, who has watched them reverently throughout. 'Of course we shall come back tomorrow.'

Then she pushes us all out into the street. Claudia barely lingers long enough to say goodbye before rushing off to the gym that's supposed to be Marcella's garage, where she's going to meet her friends. Tina flounces back home in a threatening silence. She doesn't want to watch videos about God's miracles, clearly. She no longer really wants to be a godmother at all, for that matter, even if once she thought it was a great idea. Still, she's too far in to go back now, and I think she might as well get on with it with good grace.

But that isn't going to happen. Tina storms into the kitchen and bangs about laying the table. Then when we're all seated for lunch she announces that she doesn't believe Jesus is the Son of God anyway—he's just an historical figure.

'He's a prophet all right, but he's not *God*.'

Immediately Giuseppe is shouting. 'So what are you then, a Mussulman?'

'No, I'm a Christian. A Catholic,' says Tina in confusion. 'I don't know what I am.'

'You're in need of the mercy of Jesus!' shouts Giuseppe helpfully.

It seems we're in for a long evening. Part of me is horrified at the tack Tina is taking, but, I have to confess, another part is secretly enjoying the new drama. Tina's now claiming that she doesn't believe in saints and miracles either. And she certainly doesn't want to go to confession. Confession is another thing she doesn't believe in. Why should she tell all her private thoughts to a stranger?

'Well, not *all* Concettina,' says Marcella soothingly. 'Only since the last time.'

'Ma, that was ten years ago!'

Marcella turns pale. 'Dear God!' she exclaims, aghast.

A stunned silence follows. We sup our *minestra*, a simple soup with tiny flower-shaped pasta floating on the surface like delicate Chinese water lilies. The silence continues as Marcella clears away the soup plates and brings out the next course.

'You don't go to church no more?'

Tina turns to me. 'I don't frigging *believe* this. Now they think I've been going to church regularly!'

I say nothing, just dig into my *cuscus con pesce*. I've wanted to try it for weeks. Couscous came with the Arabs and is still considered one of the finest dishes in Sicily. Marcella's couscous comes butter-yellow, topped with generous pieces of flaky white fish and accompanied by a bowl of deep orange-red spicy sauce. I try to give it the attention it deserves as the conversation gallops away into Italian. Marcella's fingers are flying around as she crosses herself. There's a whole lot about *Cristo* again, and a few saints get dragged into the melee.

Giuseppe has given up roaring and bellowing and spoons up his couscous with a flushed face.

Suddenly Tina says in English: 'But I believe in *God*, of course. That's all.'

Marcella clutches at this ray of hope. She replies optimistically that as long as Tina believes in God there's really no problem. But Tina is off again into a self-righteous spiel about hypocrisy and lying and how can she go to confession and she never said she was a Mussulman anyway. She looks trapped and harried, and not only by her parents. Tina, I think to myself, has that endless Catholic guilt, that heightened awareness of retribution and sinfulness that will dog her all her life, even though she barely qualifies as a Catholic any more.

But what do I know? The Calasciones are in full Sicilian spate as I clatter around the kitchen making the coffee. I spoon out the grinds, measure the water and twist the lid on the metal pot. When the brew is ready Tina and her parents knock it back like medicine without seeming to notice, and then rage on. I sidle my peaceful Protestant soul out of the room and retreat to the balcony. The confirmation has been called into doubt once more, what with a godmother who might be a Moslem and certainly doesn't want to go to confession, an absolute requisite prior to the ceremony.

Maybe it's never going to happen. Maybe, I think as I sip my coffee, I'm going to miss out on a fine festival. And surely for a confirmation banquet you'd have a *cassata*—I wouldn't want to miss that. But these are selfish thoughts, and soon I turn to considering Tina. She's invited me to Sicily and exposed her family history, and on our little jaunts around the country we've grown close. Now she seems to be disintegrating into erratic behaviour under the relentless pressure of family expectations. She needs to be rescued, to get back on track, because if she leaves Sicily without a confirmation it will be an enormous blow to her fragile self-esteem—and an ongoing reason for parental complaint.

It's time to call on St Anthony, because if anything is lost, it's the lost cause of this confirmation. And failing St Anthony, I'll have to have a good talk to Tina, I tell myself. Something will have to be done.

5

POWER AND GLORY

Palermo is a terrifying city of belching traffic and buildings on the verge of collapse. Elegant Renaissance mansions crumble away, their blackened facades rotted by grime. Streaks of brown rust bleed from dilapidated balconies like the wounds of Christ in a hundred churches, and balconies themselves have dropped off houses, leaving twisted metal supports protruding from the walls like giant metal claws. I follow a map from one *piazza* to another and find waterless fountains strewn with litter, telephone lines sagging dangerously overhead, posters peeling from telegraph poles. Cars with battered fenders and missing wing mirrors are parked every-where, turning squares into wrecker's yards. Blackened streets choke on the exhaust fumes of a thousand honking Fiats and spluttering Vespas driven at reckless speeds by impatient teenagers. Police sirens wail as if lamenting the city's decay, and *putti* cling onto church fronts with mouths agape, astonished at the dilapidation.

Tina and I trudge around Palermo in a state of exhausted

alarm, then stumble inside a grimy church and gasp in aston-
ishment at the riot of colour inside. We stray into the hidden
courtyards of tumbledown palazzi and find wrought-iron
benches and palm trees. Above the litter of the fountains,
Roman emperors salute in fine polished marble. Behind the
grime Tina points out a fanfare of baroque moulding or a
saint waving from a rooftop. Palermo has moments of pure
undiluted poetry: a row of grinning skulls above a doorway,
sleek ravens in a cage outside a bar, a magnificent ceramic
vase sitting behind the lighted window of a sooty building.
In the disastrous architectural muddle of the cathedral the
Gothic entrance porch stuns me with its sculpted saints and
birds perched on leafy tendrils of stone. Down a tiny alley we
walk past an altar set into the wall, with a statue of the
Virgin lit by naked light bulbs. Beside the figurine there's a
bunch of fresh gladioli with crimson, curled petals, speckled
with droplets of water. Sweet scent lingers in the air like a
promise.

Palermo is a glorious, breathtaking, shocking city. It
seems the ugliest place on earth, but it hides a tender and
tantalising beauty. Traffic roars, dogs howl, police cars wail.
Then we step through a church door and silence envelops us
like a caress. Instead of blackened walls there are pillars of
soft grey stone. I sink down into the pews in dislocated
bewilderment. We've strayed into the Chapel of San Cataldo,
right in the heart of Palermo. Its thick walls muffle the
assault of the city, and cool light filters through the windows
to produce an aquarium calm. The brickwork is austere
except for a few palm-leaf flourishes on the tops of the
pillars in the nave. It seems a holy and contemplative place,

far from the extravagant excesses of a later era when baroque busybodies set about redecorating Sicilian churches. I like San Cataldo, maybe because it was founded by the Normans and has a feel of northern Europe about it; of cold grey skies, grey seas and misty fields. Only the floors are indulgent with an interlocking pattern of stars, diamonds and zigzags. When I suggest to Tina that this geometry seems very Islamic she raises her sunglasses with the cool boredom of a movie star and silently points at the inscriptions from the Koran that decorate the walls. And then I notice the arched and latticed windows and the Arab-style cupolas that bulge from the roof in a splash of red, as extraordinary as finding a camel in the meadows of Normandy.

The Normans had arrived in Sicily and were to preside over its finest hour, although they never threw off the influences of those who came before them. Arab control of the island began to crumble under internal discord, since the Arabs, far from being homogenous, were actually made up of rival Spanish Arabs, Berbers, Yemenis and North Africans. The Normans took advantage of their petty squabbles to storm Messina and Palermo and by 1091, after a thirty-year struggle, the whole of Sicily lay under their rule. They stayed on in a blaze of glory to create one of the island's most peaceful and prosperous eras and to build a lasting and vigourous artistic legacy. Palermo was one of Europe's greatest cities, full of exquisite monuments and countless pleasure gardens, surrounded by groves of lemon and orange trees. It became a leader in European silk production thanks to the demand for rich fabrics at the Norman court. Other luxuries included graceful public baths where, according to the fourteenth century writer Boccaccio, bathers sprinkled themselves with jessamine and extract of citron blossom, nibbled on crystallised fruit and sipped expensive wines. Contemporary travellers often compared the Sicilian capital to paradise.

If this luxury sounds faintly oriental it's no surprise. The Arabs might have been conquered but few of them actually left, and Arabic continued to be widely spoken. A number of influential positions in government were still held by Arabs, and the entire financial system was largely copied from the Islamic model. Several Norman kings actually used Arab titles on their coinage, and lived like emirs in palaces full of Moslem concubines, eunuchs and Negro bodyguards. Ibn Jubair, a contemporary Spanish Arab traveller stopping off on his way home from Mecca in 1184, was 'deeply impressed by the contentment of the king's Moslem subjects' and said that King William II resembled a Moslem himself, and could even read and write Arabic. The tolerance of the age is astonishing.

To see the ultimate glory of this cultural fusion I trek off to the Palatine Chapel, the ever-patient Tina in tow. This private chapel of the Norman kings is where some of the earliest and best Islamic decoration in the world can be found. Its ceiling shows figures wearing turbans or three-pointed Muslim crowns and musicians playing Middle Eastern instruments. Other mosaics are full of motifs common in Persian and Arab art: peacocks, birds holding leaves in their beaks, palm trees, falcons attacking animals, octagonal stars. The floor is made of inlaid marble and porphyry, the walls partly covered with marble and enamel, the aisles lined with

Corinthian columns. The walls and parts of the ceilings are lavishly covered with the Byzantine-style mosaics so beloved of the Normans, a million tiny tiles of glittering gold and blue. Around the cupola King Roger II ordered a dedication to be inscribed in the mosaic: *Roger mighty ruling king*. It was no idle boast, for Roger II was immensely tall, had a loud voice to match, and spent most of his life challenging the authority of popes and emperors. He reformed Sicilian law, patronised the arts and spoke fluent Arabic and Greek.

The chapel alone was enough reason for King Roger to feel smug; this is truly one of the world's most exquisite buildings. Jaded tourists troop in chattering noisily and then fall into a stunned silence. When I wander into the Palatine Chapel I forgive Palermo its noise, pollution, corruption and decay. I feel as if I've stumbled into a fallen piece of heaven, here in the nightmarish madness of Sicily's capital, and momentarily sense the presence of God.

Palermo is another escape for Tina, another sightseeing opportunity for me; most of all I want to investigate the capital's markets and restaurants, which are reputedly the best on the island. We've journeyed up here on the train and have found a *pensione* not far from the station in the heart of Palermo's old city. It occupies one floor of a grand old apartment building in a narrow alley. The ancient creaking lift doesn't look as if it has been upgraded since the 1930s. A massive iron grille has to be hauled open with a rattle, and then we push through wooden saloon doors before clanging the grille back into place and latching it together. Only then does the lift, jerking and groaning, haul us up to the third floor. Tina says it makes her feel like a detective in a black-and-white French movie.

The owner of the *pensione* is slightly deaf and very short-sighted. The only beautiful thing about her is her name, Rosalia. Her glasses are as thick as ashtrays and her grey hair sticks up everywhere. I can't imagine what her age might be; anything from an unkempt sixty to a well-preserved eighty. When she can tear her eyes away from the shrieking television she makes haphazard attempts to keep the place dusted, but she doesn't put herself out to make it homely. The front door is always locked and bolted, and each time she has to let us in she mutters and fusses before scurrying back to her television.

I give Rosalia my New South Wales driver's licence for registration purposes. Registration forms have to be lodged with the police, a tedious bureaucratic requirement that most hoteliers hurry through, but Rosalia is determined to fill in every last box and question, even though the forms and my licence seem to bewilder her. The pen scratches away hesitantly, and a fly buzzes against the window.

Finally, Rosalia is satisfied, and reluctantly hands back my licence. I feel as if I've been given a pass into a magic kingdom, but actually the *pensione* is old and shabby. Rosalia sits at the heart of it in a dim TV room with horsehair armchairs, wearing a see-through nightie that reveals sensible underwear and great sagging breasts. The bathroom is shared, although the shower gushes hot water—and besides, there's only one other guest. He seems to be a permanent resident, a middle-aged man with a sad face and slicked-back hair, who shuffles around all evening in beige pyjamas and fluffy slippers. He stares at us mournfully with eyes as black as pools of oil.

My room has a surprising amount of heavy wooden furniture: two bedside tables, a dresser, a wardrobe and a chest-of-drawers with huge metal keys. The brass bed has a mattress that sags in the middle like a trampoline; only by dragging it off the springs and onto the floor can I achieve the hardness I like. In one corner there's a sink with a fine crazy paving of cracks in its green enamel and a tap that hesitantly coughs up rust and sometimes surprises me with a trickle of clear water. More importantly, there's a writing desk; a huge massive expanse of battered wood with pigeonholes running along the back of it, more than enough space for a tumble of books and papers. A door communicates with Tina's room, the mirror image of my own.

Our shouted conversation with Rosalia has put Tina in an unaccountably good mood, and now that we're far from Montalto it seems a good moment to broach the subject of the confirmation. Wouldn't it be easier, I suggest, if she over-looked her revolutionary ideas on religion for the next couple of weeks? Does she really have doubts about Jesus? I don't think so; although it's a good way to rile her parents, it doesn't serve much useful purpose.

'Forget Jesus, forget your parents! They don't have anything to do with the main issue. All you have to do is go to the confirmation and act as grandmother.'

'*God*mother,' says Tina, giggling.

'Whatever . . . It's not as if Claudia expects you to be on hand day and night doling out religious guidance! She's probably just glad you live in Australia and she'll soon be out of reach of the moral lecturing you're supposed to dispense . . .'

Tina doesn't say much as I rant on, but she doesn't protest either. I have high hopes: Tina's is a mind that jumps from one thing to another and is easily influenced. She hums away to herself in the cool confines of the room, then sits down at the writing desk with her diary. Her pen scratches away on the paper, and outside the door the television mutters and laughs. I shrug to myself and lie on the bed, shaking out the *Giornale della Sicilia* in an attempt to interpret its stories of corruption, scandal and Mafia killings.

'It's the frigging *confession*,' says Tina. 'Would you want to tell all your sins to a stranger?'

'I dunno. Maybe I would. There's nothing like getting things off your chest, is there?'

With what I imagine to be great cunning I point out that Padre Perrino isn't even going to care. He'll have heard it all before, won't he: sex, lies, impure thoughts, whatever it is that Catholics worry about. It isn't as if Tina has gone out and assassinated a Palermo judge on the steps of the courthouse with a stolen army pistol, is it? (I've just read about that in the newspaper.) And here's my idea: she can go to confession in some other village, with some other priest, someone who doesn't know her or her family or anyone in Montalto. It'll be like confiding to a stranger on a bus, the sort of thing you do sometimes when you're travelling.

'Huh,' says Tina. She pretends not to sound impressed but I can see she's looking thoughtful.

I decide not to press the advantage, but just let the idea drop like a stone into a pond, hoping it will spread ripples over the next few days. Throwing my newspaper aside, I wrench open the louvered shutters that lead out onto the trembling balcony beyond. I lean gingerly on the rusted railings and look down into the alley. Over the next few days I spend quite a bit of time perched here, fascinated by the neighbours. A grandmother often sits on a low wooden stool outside her door, peeling potatoes one day and washing clothes the next, letting the suds run down the centre of the street. She hitches her skirt up around her thighs and wears Wellington boots. Her husband is skinny and forlorn, and dodders around the neighbourhood streets with a walking stick. He wears a grey suit and a dark tie. Whenever I say hello to him he looks startled and bewildered, and never answers. They're like lost characters from another age, and yet someone in the household owns a gleaming black BMW. It doesn't have any of the dents or dust of most Sicilian cars. It's perfectly clean, the panels polished like onyx, the seats upholstered in soft grey, the windows tinted against the sun. One day I see the old grandmother climb into the passenger seat, and it looks like some crazy mistake, some accident of time travel. I sit high up on my balcony, squinting down in wonder.

Apart from the neighbours, there isn't much activity in the back alley. Sometimes a woman in black wanders by with a bag of vegetables for lunch. Ten minutes later comes the chattering of a Vespa as its rider, girlfriend clinging to his back, takes a short cut to the Via Roma. Then the alley falls silent once more. Later in the evening it echoes with the yells and laughs of invisible children. At midnight I lie in bed and listen to bin lids banging. Sometimes I get up and watch a shuffling old man poke among the refuse, scrounging empty bottles and putting them in a rough hemp sack. *Bang, bang. Rattle. Clink.* I wait for the noise in anticipation, and only after the tramp has gone do I roll over and fall asleep.

I awake in gloom and throw back shutters to an explosion of sunlight. We have an early breakfast at a local bar, then bursts of sightseeing or aimless wandering. Then I return to the massive writing desk to scribble notes as Tina dozes next door. After a late lunch we retreat to our shuttered rooms once more as the afternoon sun reaches its glaring zenith. An evening perambulation, and perhaps a pizza with curled ham crisp at the edges and oozing splinters of cheese. Our frequent comings and goings annoy Rosalia, I know, but after all, there's never anyone else about. Soon she's back to her sofa. The television roars. Pipes gurgle. Bin lids bang as I fall asleep.

One evening another guest arrives, a handsome young northern Italian with a square, stubbled jaw and melting eyes. He breezes in with impeccable self-confidence, carrying a kitbag and wearing a dazzling pink shirt. He reminds me of a slender statue of the Archangel Michael in the local museum. The archangel's wings are curved and powerful as a bird of prey's, the face is sulky, and the boy stomps on a lion with one foot—a cross and petulant youth full of repressed violence. There are plenty of Michaels riding around Palermo on their Vespas, in sunglasses and two-day stubble. They simper and pout at the girls and probably defer to their mothers, but I can't help feeling they've already been sucked into the city's petty crime rackets and—who knows?—will one day be shooting judges.

The new guest has the same dangerous beauty. His arrival sends a frisson of shock through the sleepy *pensione*; he's so vibrant and sexy and purposeful. Rosalia clucks and fusses and writes down all his information on her forms. (His name is Antonio Runci and he comes from Milan.) Tina smoothes down her summer dress and shakes out her curls and raises her eyebrows at me. The long-term resident stares and shuffles his fluffy slippers in anxiety before creeping off to his room.

Antonio Runci sings in the shower, and it's like a blasphemy in the silence of the building. He pads through the corridors like a caged panther, and winks at me as he goes to his room.

In the morning he's gone, and the *pensione* slides into somnolence once more.

I head out of Palermo with Tina for a day trip to Monreale up in the hills nearby. Monreale is a town well known for its cathedral. In fact, the cathedral is the most famous in Sicily and one of the most splendid churches anywhere in the world. That doesn't make it easy to find since, in a fit of modesty, Monreale town council hasn't erected signposts directing visitors to the landmark. Every obscure town in Sicily has signs pointing to its cathedral, I tell Tina crossly, except for the one town that actually has a cathedral worth seeing. I get hopelessly lost in a confusing maze of one-way streets, half of which have been invaded by a weekly market. Leaning out of the passenger window, Tina says it's impossible to see the cathedral's spire, since her view is blocked by piles of aubergines and the black-clad rumps of Monreale matrons doing their shopping. The car is exceedingly hot. The streets are exceedingly narrow and become progressively steeper. I inch my way past cars abandoned by drivers tempted into a bit of shopping but untroubled by the obligation to find a parking space. Eventually we pop out onto a hillside above the town. We can see the cathedral now, squatting among a tangled mess of houses. It doesn't have a spire. It's also a long way back down the hill.

Driving in Sicily sends me into a panic, and I feel like stopping the car and lying down on the grass and staring at the clouds. That's just what William II (the Good) did after some hard hunting in these very hills in 1174. He was catching a bit of shuteye when the Virgin Mary took it upon herself to tell him about some treasure hidden nearby. The treasure had been buried by the king's father William I (the Bad), who was a bit of a manic depressive. Fearful of plots, he'd secretly buried most of his wealth around the countryside. Now, following the heavenly instructions of his dream, his son dug it up and dedicated the vast horde of gold to building Monreale cathedral. It wasn't to be any old church but a demonstration of the wealth and artistic vitality of Norman Sicily. The greatest architects and craftsmen of the time were summoned to the court from Greece, Arabia and Italy to work on it. When it was finished in 1176 Pope Alexander III felt moved to declare: 'No similar work has ever been created by any king since time began.' It was certainly the pinnacle of Norman art in Sicily and one of the triumphs of medieval Europe. The cathedral also represented a dazzling age that was shortly to disappear along with the Norman dynasty. William II, beavering away on his cathedral, forgot to have children, and would soon die prematurely without any heirs.

Like much of Norman Sicily, Monreale cathedral incorporates the finest of the island's many cultures. When we finally battle our way back down the hillside and park the car, I discover that some of these inclusions are quite literal—the columns of the aisles are stolen from Roman monuments and adorned with the heads of Greek goddesses. The ceiling's star motifs are Arab, just like the royal lions of the throne and tympanum and the geometric floor patterns picked out in coloured serpentine, jasper and porphyry.

It's only later that I notice these details, because as I step over the threshold I'm overwhelmed by the bold mosaic work that covers every inch of the walls. Surrounded by a three-dimensional wonder in aquamarine, green and gold, I feel as if I've stepped into a precious, illuminated manuscript that's been turned into a pop-up book. The mosaics are less stylised than those in the Palatine Chapel, more dynamic and realistic, as if Sicily has slowly taken over. They're even slightly amusing. Camels lope along with huge grins on their faces, an agile Noah leaps from the Ark with beard flying, and a worker with a pickaxe floats in the air over the Tower of Babel. As for the mourners unwrapping Lazarus, who has just clambered out of his tomb, they seem to be holding their noses against the putrid smell—or are they wiping tears of joy from their eyes? This is the Bible turned into a comic strip. Around the nave Eve is tempted, Abel murdered, Sodom destroyed and Abraham sacrificed while Jacob hesitates at the bottom of his ladder. In the aisles, Christ busies himself preparing for New Testament miracles among a gaggle of lepers covered in hideous black pustules, a blind man falling over things, and a madman in a straitjacket and chains.

We sit down on wooden chairs and gaze at the vast Christ Pantocrator that dominates the central apse. Every golden glint on his tunic, every fold in his blue robe is lovingly detailed. He faces the length of the cathedral, one arm upraised in blessing, fingers long and tapering. An expression of infinite compassion transforms his gaunt, ascetic face; the soulful heavy-lidded eyes seem to look right at us. Tina is silent beside me. All we want to do is sit and stare back, and marvel.

Outside, the sun explodes in my eyes like a photographer's flash. Noise, heat and dust close in. No hope of the Virgin Mary turning up in Monreale these days, I think to myself, even in a dream. Cars honk and tailgate all the way back to Palermo, where we're sucked back into the maw of the grimy city. I sit timidly at red lights as the rest of the traffic speeds on around me and wonder at the paradox of Sicily, caught between extremes of the sublime and the ridiculous.

At lunch time the next day, encountering unexpected rain, I return from some sightseeing to the *pensione*, where to my amazement I see Tina and Rosalia deep in giggly conversation. Rosalia has abandoned her nightie. She's actually made a bit of an effort with her appearance: a bright crooked smear of lipstick, a pink slide in her hair, a comfortable but presentable cardigan. Her glasses have been polished to a shine. She has blue eye shadow the same colour as her cardigan, and too much powder on her cheeks, accentuating her wrinkles.

Rosalia has barely spoken to me for days, but now she

seems positively glad to see me, raking my arm with her fingernails. She's clutching an enormous wineglass full of plonk and I think she might be a bit drunk. This is confirmed when, in a burst of rash friendliness, she invites us to have lunch with her. She's just cooking some simple *pasta a picchi pacchi*, she says, and look at the rain, you could drown in it if you went out again.

I'm flattered by this new side to Rosalia's character. I love *picchi pacchi* too, as much for its delightful name as its strong flavour. We follow Rosalia into her kitchen, where she pours us some wine and sets about shredding basil leaves with startling ferocity. Then she hacks away at an enormous handful of garlic cloves. By this time I'm used to the alarming amounts of garlic used in Sicilian cuisine; indeed, I've come to positively enjoy it. At the rate Rosalia is chopping we'll all be reeking like peasants tonight. Who cares; I find garlic quite fascinating. The garlic on the table looks shabby and misleading, hiding behind its discouraging grey-white skin and uninspiring shape. It's the Cinderella of the kitchen, never able to match the taunting scarlet of its step sister, chilli, or the fibrous strength of ginger, which twists itself into interesting free-from shapes. But then Rosalia picks up a knife, and slices it in half, and garlic is suddenly triumphant, aggressively assaulting the senses and demanding attention.

Rosalia's kitchen is much the same as the rest of the *pensione*, an enormous room with a dizzying ceiling, an ancient stove and a refrigerator that ought to be in a museum. There are a couple of battered old dressers of Gargantuan proportions that look as if they've been looted from a medieval castle. They're weighed down with bags of mushrooms and tomatoes, jars of oil and bottles of wine as if Rosalia entertains on a lavish scale, although I've never seen a soul come or go. An enormous green platter stands on the windowsill, piled high with lemons, splashing the old-fashioned room with bold colour.

Rosalia takes anchovy fillets out of an enormous jar and starts mashing them with a fork. The plate jumps and clanks on the tabletop. Then she throws her onions, garlic and basil into a pan where they sizzle gently as she adds the anchovy paste. The sharp tang hits the back of my nose as we make desultory talk about Palermo. Rosalia takes a sip of her red wine and looks out of the window and takes another sip. Her hand trembles as she sets it down. There are no rings on her fingers, and no nail varnish. Her hand looks cruelly naked as she starts ripping the skins off blanched tomatoes and dicing them up.

Rosalia asks Tina to put the *maccheroni* on to boil. Here in Sicily *maccheroni* is a general term for any kind of dried pasta; Rosalia's *maccheroni* is actually spaghetti, and Tina drops handfuls of it into a pot, pushing it down into the water with a wooden spoon.

'So what about Sicilians?' I ask Rosalia. 'I'd like to know more about them.'

She cocks her head to one side thoughtfully. Behind her the tomatoes are now simmering along nicely in the pan along with the other ingredients, and the smell is making me hungry. Tina has wandered over to the window, where she seems mesmerised by the rain.

'The Sicilians! I'll tell you what you need to know about them for all those notes you scribble in your room. The

Sicilians are sad about everything.' Rosalia peers into the bubbling pot of sauce. She sprinkles in some salt and a few twists of ground pepper.

'Sad?'

'Oh yes! That's their leading characteristic. They're sad for the past—nostalgic, you know. They go away to America and your Australia and they're sad because they aren't in Sicily. But they're sad if they stay, because Sicily is a sad place. See? That's all you need to know about Sicilians.' She shrugs her shoulders and gives me a grimace.

The *pasta a picchi pacchi* is ready. The sauce has been mixed into a great pot full of spaghetti and Rosalia doles it out on a plate the size of a cartwheel. It smells magnificent.

'You're not Sicilian?' I ask, puzzled by Rosalia's accusing tone. But Rosalia hunches her shoulders and doesn't answer me, gazing down distractedly at her spaghetti. Tina slides into the chair beside mine.

We tuck into the meal in silence, as the rain splatters on the window and spaghetti sauce oozes across our plates like blood.

Many people, even Italians, believe that Marco Polo brought spaghetti to Italy from China in 1295. He didn't. Marco Polo has gained an absurd legendary status and is quite wrongfully attributed with all sorts of things. Frankly, the man's not to be trusted. For a start, he forgot to mention the Great Wall, chopsticks and tea drinking, three things you'd imagine he ought to have noticed while on a business trip to China, especially as they were all unknown in Europe at the time. What's more, he never mentions noodles in his *Travels*, even though the Chinese had been eating them for more than a thousand years. You'd think that if he'd carted noodles back to Italy he would trumpet them in his book. Of course, maybe he was just too modest to boast about his noodle imports. Perhaps he was too busy writing about the other things he came across, such as men with dog's tails and eagles large enough to carry away elephants.

I told you he was unreliable. So let me tell you this: merchants in Genoa were already referring to pasta in 1279, when a basket of macaroni is listed among other items in the inventory of one deceased Ponzio Bastone. This is the first written evidence of the presence of pasta on the Italian mainland, a full sixteen years before Marco Polo's return from China. In fact, the whole myth of spaghetti's Chinese origin was traced by one Italian historian to a single article entitled 'A Saga of Cathay' that appeared in the American *Macaroni Journal* in the 1920s.

'So much for the great Marco Polo!'

In Palermo I'm developing a pasta passion that starts in Rosalia's kitchen and moves on to local restaurants. Right now Tina and I are sitting in a cheap trattoria near the cathedral with battered metal tables under a yellow awning, watching women with poodles totter along the pavement. Our waiter has heavy jowls and a bristling grey moustache and looks like Saddam Hussein. He flicks at flies and dust with his tea towel and lounges against a mammoth pot of marigolds, and whenever he meets my eye he smiles encouragingly. When our *pasta con le sarde* is ready he presents it to us with the flourish this extraordinary dish deserves. 'Discordant but exhilarating' says one Italian cookery writer of the rich ingredients: pine nuts, dark green fennel leaves, and elegant silvered fresh sardine fillets from which the dish derives its name. Black, corrugated raisins stud the pasta and I'm glad to see they're comfortably fat, hopefully indicating they've been soaked in water to draw off their excess sugar. Everything has been piled on top of long strands of pasta glistening with red tomato sauce.

'So pasta didn't come from China. Where did it come from?' asks Tina, spearing a sardine and, for once, encouraging me to talk about food.

Well, I tell her, patriotic Italians like to claim pasta has existed in Italy since the earliest times, relying on a convenient lack of convincing evidence to support their case. All I'm going to say is this: the first records of 'modern' dried pasta came out of Arab Sicily. Maybe the Arabs brought it there, though that's unclear. Various types of noodle called *rishta, itriya, sha'riya* and *fidawsh* were eaten in Persia and frequently mentioned in Islamic cookery books, in which they're cooked in meat stock and served with lentils and meat. Some historians claim pasta was developed by the Arabs as a method of transporting non-perishable food across the desert.

'Nobody really knows,' I sum up to Tina. 'So all I can say is pasta seems to have originated in Sicily during Arab times.'

Only one thing is certain: pasta is Sicily's greatest contribution to world gastronomy. The dish we're eating right now, *pasta con le sarde*, is a traditional recipe from western Sicily supposedly invented during the Arab occupation and therefore perhaps one of the earliest pasta dishes ever. As we tuck into our lunch under the watchful eye of Saddam Hussein there certainly seems something vaguely Islamic about the skinny strands of pasta coloured with saffron, not to mention the toasted pine nuts and raisins. But I'm wary of drawing too many culinary conclusions, since all the ingredients of the sauce, except for the tomatoes, have been available since classical times. In fact, the Romans had a habit of using pine nuts and raisins, and Apicius suggests a sweet-and-sour sauce made with pine nuts, raisins, mint, honey and vinegar. The recipe isn't much different from *pasta con le sarde* and appears strikingly 'Arab' in concept.

How it started is still a bit of a mystery, but by Norman times pasta was being produced on a large scale on the island. It's mentioned in a survey known as *The Book of Roger* after King Roger II, who ordered it. 'To the west of Termini lies the town of Trabia . . . where they manufacture *itriya* in such great quantity as to supply both the towns of Calabria and those of the Muslim and Christian territories as well, to where large shipments are sent.' *Itriya* is the Persian word for 'string', and from the context it's perfectly clear that it was a type of pasta. Long, skinny strands of pasta are still called *tria* in Sicilian dialect. Spaghetti, of course, is Italian for 'little string'.

By the twelfth century, pasta was being exported north-wards to other parts of Italy, but being very expensive was slow in catching on, and eaten only by the aristocratic classes. Sacchetti's *Trento Novelli* of 1397 contains a scene in which a Florentine lord upbraids his steward for ostentatiously eating pasta in the face of people's poverty. Even in eighteenth-century Britain someone who travelled widely and acquired foreign tastes was known as a macaroni; a pejorative term, of course, but also one that implied wealth and elegance, as in the song about the famous Yankee Doodle dandy. Even the name macaroni, it has been suggested, was derived from the exclamation of a Neapolitan prince on first trying the dish: *Si buoni, ma caroni!* ('Yes, good, but so expensive!')

Our *pasta con le sarde* certainly hasn't come cheap. Tina doesn't like it much. I find it intriguing and worth the try, although sardines have never thrilled me. Saddam Hussein whisks our plates away and seems to hesitate in shocked disapproval at the fennel I've left on the side of mine; it's one of the few things I really can't abide. He recovers in time to take our order for *secondo*. The fact that pasta remains a *primo* not to be indulged to excess is perhaps a reminder of its formerly expensive place in the kitchen. Pasta can sometimes still seem luxurious. In Mazara I had *stracciatella con polpettine e pastina*, a light soup containing tiny grains of *orzi* pasta, as well as beaten egg, carrot, onion, courgette and miniature dumplings made from sausage meat and turkey—a glorious little dish that costs more than an entire meal. In Lípari I had another pricey pasta, skinny *taglierini* noodles cooked in fragrant saffron and covered in a buttery sauce containing tomatoes, garlic, dry white wine, bream and swordfish fillets. The chunky sauce is a fine counterbalance to the delicately thin pasta, the harmony and aesthetics perfect, the pasta worth every penny.

One of the great glories of pasta is that it can be either refined or simple. Rosalia's *pasta a picchi pacchi* is inexpensive but delicious, and the spaghetti we had at Carmela's house in Montalto was even simpler, with nothing more than olive oil and garlic for dressing. I travel around Sicily indulging in my pasta passion. Marcella drizzles butterfly-shaped pasta with a sauce of garlic, green olives, parsley and zippy dried chilli to produce *farfalle con pepperoni arrostiti*. She tops the whole thing with slices of roasted red and yellow peppers to add glossy colour and crunch, letting the sweet smoky juices soak into the pasta. In Marsala I have gnocchi bursting with puréed potato and covered with tomato sauce and mozzarella, then baked for the briefest time so that the cheese melts richly over the pasta. In Selinunte Tina indulged in a slightly more carnivorous pasta, *ravioli di zafferano*, filled with spinach, sausage and tomato in a splendid trio of colour.

This is the power of pasta; it can be as simple or as complex as you want, and its variations are practically end-less. You can boil it, bake it, stuff it, have it hot or cold, do just about anything with it except eat it raw. Whoever created it mightn't have realised its amazing versatility, because pasta got off to a slow start and didn't really come into its own until the nineteenth century. But there in Sicily, way back in the Middle Ages, was born one of the greatest culinary inventions ever to emerge from the kitchens of man. Or woman, of course.

But certainly not of Marco Polo.

Down near the harbour, Palermo's old town disintegrates into a seedy quarter known as Vucciria, where the air is thick with vice and corruption. A local crime boss named Tano kept his four sisters immured behind the walls of Vucciria because, according to gossip, he loved them so much he couldn't contemplate them meeting other men and getting married.

Recently Tano was killed in a gangland murder, though I don't know what became of his sisters. On street corners huddles of men in black jackets sneer at passers-by and are probably dealing in drugs or forged papers for hapless Tunisian immigrants. They leer at Tina and wolf-whistle as she hurries along the footpath. We edge past a man with a scar on the back of his hand and shifty eyes, who offers me an ancient Greek coin, probably stolen.

The only reason we're wandering nervously down these alleys is that Vucciria is home to Palermo's best market. It used to be the best in all of Sicily, but most people lament its decline, even though 'when Vucciria dries up' is a Palmeritan expression similar to 'hell freezing over'. I don't know what the market used to be like, but it still seems to be thriving nicely, piled high with glorious lemons, stacked like a treasure trove from the palace of an Arabian prince. I inspect baskets of twitching snails the size of my thumb, coarse hemp sacks full of chickpeas and white kidney beans, and platters of sugared pineapple discs and candied orange peel. Twisted plaits of garlic hang from the backs of wooden chairs. The pavements are heaped with purple-striped *borlotti* pods, a variety of bean prized by Italians but hardly ever seen anywhere else. The bean inside is a beautiful deep red-purple, though the colour disappears on cooking, leaving a creamy brown-skinned bean frequently used in soups and pasta.

'Eh Franco,' shouts an old woman. 'I hear your cousin is down from Padua for a visit, and how much are these lemons? Sixty *centesimi*! That's a thousand two hundred lire in old money, you thief!'

At every corner, stall owners wash and polish their wares until they come up shiny as soldiers' boots. We pass piles of glossy peppers red as lava, gold as Byzantine mosaics, passionate purple. Local women hold them in their cupped palms carefully, checking them for weight and a skin thick enough to roast. Cardinal-red tomatoes are lined up in rows and bought by the crateful, succulent aubergines sit plump as bowling balls, and figs from Africa (it isn't quite the fig season in Sicily yet) tumble across wooden trestles. Even the flowers—roses, carnations, lilies—are stunning, every petal perfection.

'Holy Mary, yesterday I only paid fifty *centesimi* for lemons at a stall on the Via Roma. Has there been a disaster, an invasion of locusts, to raise the price so dramatically?'

I love these Sicilian markets; they're a celebration of the glories of food and the joy to be found in freshness and variety. Sicilians and Italians in general still don't care much for lonely supermarkets and have little interest in ready-made convenience foods; they have fewer supermarkets and smaller fridges than anyone else in Europe. Fresh is best. The only fast foods you can find in Vucciria are cooked artichokes and potatoes bought straight from bubbling cauldrons, deep-fried calf spleen, or aubergine slices and lamb from charcoal grills ready to be taken home as *antipasti*.

'Fifty? *Bene*. God bless you. I have to say you have the best lemons in all Palermo, Franco . . .'

The rhythm of nature and the song of the seasons direct eating habits in Sicily; Sicilians are tuned in to their geography and the agriculture, to the fluctuating supply of whatever fruit and vegetables are locally available. Sicilians know that the most flavoursome potatoes come from Avezzano in Abruzzo, the juiciest onions from Tropea across the Straits of Messina, the choicest cherries from Marostica near Venice. Better yet is the produce straight from local farms. The potatoes in the Vucciria market still smell of the soil they were planted in, the zucchinis come with blossoms attached, the tips of the curling chilli peppers are bright scarlet. In Vucciria I watch Sicilian matrons buy handfuls of orange and cream mushrooms with slow care, no doubt imagining how they'll sautée them in garlic and parsley. As for the parsley itself, they know the stems are less strongly flavoured than the leaves—perfect for adding to light soups. Shoppers caress the plump flesh of aubergines, touch flaking garlic skins to check for freshness, inspect the outer layers of fennel bulbs for a healthy glow. Mottled purple bruising at an artichoke's base means it has been affected by frost, any Sicilian knows that. But that's a good thing with an artichoke, only adding to its sweetness.

'You know, Franco, I'm making *macedonia di frutta* for my sister who's coming up from Agrigento. Did I tell you she was bitten on the leg by a dog while she was *in church* if you can believe such a thing . . .'

And I drift away, a smile on my face, knowing that markets aren't just about food but about sociability. These old ladies can spend hours here, chatting and shopping, and will never know the alienation and loneliness of supermarkets. Marcella once mentioned that almost the first thing she does when getting back to Sicily, after six months of antiseptic, antisocial shopping in America, is to head for the market.

Thinking of Marcella, I realise we ought to be heading

back to Montalto. Tina reluctantly agrees, knowing that the confirmation is set for Saturday. In Monreale, perhaps moved by the mosaics, Tina told me she might as well give in and perform her godmotherly duties without any more fuss, even if it does mean watching endless videos with the priest and going to confession. With the event now rapidly approaching, she seems eager to get it all over with as soon as possible.

'It won't be long now, will it?' she says.

'No,' I answer comfortingly, not knowing how wrong I am.

We say our farewells to Rosalia, who seems a bit sad to see us go. We leave her to the blaring television and speed back eastwards along the motorway. The car is perfumed with bright lemons, bought from Vucciria in a sack, and aubergines tumble at our feet.

The next day I'm driving more sedately with Marcella beside me, down a narrow rutted lane to a house at the bottom of the village. We're on another shopping spree, another search for freshness. We pull up at a shed lined with deep, tiled sinks in which *stoccafisso* is soaking; the cod introduced to Sicily by the Normans. Cod was among the few unadventurous products the Normans brought to Sicily with them from their cold northern seas; salted and smoked herring and fish rolls (*involtini*) were others. While the Norman imagination soared in art and architecture, in the kitchen it collapsed like an overcooked soufflé; the Normans weren't inspired by food. Still, their tolerance of Islamic culture extended to the kitchen, and Norman cookbooks were greatly influenced by the Arab cuisine of their territories in Sicily and Antioch.

Despite the few innovations of Norman times, Sicilian cuisine remained fine and varied.

I peer in at the dried half-fishes the length of my arm as they soak in brine. Marcella pokes through them with a finger and they turn lazily in the currents of water she stirs up. Cod was probably the first commercial fish in Europe. Before the twelfth century fish had been something of a luxury item, difficult to transport and keep fresh. One reason for the popularity of eels back then was that they could live for several days out of the water. Improved drying and preserving processes meant increasing fish commercialisation, but it wasn't until the mid-fourteenth century that a Dutchman invented a system for gutting, salting and storing fish in barrels on fishing smacks at sea. Much of the wealth of northern European ports was built on the discovery, which enabled cod from the recently discovered Newfoundland banks to be easily transported back to Europe. Cod was preferred because it was both easy to catch and kept exceptionally well—anything up to several years—when dried or salted.

Cod was in great demand in medieval times, when the consumption of meat was forbidden on countless religious feast days. It became popular in Sicily, too. It might seem strange that this Mediterranean island acquired a taste for a northern fish, but its supply was both cheaper and more certain than anything that could be caught locally. These days, cod is still often served on Fridays in Sicily (a meatless day in the Catholic tradition) and is considered a delicacy. Thanks to overfishing of the Atlantic cod banks, however, it's no longer cheap.

Cod has one drawback: it isn't terribly easy to prepare. 'Beat it soundly with a Mallet for half an hour or more and lay it three days a soaking, then Boyle it on a simmering Fire about an hour,' begins one recipe from 1682. Fortunately the cod we're about to buy has already been beaten and rehydrated. Marcella rejects several of them—they're too yellow—before selecting one that's suitably pale. She lifts it out by the tail, and I see it's been almost completely flattened in the drying process. Most cod is dried in the Netherlands these days, Marcella tells me; all they do in Sicily is soak it. I'm not sure if she disapproves of the foreign processing or of the little the cod-seller has to do for his money. I wait outside in the back yard, a riot of roses and lemon trees heavy with fruit, as she haggles over the price.

Back at home, Marcella soaks the cod some more in a bucket in the kitchen, picking at its edges and nibbling at it. It's the only way to know if it's ready, she tells me, since soaking depends on the fish's thickness, its saltiness, how you want to cook it. Apparently satisfied, she prepares a traditional eastern Sicilian dish of *stocca alla messinese*, a rich tomato stew containing onions, carrots, celery and potatoes as well as the fish. The cod is slightly chewy but more tender than I expected, almost creamy, and lacking the highly salty flavour I anticipated. The sauce is a deep red flecked with yellow, full of mottled green olives and piquant capers, and we soak it up with crusty bread. Tina slumps in her chair looking relaxed, drinking a homemade rosé that's almost orange, the mellow colour of distilled sunlight. The break in Palermo has done her good and so far she's maintained a truce with her parents, behaving with the calm and poise of a mosaic saint.

When we've mopped up the last of the rich juice with our bread crusts the talk turns to Maria, a dear friend who Marcella saw a lot of during the days we were away in Palermo. They were schoolchildren together, and confirmed together, and Marcella was a bridesmaid at Maria's wedding fifty years ago. Anyway several years ago, Marcella explains to us, Maria was diagnosed with breast cancer, which had already spread throughout her body. The doctors said nothing could be done. Marcella thought otherwise, and wrote to another friend, a woman who runs a souvenir shop in San Giovanni on the mainland. In her letter she asked that special prayers be said for Maria over the tomb of Padre Pio, a local monk recently canonised by the Vatican.

Marcella explains to us that she has great faith in the holy monk because she knows a Pennsylvanian woman who was cured through his intervention. As she scrapes up her tomato sauce with a crust of bread she tells us that San Giovanni is a beautiful place, for she's been there herself several times.

'Very restful. It isn't a peace of this world but of another,' Marcella says, licking her fingers. 'Standing in front of the tomb of Padre Pio is an unbearably moving experience.'

Well, a few days after she wrote the letter, Marcella was driving along the road to Patti when suddenly she smelt a delicious perfume, a perfume of roses and all the flowers of the world, that filled the car. Marcella slowed down and looked around her. She could still smell the fragrance, and wondered whether there was a perfume factory somewhere. She shouted to a local farmer in his olive field, but he assured her there was no such place near Patti. It was only when she had reached home that Marcella realised the significance of the heavenly fragrance, because there in the letterbox was a message waiting for her.

'The monks of San Giovanni had said a special prayer over Padre Pio's tomb, and I felt sure the Gracious Lord was watching over Maria!'

Marcella pauses to bring out the *provoletta*, shaped like a giant pear and covered with waxy, soft yellow rind. She cuts it in half and we use our knives to slice portions off the pale, almost white flesh. The meal is rounded off with Japanese medlars. The egg-sized fruit is soft and should be eaten almost overripe; hard medlars are acidic. The velvety orange skin is mottled with brown spots. I peel off the thin skin with my fingers, revealing a paler orange, grainy flesh. Large seeds fall out; underneath their papery brown coating they're a startling pale green. Medlars are a symphony of colour, a beautiful juicy sweet fruit with a taste that recalls apricots. Tina loves them, and eats one after another. Like everything else, they've been bought straight from the market, carefully selected by Marcella—a triumph of considerate shopping.

'So everything was OK, Ma? You know, with Padre Pio and all?'

Yes, says Marcella. That very same night of the strange fragrance, Maria had a vivid dream in which she saw the face of God, so large it covered the whole sky. She felt a calmness and happiness such as she'd never felt before washing over her, and was so transported she could hardly speak. Finally, she plucked up the courage to ask God for a few more years to look after her five-year-old granddaughter. According to Marcella, God didn't seem at all put out by the demand. On the contrary, he kindly asked exactly how many years Maria needed. She managed to stammer that a couple would do.

'Of course, when I heard this I was distraught! Imagine only asking for a couple of years! As if Maria couldn't have asked for more!'

Giuseppe suggests sourly that Maria might have been a bit intimidated, what with the face of God bending over her. Then he's away from the table; he never lingers after meals, but is impatient to be off to the piazza. Tina, Marcella and I are left behind to finish off with coffee and homemade chocolate balls. Now that I've settled into the swing of life in Montalto, it's become a familiar routine. My friendship with the Calasciones is growing, and Marcella especially is opening up to me during these after-lunch coffee sessions. She tells me about her family and her childhood, and her talk becomes increasingly more revealing. Sometimes I think I'm merely a go-between, a method by which Marcella can talk to her daughter about her troubled life; a filtered plea for understanding. It's a good sign that Tina lingers, trying to understand her mother and her past.

When the coffee is ready Marcella picks up the thread of her story. After the dream Maria's cancer really did go into remission, and for the last two years she seemed so well as to have beaten the cancer entirely. Then only a few weeks ago Maria had another dream in which the Virgin Lady appeared to her and told her that they'd soon meet face to face in heaven.

'Instead of being afraid, Maria was filled with calm.' Tears seep from Marcella's eyes as she recalls the conversation. From that moment on the cancer had returned with a vengeance, spreading so rapidly that there now seems little hope for Maria.

'That's why I've been spending so much time with her. Soon Maria will be with the sweet Mother of God, full of heavenly gifts . . .'

We finish our coffee in silence and sighs, and for the rest of the evening Marcella is sunk in melancholy. The next morning Maria herself telephones Marcella to tell her she's going into hospital in Barcellona. Marcella isn't to worry, there's nothing wrong, only she feels so weak.

Marcella is on the verge of hysteria; she heard a dog barking the night before, always an augur of death in Sicily. After a fretful morning Tina drives her mother over to the hospital, where she spends the afternoon by Maria's bedside. In the late afternoon her friend slips into a coma. All the while, Marcella tells me later, there are tears pouring down Maria's cheeks, so many that they soak the pillow. Marcella has never seen so many tears.

Late at night one of Maria's sons persuades an exhausted Marcella to go home. Marcella roams the rooms of Aunt Rita's house distractedly, looking old and lost. I'm sitting with her in the kitchen two days later when the phone rings once more: Maria has passed away.

Marcella hangs up. She sits down and starts to sob.

And I think: not only has her best friend died, but soon in the middle of all her grief she will realise the confirmation will have to be postponed again, and there'll be another family drama. It won't happen at the weekend now, since Maria's son has said the funeral will be on Saturday. The priest will be busy, and half the village will be in mourning.

Then Marcella starts to talk to me about her friend, about their lives and how they've intertwined over sixty years. Marcella is a sad woman whose husband and daughters will never offer her comfort—and, more cruel still, she accepts that she has only herself to blame. In the dusk of her life she's alienated from her family, drifting between two countries, slowly losing all the ties that bind her to either.

I sit and hold her hand as she weeps.

There's only one thought that really comforts Marcella. Maria, she's been told, died beautifully, like a saint, with her long hair spread out on the pillow, and the smell of perfume in the air.

6

ASHES AND DUST

A gaunt grey horse bolts across the field, pink lips curled back in a terrifying snicker, long black mane flying. The horse is huge but emaciated. The ribcage stands out starkly, and every tendon and muscle on its neck and flailing legs is painfully stretched. The animal is ridden by a glaring skeleton carried away by the thrill of the gallop; his left hand is raised high, about to smack down on the sweating flanks of the horse, urging it onwards with even greater speed. In his other hand the skeleton holds a bow from which he lets fly deadly arrows at a crowd of panicked nobles. Some have already fallen, their shrunken faces grimacing in terror. They cower under the horse's hooves in a great tumble of embroidered surcoats, ermine hems, mitres and velvet gowns. Behind them, oblivious to the unfolding drama, two musicians play on a lute and harp while an aristocrat fusses with the hunting falcon on his gloved wrist. In another corner a huddle of peasants and nuns in wimples has been ignored; the speeding rider has already galloped past. There's a certain

Sicilian satisfaction in knowing they've gone unnoticed while landowners, barons and princes of the church get their come-uppance. Ironically, though, those who've been spared look unhappy, old and sick. They turn to the wild mounted skeleton almost longingly, hands clasped, faces beseeching, praying for the release of death.

Those who crave it are ignored; those who least expect it get struck down. No wonder the fresco is called *The Triumph of Death*. The masterpiece, executed on four massive slabs of flat stone during the mid-fifteenth century by an unknown artist, hangs in the Palazzo Abatellis in Palermo. It's just one of the many places where death turns up in Palermo in images of terrifying immediacy and power, nowhere more so than in the Capuchin crypt, a place that has become something of a ghoulish tourist site. There are eight thousand preserved bodies in the crypt, dressed in their best finery, belonging to notable members of local families who died between the seventeenth and nineteenth centuries. Many are eviscerated and embalmed in vinegar and herbs, others have simply dried out in the arid air of the catacombs until leached of all their moisture. They stand pinned to the walls of the crypt, different passageways being reserved for different professions and social ranks: clergy here, doctors there. A fat bishop with brooding eyelids and a crumbling chin stands with a silk mitre on his head, surrounded by priests. Virgins line up along one corridor, wives along another.

Many of the corpses are identified by name and even have their addresses pinned to their clothes, which must have made it easier for relatives to find them when they came for a visit. After a while, as the clothes slowly faded and rotted and their features caved in, these dead kinsfolk would have been difficult to recognise; many have the same leathery, shrivelled look as the dried cod cooked by Marcella. Mice and the passage of time have nibbled away at the bodies. Arms and legs have dropped off and are fixed on again in a grotesque puppetry of flesh and wire. Some bodies have been sewn up in burlap sacking to stop them disintegrating. The mortal remains of Salvatore Manzella are bundled up in a white tunic, sewn with twine down the front to stop him splitting open—rather appropriately, since in life he was a noted surgeon of his day. Others have done a little better. Antonio Prestigiacomo received an arsenic treatment that managed to preserve him hair, eyes and all; he stands in a niche in his greatcoat, goggling out across the corridor. Giovanni Carrao, a murdered hero of Italian unification and one of Garibaldi's generals, lies in an open coffin, showing off his still magnificent sweeping moustachios. A two-year-old baby in a little lace cap lies in her cradle, almost perfectly preserved by a series of special injections; the 'dear loving little angel', says the card, is Rosalia Lombardo, the daughter of a wealthy Palermo merchant.

Death is an art form in Palermo's museums, a lurid spectacle in the Capuchin crypt, whose corpses are a worthy symbol of the decay and fascination with death that seems to haunt Sicily. In Montalto, death is also a public event. It's only the day after Maria breathed her last and already notices are pasted up all around the village, complete with black borders, crosses and heart-rending poetry. *A dear granddaughter left bereft. A husband's heart laden with sorrow.* Maria's face peers out from the black-and-white posters, eyes staring at the

camera, crucifix at her throat; she has long hair piled
on her head and the ravaged beauty of an ageing French
film star.

Maria herself has returned home. She lies in an open
coffin in the front room of her house, hair tumbled across
her shoulders, wearing a white shift. Her feet are pointed
towards the door according to tradition; Sicilians consider
sleeping in this manner an ill omen. Candles flicker around
her body. The room has been transformed into a temporary
chapel complete with coloured light bulbs, plastic chrysanthemums and suitably tragic saints. Friends and relatives
have turned up from as far away as Messina and Palermo,
and half the village has filed into the house to farewell her,
kissing the old woman on the forehead. Maria's relatives
sit on rigid chairs, unkempt and unwashed as mourning
demands, faces shadowed in the gloom of the shuttered
house. They'll sit there all night, praying and lamenting.
Maria's bewildered husband is unshaven and already red-
eyed with exhaustion. He seems pathetically grateful when
he thinks, in his confusion, that I've come from Australia for
his wife's funeral.

Marcella is hovering outside Maria's house looking frail.
She's encased in black, from stockings to collar.

'I put on black fifty years ago when my father died,' she
says to me sadly. Marcella was in Geneva at the time, working
as an au pair, and when she heard the news of her father's
death she went to her room and put on a black skirt and
sweater. Then she told her employer she was going out to the
house of her sister, Tina's Aunt Rita. Her employer told her
cheerfully that she hoped she'd enjoy the evening.

'She thought I was going out on a date, maybe black was a stylish colour for her!'

These days Marcella doesn't have much patience with the tradition: she's come a long way from the Sicilian habits of her youth. She points out her cousin Grazia in the crowd of mourners in Maria's house. 'Thank goodness Grazia doesn't wear black all the time, even though she's a widow,' Marcella comments. Although strangely enough she's very conservative in other ways. Now that her husband has died, she feels it wouldn't be proper to go to the cinema any more.

'Which is a shame, because Grazia always liked the movies.'

We're standing outside waiting for Tina. Groups of people wearing black mourning buttons are hovering around recalling Maria's many virtues. She didn't miss mass for ten years, remembers a cousin, not since her son was in that tractor accident. A neighbour, who is crumpled on a bench dabbing at the corners of her eyes, says she once saw Maria putting twenty thousand lire on the offering plate. And of course there was that time the Martellos' house burnt down and Maria took the whole family in for three weeks, may the Lord rest her kindly soul.

The conversation moves on to Maria's last moments on earth, which can be little more than hearsay, if you ask me. Everyone wants to know exactly how the old woman died and what she said and did right up until she drew her last breath. Talk then turns to how Maria's body was kidnapped from hospital. The family bribed a doctor to pretend Maria was still alive and to sign a discharge form so she wouldn't have to suffer the indignity of an anonymous morgue. Two of her sons took their mother under the arms and dragged her out to the car while hospital staff turned a blind eye. The sons drove the dead body back to Montalto, which is only natural, because how else would Maria be able to enjoy the comforts of the family home and a proper wake?

Tina never knew Maria well and, distanced from the emotions of her mother, she finds this talk rather amusing, if a bit gruesome. Perhaps in spite of herself she's a Sicilian after all, familiar with gossip and death. I leave her discussing the corpse with Claudia's brother and sidle off to investigate the food, that other mainstay of Sicilian life. The tables and side-boards of Maria's house are piled high with dishes brought in by friends and neighbours: baked macaroni, cold lasagne, roast chickens, *antipasti*, cakes. A funeral seems an important enough occasion to warrant a cassata, I think to myself a bit irreverently, but once more my hopes are dashed. I compen-sate by nibbling on *ossi da morto* (bones of the dead) in the shape of femurs and skulls; glorious little offerings made with sugar, egg whites and chopped almonds. There's also specially-baked bread called *armuzzi*, a dialect word meaning 'souls of the dead'; the dough is formed in the shape of a pair of hands crossed over the breast, the way corpses are laid out in their coffins.

I'm munching on a pastry when Marcella pops up beside me with Tina to point out Maria's sister, who has come from Palermo for the funeral. She doesn't look any different from the other women at the wake, perhaps because she, too, is dressed in black, her head covered with a black shawl. She's thin and brittle and looks ill at ease. Marcella thinks she's here to gloat, if not actually to dance on the grave. She's feuded with Maria for the last thirty years, all because of their grandfather's goats. Despite herself Marcella finds it all a little amusing now, because like most family feuds it had such ridiculous origins. Back in the seventies, Maria and her sister Caterina fell to discussing their grandfather's farm and how many goats he owned before he died. Maria claimed he had fifteen, Caterina only twelve.

'Ma, they couldn't have fallen out over something like that.'

But they did, according to Marcella. In fact they argued furiously about it and one thing led to another. After that they were always impassioned rivals. What one had, the other wanted too, only bigger and better, and as both did very well for themselves the competition escalated. When Maria bought a fur coat, her sister had to go out and buy two fur coats. And the food! The food! Holy Jesus, says Marcella, there was so much food on the occasion of family visits it was incredible. Maria went out and bought a whole new table, much bigger, just to accommodate the family spread when Caterina came with her children. And soon Caterina bought an extension for her table too. Gigantic lasagne used to be served, just for the *primo,* in a dish as big as a flagstone. That would have been enough for the entire evening, but then would come more pasta, and meats, whole chickens and salads and heaven knows what.

'There was a lot of envy. Caterina couldn't stand Maria having anything she didn't have.'

Anyway Caterina was pathologically jealous of everyone. If her husband ever talked to a strange woman, say at a dinner party or something, she'd quiz him afterwards: 'Who was that woman? Why were you talking to her? What did you say? Are you having an affair?' She was convinced they were starting an affair.

'And if her husband was seated beside another woman at the table, that was like World War Three!' says Marcella in wonder, biting into a *fava dolci*.

I watch Caterina drift around the room. She doesn't look much like a retired businesswoman, more like one of the peasants I pass out in the olive fields, desiccated and wrinkled, although you can see the family resemblance in the photos of her dead sister. Maria must have been beautiful once and you can tell Caterina was too, only more angular and remote. Nobody talks to her much. She seems to hide behind her black head shawl as if warding off conversation. Her face is lined and tear streaked, and she looks old and confused. It's as if all purpose has gone out of her life, and maybe it has. Caterina has been robbed of her sisterly bickering and impassioned rivalry. Of all Maria's relatives, it's suddenly Caterina I feel sorry for the most.

Next day we troop back to Maria's house once more. Padre Perrino arrives late with a black stole over his surplice. Acolytes walk beside him carrying a cross and a basin of holy water, their faces intense with the studied solemnity of youth. Water is sprinkled over the coffin as the priest intones the *De Profundis*, and then Maria is carried down to the church followed by the priest and a flock of silent villagers to the sounds of the *Miserere*. I squeeze into a pew with the Calasciones not far from Lucia, who is poised, teary-eyed, at the feet of St Anthony. Maria must have sat beside Lucia many a time saying her prayers, but now she's laid down in the centre of the church with her feet towards the altar.

Come to her assistance ye Saints of God, come to meet her ye Angels of the Lord . . .

The candles around Maria's coffin gutter and smoke through the Vespers for the Dead, the psalms and responses. The medallions on Lucia's bosom heave in grief. Over on the other side of the church I spot Claudia and her family draped in black. Claudia is eyeing a young man in a suit and slicked-back hair, and after a moment I realise it's Carlo from Marcella's garage-gym.

Eternal rest give unto them, O Lord, and let perpetual light shine upon them . . .

Marcella shrinks back in the pew, voiceless. Tina's face is ashen and she hasn't spoken either, I think because she doesn't know the responses in Italian, maybe not even in English. I'm feeling a bit uncomfortable, an interloper in this moment of emotion, a witness to the end of a life I was never privileged to share. An acolyte stands at the head of the coffin with his cross, the priest at the foot, praying that Maria might escape a vengeful judgement. The congregation launches into the Lord's Prayer as the coffin is sprinkled with more holy water and smoked with incense. The service is interminable; mass and absolution follow, and by the time it is over the candles have wept wax into hot puddles on the floor.

O God . . . we humbly present our prayers to Thee for the soul of Thy servant Maria . . . to command Thy holy angels to receive it, and to bear it into paradise . . .

This is an ageless ritual. I can see the comfort in its lilting cadences and familiar promises, but it leaves me only sad:

I can't will belief, although I often envy it. When the service ends Marcella and the mourners seem calmer, more digni- fied. They follow the coffin up towards the cemetery, hauling gigantic floral wreaths, white against black dresses. Mon- talto's graveyard, like every other in Sicily, is perched high on the flanks of the hillside and dominates the village. A spectacular view sweeps over the town's rooftops and down to the coast. Marble glitters in the mid-afternoon heat. The flowers on the gravestones have shrivelled to brittle brown and the photos of the deceased are cracked and yellow. Poppies, thistles and dandelions struggle up from gaps in the concrete terracing.

'You wouldn't believe someone's paid to look after this place,' whispers Tina.

The observation seems to cheer her up a bit, and she smiles at me. We stand in the back ranks of the funeral party as the priest reads the service over Maria. It's surprisingly short compared to the one in church. I hear a dull thud and rattle as the undertakers shovel earth on top of the coffin. Someone in the family gives a low dismal keen and the crowd shivers in sympathy. Perspiration is trickling down my temples and I feel slightly sick. I've never been to a funeral before.

May her soul and the souls of all the faithful departed through the mercy of God rest in peace . . .

Down in the valley the bells of the church are tolling. The mourners straggle along the path, crossing themselves, and then stream down towards the village. Padre Perrino flaps away in billowing black, his acolytes tripping after him. Lucia leans on Marcella's arm as they follow him out of the gates.

Maria remains behind, covered by a mound of flowers.

***

Time is one of the greatest luxuries in the modern world, and travel is an opportunity to shamelessly indulge in it. In Sicily I have all the time I want, and the most delightful way of spending it is over a leisurely breakfast. The morning after Maria's funeral I wander down as usual to my favourite café in the piazza—not the one that Giuseppe haunts, but a quieter and more atmospheric neighbour. I order an icing-dusted croissant filled with rich chocolate mousse and a superb *caffè latte* frothing with milk. The burnt-sugar fragrance of coffee hangs heavily in the air. I eat sitting with my elbow on the marble bar as the espresso machine hisses and gurgles and Mario the bartender washes cups. Mario isn't much more than twenty, the son of the café owner and a quiet fellow, almost shy. When he isn't serving customers he snatches a read from a novel propped up against a stack of glasses on the counter. I find his presence restful.

As the village men come in, Mario serves them early morning coffee in tiny ceramic cups. The black suits have disappeared, but several of them are wearing black armbands. I watch as the men trickle sugar from little sachets into the thick, strong brew. The white crystals float on the surface, an indication of a good *crema* on top of the coffee, which holds in the coffee's flavour and aroma. The sugar sinks out of sight when the coffee is stirred, and then the drink is downed in almost one gulp. The residue leaves a pale brown froth that creeps down the sides of the cup slowly, as it should; a *crema* that disappears rapidly indicates stale or inferior quality beans or excessive roasting. As if to prove the point, Mario leaves the empty cups standing as the foam slides towards the bottom, then whisks them away and wipes down the counter for the next customer. People turn up in Montalto's bar all the time, another good sign. An espresso machine has to be constantly operated, otherwise dregs and oils from the coffee beans accumulate, causing the drink to taste stale or slightly off. No espresso purist would ever go into an empty bar.

I watch Mario springing into action as regular customers come through the door. The espresso is aptly named, since any bartender with an ounce of self respect prides himself on the speed with which he can process orders. By the time the villagers have settled on a bar stool he's delivering their coffees: a *doppio* (double dose) for the man in a pinstripe suit, a *basso* (extra strong) for the workman in paint-splattered overalls, a *macchiato* (slightly stained with milk) for Claudia's sprightly grandfather out on his morning constitutional. Mario makes it seem so easy, a delightful ballet of steam and metal levers. The order is hardly out of a customer's mouth before Mario is twisting the strainer off the machine and banging it against the sink to knock out the dregs of the previous cup. He clamps the strainer onto the grinder and fills it with pulverised coffee, making sure it's pressed flat but not packed down so tightly that water will pass through it unevenly. Then the strainer goes back on the espresso machine and steam is driven through the powder. This is the most vital part of the whole operation. If Mario is distracted and leaves it too long, the coffee will have a bitter flavour and be a bit thin; if he takes it off too quickly, it will be thick and sharp. About twenty seconds is enough. When the dark liquid oozing out of the machine reduces to a dribble, Mario removes the cup and slides it onto a saucer towards the waiting customer.

I sit and sip and watch. It strikes me as funny, really, that people drink coffee at all, because its strange flavour is completely unsuited to the average palate. The first Europeans who came into contact with coffee thought it appalling: 'bitter and evil', a 'hellish black brew', a 'cup of poison' they all complained. The *Women's Petition Against Coffee* of 1674 ranted that it was nothing better than 'base, black, thick, nasty bitter stinking, nauseous Puddle water'. And it is! Few people actually like coffee the first time they try it, and children usually have to be weaned onto it by drinking it with plenty of milk and sugar, a habit a lot of adults never shake off. Coffee is like a medicine: not always very nice when it goes down, but at least beneficially stimulating. Sometimes I think its real saving grace is its smell; like sun shining on antique wood or the comforting smokiness of a campfire in the desert. The aroma of coffee is beyond compare, even if its taste is often wanting.

That coffee possesses such an exotic aroma is only right, since the drink is another way in which we've been inspired by the Arabs, although it came far too late for them to have introduced it during their occupation of Sicily. One legend has it that Solomon invented coffee on instructions from the Archangel Gabriel, but more likely is the legend that it was a goatherd who first noticed that his goats were friskier after they'd been nibbling at the coffee plant where it grew wild in eastern Africa. Arab physicians soon concluded that the plant's berries contained a mild and apparently harmless stimulant. In the beginning coffee wasn't ground; the whole berry was simply infused in hot water. It became a drink of the religious orders of Sufism in Yemen because it helped devotees with their demanding hours of meditation and prayer. 'They feel the slight exhilaration strengthens them for their religious observances and worship,' commented a Turkish visitor of the strange new drink. Not only that, physicians were claiming the infusion was good for coughs, colds and the kidneys, haemorrhoids, melancholia and headaches. Doctors also promoted coffee as an aphrodisiac, as well as a painkiller particularly efficacious during menstruation. As a result, a Turkish husband's refusal to keep an adequate supply of coffee beans in the house was thought to be legitimate grounds for a divorce. By the sixteenth century coffee was grown on a commercial scale and widely consumed throughout the Middle East.

In Sicily, like most places in the Mediterranean, coffee is still taken very much in the Arab way: strong and sugary and consumed in minute quantities. ('It is drunk . . . as a delicacy and in mouthfuls,' commented Prospero Alpino in 1580 from Egypt, in the first ever description of coffee by a European.) Not that strong, sweet coffee has ever been to my taste; I prefer my sugar in an accompanying *cornetto*. Mario, in a good natured way, always smiles in amusement when I ask for a *caffè latte*, something any self-respecting Sicilian wouldn't dream of drinking until well into the afternoon, if at all. He froths the milk with kind patience, as if humouring a madman.

My *caffè latte* is smooth and creamy and altogether perfect, and I tell Mario so before he shuffles back to his book. I'm more than content on this sunny morning in

Montalto with my *caffè latte*. On the morning after a funeral I can't help but feel it's good to be alive. Mario is asking me anxiously if my *latte* isn't too hot. Obviously I'm taking far too long to drink it; the perfect espresso is served just warm enough to consume immediately. But I'm happy to linger, watching the villagers come in and out, watching Mario work his levers as the steam hisses around him. I open my notebook and start jotting down observations. Where would writers be if coffee hadn't been invented? Balzac got up in the morning and had coffee with barely any water on an empty stomach, much to the profit of his memories and ideas. 'The mighty labour begins and ends with torrents of this black water,' he wrote gleefully in his diary—surely a sentiment shared by many a writer since. Composers, too. Beethoven was fanatical about coffee (he used exactly six beans to every cup) and Bach wrote a whole *Coffee Cantata* in celebration of the exotic brew.

I delight in coffee lore. Even if you're only spooning some Nescafé into a mug you're participating in a grand historical adventure. Pour some coffee from a flask on a windswept Tasmanian beach, with the cold nibbling at your fingers and the gulls scolding overhead, and even Nescafé can taste like ambrosia. I have no patience with coffee purists, although I enjoy fine coffee. I savour coffee and feel its history and passion: the spicy smell of the souk, the smokiness of Bedouin tents under a starry sky, an elemental nuttiness that makes me dream of hot deserts.

An hour of reverie and quiet enjoyment over a cup of coffee is never time wasted. I sit in Montalto inhaling the aroma of Arabica and watching Mario work his magic behind the bar. Coffee cups rattle on saucers, and the espresso machine hisses and bubbles as it yields its liquid treasure.

The road inland from Montalto climbs into the hills, twisting through rolling farmland in a chequer of brown and green fields. Cows with clanking bells stand and stare at Mt Etna smouldering on the horizon. And always the Impressionist blur of flowers in the hedgerows: honeysuckle and iris, an explosion of yellow acacia, splashes of wild peonies. The sun is shining and the worst of the sirocco has abated. This is a happy landscape and beautiful weather for getting over the gloom of a funeral. Beside me, Tina hums a little and the warm breeze through the window ruffles her hair. The confirmation having been postponed until next weekend, Tina has proposed sightseeing around the southeast corner of the island. I think it more likely that she wants to escape from her dolorous mother and unpredictable father, but the plan suits me well enough, since there are several towns in the southeast that I'd like to visit. We head happily along country roads and the morning is still young as we slide into Nicosia, where the car barely scrapes past the sides of the houses in the narrow streets. An old man with a stick takes refuge in a doorway as we drive past with tyres squealing on cobblestones worn smooth by the centuries.

Before the coastal highway was built, Nicosia was a trading town of considerable importance on the inland road between Palermo and Messina. That was centuries ago, and nothing much has happened since then but a slow slide into dishevelled obscurity. A Norman castle collapses quietly on the hilltop. Glaring gargoyles sometimes give up the effort to cling on to the balconies of the upper town's crumbling palazzi, and drop off into the street in disillusionment. The bells that fell out of the tower of Santa Maria Maggiore still lie forgotten at the church door. The vestry is full of stacked floor slabs, vases, tables and moth-eaten rolls of carpet, while in the nave a few women in black have fallen asleep in the pews under the statue of an old prophet holding a skull in his outstretched hand.

The only proud reminder of Nicosia's days of glory is the massive cathedral, square and gaunt, which dominates the centre of the old town. Half the interior is gloomy, the other half ornate with twisting, multicoloured pillars in green and pink like huge chunks of rock candy. Glass caskets full of skulls and bones sit around the aisles on dusty shelves, and rows of blue bottles and small containers hold teeth and more bones. Halfway down the nave the elaborate casket of a local *beato*, Felice da Nicosia, displays his arm bone and vertebrae on a small cushion. A woman with a green ribbon in her hair stands motionless near the casket, praying and occasionally kissing the tips of her fingers. The noise of traffic and people talking in the piazza rumbles faintly in the still of the church, as if coming from a very great distance. Even the flies have fallen into apathy and sit sulking on the altar cloth.

Outside, the vast, battered doorway of the cathedral's entrance is flamboyantly imprinted with the emblems of the Aragonese monarchy, a sign of Sicily's ever-changing power politics. The Spanish turned up on the island almost by accident in 1268. For a while a succession of Aragonese princes lived on the island and ruled it relatively efficiently. They built many splendid mansions in Palermo. One was the

Palazzo Abatellis, a fine, late-fifteenth-century mix of Gothic and Renaissance styles, topped by towers and rows of gargoyles. It's now covered in holes and soot and has been turned into a museum; inside there's an exquisite bust of Eleanor of Aragon by Francesco Laurana. The face is luminous, with perfectly smooth, pearly skin marred only by an accidentally damaged nose. The bust has narrow, tight features: a mouth that would be mean but for its slight smile, a long nose, and close-set almost oriental eyes. The hair is caught back in a severe net. Eleanor of Aragon seems like a strong woman, not without wit or humour.

When Spain was united in 1469 the Aragonese were replaced by Spanish viceroys and few were as appealing as Eleanor. The Greeks, Arabs and Normans all came to Sicily to settle, but the Spanish ruled the island from afar for the first time since the Roman Empire. Like the Romans, they came to exploit Sicily, particularly for its wheat and cloth. With the centre of political power in Madrid far to the west, Sicily became a rather minor corner of the huge Spanish Empire, pushed to the periphery of European affairs for the first time in centuries. Spanish rule is generally seen as unenlightened, conservative and corrupt. Feudalism was maintained, an often absentee aristocratic class grew idle and indifferent, and Sicily went into severe economic decline. A tyrannical Spanish clergy also introduced the Inquisition and managed to isolate Sicily so effectively that even the Renaissance had virtually no impact on the artistic and intellectual life of the island.

As we head out from Nicosia in an explosion of sunlight it's a Spanish landscape that spreads around us. We drive past

somnolent villages, ruined farm buildings and abandoned
railway viaducts. In the distance, hazy views of Mt Etna
shimmer like a mirage. Every rocky outcrop is crowned with
a withdrawn town full of hostility and suspicion. At
Calascibetta the notes of the houses reach a crescendo in a
church teetering on the edge of a cliff. Not long afterwards
we park in the old town at Enna, almost in the dead centre of
the island. The town sits on top of an imposing great lump
of pale rock, brooding over the landscape below, an architecture of insecurity wedded to an uninviting geography. Enna
ends in a giant fortress, bristling with towers. These days
locals walk their dogs—we see a Rottweiler, a golden
retriever and a piddling beagle—around the ruins.

A gloomy flight of steps leads up to the top of the castle's
tallest tower, where there's a sudden dazzle of sunlight from
the ramparts. Tina and I are peering over the battlements
when someone behind us offers to take our photo. I turn
round and see a dark, Sicilian-looking man. I can tell he isn't
really Sicilian; he's far too breezy and self-assured. In the way
of Americans he announces that in fact he's from Santa
Monica, California, on holiday to visit relatives in Palermo.
His name is Chris Liotta.

'A photo would be good,' says Tina. 'We don't have a
photo yet.'

'We just got married, we're on our honeymoon,' I explain,
pulling Tina in close.

She giggles at my joke, which I'm sure makes her seem all
the more like a bashful bride. I have the photo now: Tina and
I with big grins on our faces, looking suntanned and relaxed.
Half of Sicily recedes behind us in a blue haze, melting into

the summer sky. A moment of friendship, a moment to remember.

As we clatter back down the steps of the tower Chris Liotta fusses and fiddles with his own camera. He wants to know if we've been to Piazza Armerina yet to see the Roman mosaics. And what about Siracusa? We should definitely go there. He himself was there only yesterday and found it well worth a visit. And Palermo of course. I can tell Tina, like me, is listening with half an ear and calculating her escape. The American is one of those people for whom there's always something better somewhere else. Now he's telling us that there's even a church right here in Enna that's more interesting than the cathedral, only most people don't know about it: the Church of San Salvatore. He was there only this morning. How about us?

'Yes, we were there only an hour ago, and the priest even opened up the crypt and showed us the mummies!' I tell him.

Tina grips me by the elbow and hurries me away. 'What is your problem?'

I say nothing, sulking.

'I know what's wrong with you,' she says. 'It's time for some food.'

She's right, of course. Tina can skip lunch with impunity, or nibble on a carrot and call it a meal, but hunger makes me tetchy. Leaving Chris Liotta to his sightseeing, we find a restaurant with starched white tablecloths and gleaming sets of glasses, two to a place setting. The interior is dark and cool after the golden glare of the street. The chef, who pops in and out of the kitchen to greet his regulars, wears a white hat and apron and is reassuringly plump and jovial. The sole waiter wears a burgundy waistcoat and black trousers and looks mournful. Along the back wall there's an enormous *antipasti* buffet, and at the door a pyramidal platter of fruit and a display of desserts. *Antipasti* dishes are nearly always cold, and therefore a good way for chefs to attract and titillate customers; they're the operatic overtures of the kitchen. The restaurant we're in now has a central table covered in a snow-white tablecloth weighed down with earthenware dishes containing a triumphant chorus of food in purple, green and red.

The Spanish brought gloominess and fervent religion to Sicily, but at least they can be thanked for the glories of *antipasti*. Agriculture suffered badly after the departure of the Arabs, but the Spanish did at least introduce fruits and vegetables from their empire in the New World. American novelties included potatoes, corn, pumpkins, blackberries, raspberries, pineapples and peanuts, all mostly ignored in Italy. Much more important were those vital flavours of ice cream—strawberry, vanilla and chocolate—as well as beans, peppers, tomato and zucchini, all of which became central to the Sicilian kitchen. The latter vegetables are all common in *antipasti* recipes. So, too, are anchovies in oil, olives, ham and salami. But *antipasti* can be wildly inventive and include dishes such as tiny omelettes, a paste of crushed olives flavoured with fennel and mint, fruits in a sweet and spicy mustard sauce (*mostarda*), marinated local cheeses, or fish roe with a squeeze of lemon. Many of today's *antipasti* dishes were first described by Bartolomeo Scappi in 1570; his celebrated cookery book lists twenty-four of them at a time when Italian cooking was certainly the most sophisticated in Europe.

According to a Sicilian proverb, good things must be eaten sparingly so as not to spoil the appetite. This is probably good advice, but I'm never able to resist the temptations of the *antipasti* table. By the time I've glanced at the menu and fiddled with my fork, my eyes are already on the colourful offerings. Some anchovies slick with olive oil and lemon juice, dotted with chips of garlic and hot chilli pepper, perhaps? And a wedge of lush, cool ricotta cheese as a counterbalance. Tina is going for the sensational simplicity of juicy yellow and green peppers roasted over an open flame until the skin is charred. I hesitate over a silky, transparent slice of prosciutto ham wrapped around a bright green asparagus shoot with a tip turning to mauve. A sharp protest of pickled black olives, the unctuous rust-red of sun-dried tomatoes, a hunk of crusty yellow bread, and there I have it, a plate of *antipasti* like a Byzantine mosaic of colour, shape and texture.

I munch with delirious delight through my *antipasti*. Then I have to consider what to eat next. Enna is known for its wild game—rabbit, hare, duck and partridge—but for once I feel that nature has been ravaged enough around here. The local speciality is *pasta 'ncasciata*, a lasagne of meat, peas, cheese and tomatoes, which sounds a little heavy. Tina has tortellini in a light cream sauce. I decide to order *rigatoni alla Norma*. Unlike Marcella's version, the aubergine in this restaurant hasn't been cubed and mixed into the sauce but is cut through in slices and fanned out decoratively on top of the pasta and sprinkled with cheese. The purple sheen of its skin glistens on top of the bright red sauce.

After that, a *secondo* seems a little much. We finish off with coffee and profiteroles full of thick, creamy chocolate mousse.

Then as we collapse back in our seats Tina says we really ought to go to that church.

'What church?'

'San Salvatore. The one that the American guy was talking about.'

'Oh, all right,' I say agreeably, as I feel chocolate and caffeine carousing through my veins.

Not long after we're standing at the church door, where we find everything locked up and a notice directing us to the barber's shop for a key. The barber is a cheerful man with a beer belly and red face, and he's in the middle of cutting someone's hair. No matter, though; it's only a cousin and he doesn't mind waiting. We leave the customer abandoned on a swivel chair and the barber unlocks the church doors, ushering us into the interior, which is small and rather beautiful. There's an impressive carved ceiling and a painting of the martyrdom of St Elmo on the wall. Elmo's stomach is cut open to show the coils of his intestines, which are being winched out on cogwheels. If you ever have a stomach pain, the barber tells us, this is the saint to invoke for relief.

I don't understand all of the barber's local dialect, but I follow the dates well enough, one after another in layers of proud local history. He shows us a statue of St Barbara originally made in Venice, shipped to Catania and brought all the way to Enna on the back of a mule. Barbara, the barber says happily, was a beautiful Syrian maiden martyred some time in the third century. Her father Dioscorus locked her up in a tower to preserve her maidenhood and pagan heritage, but she become a Christian anyway. Her father wasn't too amused, especially when one day she had three windows placed in his bathhouse in order to celebrate the Trinity. In a rage at her meddling with his architecture, Dioscorus had his daughter denounced as a Christian and personally beheaded her with his own sword. In his turn, Dioscorus was killed by a bolt of lightning. Barbara was rewarded by becoming the patron saint of stonemasons, gravediggers and architects.

I listen fascinated. Martyrdoms and legends, dates and solid history; it's all the same to the barber. On the way out he shows us a gilded palanquin which is carried around Enna at Easter bearing an effigy of Christ. The barber tweaks aside the sheet that covers it, and I have a momentary glimpse of gold, tassels and a bleeding wound on the side of a ribcage. The statue seems hideous. All the best and worst of Sicilian art is found in its churches, I'm realising, and all of it's about those eternal Sicilian themes: beauty and violence, death and passion. It all seems so ordinary, too; this is nothing more than a casual part of the barber's life. He does no more than cross himself at the sight of the bleeding Christ, and then we troop back into his shop. Tina and I sit in the cool shadows, sipping Coke. The barber goes snip, snip, snip at his cousin's hair, while above him on a shelf a weeping Madonna looks on.

The sun is slanting yellow across an afternoon horizon as we squeeze back into the Fiat and head out of town along a road lined with prickly pears and a maze of drystone walls. The air smells of wild mint and rosemary, and we pass groves of lemon and almond trees. Eventually we see the twin hills of Ragusa in front of us, crowned by the old and new towns. The new town emerged after a devastating earthquake in 1693 and became a bitter rival of the old town across the valley. The modern town was well laid out and prosperous, particularly after the discovery of oil nearby; it also adopted St John as its patron in defiance of St George, who had served the old town well enough for hundreds of years. The old town, largely medieval and baroque, has been eclipsed ever since. Depopulation has left many of its buildings empty. Only the old live here now, and tourists hardly bother to visit.

Tina parks the car outside a boarded-up church whose crumbling masonry has been pasted over by election posters and death notices. Weeds sprout from the ledges and pillars of the baroque facade and rusty drainpipes lean dangerously over the street. Pigeons fly in and out of the church's gaping windows; I can hear them cooing in the interior, the sound magnified as if it's being relayed through loudspeakers. The whole town—the whole region, for that matter—suffers from the same weary decay. Ragusa's old town appears abandoned, like some magical village in a fairytale that has been lying under a spell for four hundred years and has slowly crumbled away. But people still live here. Washing flutters defiantly from wrought-iron balconies, and in the cafés old men nod off in the sun. Up in another church at the top of the town two elderly women are fixing sprays of flowers for a wedding: white lilies with yellow stamens on the altar, pink roses and carnations along the pews. In a glass casket in a side altar a skeleton moulders away, bones poking through his stockings, his ribcage revealed beneath an unbuttoned silver jerkin decorated with ribbons. The skeleton reclines on a red cushion, propped up jauntily on one elbow as if whoever it was simply passed away in the middle of a dice game.

Still, among the decay of Sicily's inland towns you never have to look far to discover the haunting beauty that imbues the island. Ragusa might be falling down, but it's also an agreeable mixture of grey, medieval austerity and sudden baroque flamboyance. The old town is cluttered with bell towers, campaniles, curling cornices, baroque doorways and dripping fountains. Buildings are covered with layers of different coloured paint, splotches of faded green and blue and pink. This is another fairytale sort of place, populated by marvellous people. A small boy leads a huge muzzled dog far bigger than he is. Old men, bodies hard and rough from decades of labour, mumble through mouthfuls of missing teeth. Kids with snotty noses and dirty clothes look as if they've stepped out of a canvas by Caravaggio, all curly black hair and luminous skin. A policeman bends over to greet a wizened man in a motorised wheelchair, kissing him on each cheek. In a doorway a middle-aged couple stand for a moment, fresh from a languid afternoon of adultery. The man presses his lips against the inside of the woman's arm: deliciously Sicilian, full of erotic longing and sadness. Overhead gargoyles hold balconies up on their shoulders, and window frames burst with baroque passion.

Ragusa smells of melted caramel and warm stone. The caramel, we soon discover, comes from a stall in the main square where an old man is selling *torrone*, crunchy nuts embedded in caramelised sugar. I watch in delight as he melts a pot of sugar syrup on a little gas burner, then pours it onto a marble slab to let it cool. He smooths it out thin and even with half an orange, then cuts it up. I buy a few squares, sticky on my fingers, and Tina helps me crunch it up, the sugary scent following us through the street. Crumbling churches, on the other hand, smell of cloves and are full of whispering women whose muted prayers hiss and rattle around the walls and rafters. *Hail Mary, full of grace, the Lord is with thee; blessed art thou among women . . .* The front of the cathedral is covered in frothy pillars and baroque decoration like spun toffee, giving the whole building a lightness quite unlike the fortress austerity of Palermo's exteriors, as if the churches of Palermo have been turned inside out, exposing their tumultuous exuberance for all to see.

By evening the sun has stained the walls of the old town pink, and long, lazy golden light illuminates the faces of the old men sitting in the cafés, lending them the same Byzantine serenity as the prophets in Palermo's mosaics. Pigeons coo and flutter from baroque perches, and a Vespa splutters across the piazza. I sit with Tina at a rickety table, feeling relaxed and happy, and order a bottle of Faro wine, rich and deep as fine rubies. The bouquet is mellow and rich, the flavour nutty. Its colour glows with an inner fire, as if the wine has distilled the character of Sicily: volcanoes and passion, beauty and blood. Tina sits, hair cascading down her back, intoxicated by the evening.

The liquid sunlight is absorbed into the sugar-stone buildings, and suddenly it's dark.

In Sicily I seem to measure out my life with coffee spoons, just like the character in the poem by T. S. Eliot, although I feel neither as middle-aged nor as melancholy as J. Alfred Prufrock. In fact, Sicily's cafés make me feel very cheerful, with their convivial atmospheres and heady smell of coffee and sugar. From Ragusa to Marsala, from Agrigento to Mazara I retreat to cafés, comforted by the espresso machine as it hisses and grumbles like a dog sleeping in a sunlit piazza. This is a good spot, because locals congregate around the espresso machine, too. Besides, coffee is always cheaper taken at the bar rather than sitting down. Stand at the bar and you can also help yourself to the *cornetti*, boiled eggs or marzipan fruits sitting out in baskets, casually monitored by the bartender who'll only ask you for money as you're leaving. But cafés in Sicily aren't just about eating and drinking. These are places to have a romantic rendezvous, soften the edges of a little business deal, ogle people passing in the street, retreat behind a newspaper or catch up on local affairs. Cafés are places where you can discuss the weather, the crops, the latest soccer results, politics and even revolution.

It has always been so, ever since cafés—or coffeehouses— first sprang up in the Islamic world as the coffee craze took hold. While there were those who drank coffee to gain religious energy, the public was now flocking to coffeehouses for the range of unholy entertainment they offered: storytellers, musicians, puppet shows and prostitutes. According to Alexandre Dumas in his *Dictionnaire de cuisine*: 'The taste for coffee went so far in Constantinople that the imams complained their mosques were empty while the coffeehouses were always full.' There was a religious backlash in the form of numerous legal and academic investigations into the new drink, which was feared as the kind of stimulant expressly forbidden by Islamic law.

Moslem rulers, too, were nervous at the popularity of

coffeehouses; large, late-night gatherings of men seemed full of subversive possibilities. In Mecca in 1511 the local governor tried to ban coffee, worried that talk in coffeehouses would foster opposition to his rule. This is the first of many recorded coffee bans, but it had no effect; in fact the governor's efforts provoked such a popular outcry that he was removed from office and later executed. Some time later Sultan Amurat II was more successful in closing down coffeehouses in Constantinople by the simple expedient of tying regular customers up in sacks and throwing them into the Bosphorus. Somehow, though, coffeehouses prospered until by the sixteenth century Constantinople had more than six hundred of them.

There are Arab-style coffeehouses in Sicily, too. Although they're modern places set up for newly arrived Tunisian immigrants they still have, to me at least, the smoky, seedy, slightly dissolute atmosphere that must have so alarmed the Ottoman sultans. In Mazara men in patched jackets sit in a cloud of cigarette smoke that curls up around posters of the plump Tunisian president and sultry Egyptian singers like incense around images of Hindu gods. They munch on *halavah*, a crunchy sesame candy sprinkled with chopped nuts, and drink mint tea. In Palermo, little piazzas of the old quarter hide cafés full of battered Tunisian fishermen and smooth young Moroccans who are taking time out from hawking bangles and fake watches. Waiters stagger out under the weight of dishes piled high with steaming couscous. A chanteuse wails in Arabic over the loudspeakers. After dinner the hookahs come out, rumbling and burping as the customers sink into a postprandial haze.

While in Ragusa I sit in another Arab-style café and play backgammon with Ali. He isn't much more than twenty, with slicked-down hair and an Arafat stubble. Ali wants to learn English, and has two big pockets in his jacket full of slips of paper—English words on one side, Arabic translations on the other. After he's memorised them he passes them from his left pocket to his right: *currency, recommend, postage stamp*. I lose miserably at backgammon, which means it's my turn again to buy the dessert, but I couldn't care less. My fingers are already sticky with honey cakes dipped in sesame seeds. I like ordering the desserts, because they have such resonant names: 'lady's lips', 'gazelle's horns'. Sometimes I go for the 'nightingale's nests', whose flaky pastry is filled with finely chopped pistachios soaked in syrup and perfumed with rose-water and lemon. The bartender slides two tiny cups of coffee towards us. *Reward, engineer, visa*. We let them sit for a moment, allowing the grounds to settle, then knock them back in a single pungent gulp. *Practical, driving licence, politics*. The little scraps of paper flutter from one pocket to another, and suddenly I have a stack of black pieces sitting on the bar of the backgammon board.

I like it that Ali sits in this café and tries to educate himself. Coffeehouses have always been associated with educated middle-class customers, even after spreading into Europe. (The working classes continued to drink tea and beer in Britain, rough wine in France and Italy.) As in the Islamic world these new meeting places for the educated weren't looked upon benignly by those in political power. In England Charles II briefly had coffeehouses shut down, fearful of their subversive overtones. In France Montesquieu observed in his

Persian Letters: 'Were I the King, I would close the cafés, for the people who frequent these places heat their brains in a very tiresome manner . . . the intoxication which coffee arouses in them causes them to endanger the country's future.' Montesquieu's prediction was to prove only too accurate, since by the time of the French Revolution cafés had indeed become meeting places for the disaffected. In Italy coffeehouses were also venues for assorted revolutionaries, artists, writers and other people of ill repute. Many became well known in the nineteenth century as meeting places for partisans who promoted the unification of Italy.

In Ragusa Tina says cafés are my natural habitat because I'm middle-class *and* a writer. Not to mention disaffected, she adds, although my disaffection is relieved by travelling rather than revolution. I'm rather startled by this comment and I compensate by gorging on peaches stewed in wine and stuffed with chestnut purée. But maybe she's right; cafés are certainly my natural habitat. You can do things in a café that you can't in a pub: read newspapers and paperbacks, have proper conversations, titillate your tastebuds. In a café you can have little chocolate cups filled with candied orange and toasted slivers of almond accompanied by another *caffè latte* coughed up with skill and artistry from an espresso machine. You can luxuriate in the coffee's aroma and listen to the soothing bubbling sound from the bar as another jug of milk is frothed.

If this is disaffection, who would want it any other way?

We arrive back in Montalto to find things much as usual in the kitchen of Aunt Rita's house: splendid organisation on a table covered with herbs and chopped tomatoes, disarray in

Marcella's hopes for the confirmation. It's a disaster, Marcella cries as she pieces together a chicken casserole. Well, maybe not a disaster this time, the Divine Lord be thanked, just an irritating setback. The organist! Padre Perrino! What about the music!

'Calm yourself Ma!'

Marcella grinds pepper over her tomatoes and herbs. Watching the sauce start to simmer on the stovetop does seem to calm her. It doesn't really matter, she says, it's just that Pietro the organist has fallen out with Padre Perrino. He's feeling rebellious, and to spite the priest he's threatening to go on strike. It would have to happen now! Not that you need an organist to be confirmed, of course, but it's a big day after all, and it would be nice to have some uplifting music, wouldn't it?

Yes it would, says Tina, shrugging at me across the table. She seems determined to keep up her promise to herself that she'll patiently accept whatever the confirmation saga throws at her. Tina seems suddenly to have arrived at certain insights, both into herself and maybe into her mother: a small step of progress in her search for understanding.

But Marcella is in a frenzy of fussing as she slaps chicken pieces into the bottom of her casserole dish, basting them with olive oil before setting them to brown in the oven. The music is a small detail, but something she feels will have to be sorted out. It all started when Pietro attended an evangelical mass only a few days ago in Campobello, a neighbouring village. He hadn't mentioned to the priest that he was going, but naturally enough Padre Perrino somehow got to hear of it anyway, and was furious.

'Why did you do a thing like that?' he apparently shouted at his organist. 'It's only a show, a spectacle! Call that a mass!'

With a certain smug cleverness, Pietro retorted that the Lord was pleased that he went. Well, as Marcella comments, Pietro is young and all he wanted was to see what an evangelical mass was like—there wasn't any need for him to ask permission of the priest. But the priest didn't see it that way.

In fact, the minister of God practically threw Pietro down the steps of the church and then stormed off in a rage.

At this, Marcella pauses to draw breath and take her browned chicken from the oven. She adds handfuls of roughly chopped potatoes and carrots to the dish and covers it with generous scoops of her nicely reduced tomato sauce. As she ladles it on she tells us that the organist is very talented and also has a fine singing voice. The pity of it is that he works in the church for nothing. Padre Perrino doesn't even pay him, another stark sign of his miserly nature, and all the more reason for him to treat Pietro well. Quite frankly, Pietro's wasting his talent in Montalto and is just not getting anywhere.

'Last year he was offered a scholarship for a music course in Verona for three months, but can you imagine, he declined because he has a girlfriend in Montalto! His mother wept. Everyone thought he was mad. Now he's still in Montalto, and what has he got to show for it?'

'Well, I suppose he has his girlfriend,' says Tina brightly.

Marcella sniffs doubtfully as she thrusts her casserole back into the oven. She doesn't hold out much hope for *that* relationship—though you never know the ways of the Lord, she adds hastily. And shouldn't the priest be more careful? Only recently she read in the newspaper that a sacristan from Pedaro on the east coast was arrested for trying to kill a priest. The priest collapsed after drinking communion wine laced with weedkiller, and the sacristan broke down and confessed to the crime. Imagine! He'd been the sacristan for twenty years. The whole problem was that the priest had refused to officially employ him, and wasn't paying enough for his services.

'It sounds just like the same situation as in Montalto!' says Marcella, poking me in the chest.

Tina gives me a wild-eyed look, but Marcella has already galloped away from the murder idea and is muttering about visiting Annunciatina, the organist's mother.

'This will be nearly two hours cooking slowly. I'll go now. Why don't you both come? Maybe you'll find it interesting!'

'Ma, what's the point in visiting the organist's mother?'

The point, explains Marcella as she shoves on her shoes and ushers us out the door, fired up with her plan, is that Annunciatina is not only Pietro's mother but sits on the church committee *and* knows the priest well.

'But Ma, doesn't that place her in a delicate position?'

Perhaps it does. But Annunciatina is a lawyer—she travels up to Palermo, where she has an office, three times a week— so she ought to be able to negotiate the stormy waters of parish politics. Her husband died some years ago when he was still very young. Annunciatina herself is only forty-five. She's a smart woman and, of course, the villagers think she's uppity and pushy, says Marcella, but all she's done is to make something of herself. She ought to be able to sort out this trivial problem, you'd think.

We arrive at Annunciatina's house flustered and expectant.

Annunciatina herself answers the door, and if she's surprised to find two breathless women and a foreign man on her doorstep she doesn't show it. Instead, she ushers us in gracefully and invites us to sit down on her black leather sofa. Her sitting room is totally unexpected: all metal and glass, glimmering and shimmering under muted spotlights. Abstract art hangs in big coloured splotches on the walls. But Annunciatina herself is unexpectedly gloomy. The trouble with priests, according to her, is that they're all useless; or at least the older ones.

'You see, in the old days Sicilians had big families, maybe five, six, seven children,' she explains, turning her eyes to me. 'And they were poor. One of the kids always entered the priesthood; it was a matter of earning income. So priests who are in their sixties and seventies, well, I'd say ten percent of them are true believers, ninety percent of them don't care at all!'

'Heaven help us,' groans Marcella.

'Who are the real Christians? The ones who've become monks, friars. But not village priests!'

Marcella crosses herself. Annunciatina might be on the church committee but she doesn't look like the kind of person who crosses herself. She lights herself a cigarette and crosses her elegant legs instead, and stares at Marcella with a kind of pity.

'Now, if I needed to go to a priest, I'd go to one who was thirty years old. Then I'd know he was a real man of the cloth.'

I glance at Tina. I imagine if Annunciatina ever went to a thirty-year-old priest it would be to defrock him rather than ask for spiritual guidance. She seems like an extraordinary woman to find in the middle of Montalto, with her chunky solid gold bracelets, chic furniture and forthright manner. I rather like this merry widow and I wonder why she still remains in this conservative little village.

'We would thank God a hundred times a day for such a priest!' exclaims Marcella.

Annunciatina says she'll speak to her son about playing the organ for the confirmation, since she understands Tina has come from overseas and has already been in Montalto longer than she intended. And now, would we perhaps like some ice cream?

No we wouldn't, because dinner is waiting in the oven. As we hurry homeward Marcella finds consolation in Annunciatina's promise; another problem solved. Everything is going well now, isn't it, she says as she lays the table.

Then Giuseppe returns from the piazza in high dudgeon, muttering and cursing as richly marinated chicken pieces are served onto his plate. The parish priest, it seems, is far wilier than any Palermo lawyer. He's tired of Marcella's harping, Claudia's indifference, Tina's confirmation certificate that still hasn't arrived, fights with organists.

Padre Perrino is refusing to hold the confirmation at all. He came by the café and told Giuseppe he was too old for such a tedious task.

He wouldn't do it. It couldn't be done in Montalto. If Claudia wanted to be confirmed, he would recommend her to Messina for the ceremony.

Giuseppe stabs his chicken as if he wishes it were Padre Perrino. Marcella and Tina sit at the table with their mouths agape like some parody of shock.

This is an enormous blow to the Calasciones, as well as to Claudia and her family. Who wouldn't rather be confirmed in their own village church, full of familiar people? But the fire seems to have died in Marcella, and the weeks of wrangling have worn down the last of the family's resistance. They're unaccountably quiet over the meal, as if the war declared by the priest has finally wrought a truce in the family. Nibbling on her after-dinner pastries, Marcella accepts the change of plans with tired annoyance.

'Well, at least the confirmation will take place in the cathedral,' she sighs. 'With the Bishop of Messina! It will be quite grand!'

And she seems to perk up at the thought.

7

LOVE BITES

I have only one week left in Sicily and sex is on my mind. I dream of bare breasts and saucy bums, voluptuous women draped in tumbles of silken cloth, pink flesh against blue satin. I'm looking for nipples and naughtiness, for passion and sensuality. In short, I want some baroque.

Right now I'm sitting in a café in Siracusa with Tina and have to satisfy myself by eating *fedde*, a traditional bun stuffed with almond paste, jam and custard. The filling oozes out between two ovals of pastry, sweet and sticky. In Sicilian dialect *fedde* (which really just means 'slice') is slang for the vulva, Tina tells me matter-of-factly. I'm discovering that eating *fedde* is a very physical experience that brings a lot of sensual pleasure. I don't think Tina agrees. Probably she finds it quick, boring and annoyingly sticky. She isn't really in the mood.

It's not *fedde* but 'virgin's breasts' that I'm really after. In his memoirs the Duke of Verdura recalls 'the famous *minne di virgine*, alias breasts of virgins—dainty little mounds of almond paste, *grandeur nature*, filled with some kind of fruity stuffing, baked in a way that made the tips turn browner . . . [They] arrived in trays lined with multicoloured paper and covered with tinsel and little sugar balls dipped in silver and gold.' The duke remembers these pastries were delivered to his Palermo house from a nearby convent, along with pistachio pies, candied fruit and marzipan.

Yes, indeed. The most amusing thing about *fedde* and virgin's breasts is that they were produced, and almost certainly invented, in Sicilian convents. This is all the more peculiar considering sugar and sweetmeats were introduced by the Arabs. Nuns in the convents of the interior later took these unholy Islamic inventions and transformed them into naughty baroque nibbles.'Reclusive sisters clothe dreams and sighs in sugar and fine flour,' wrote Paolo Monelli. Like everyone else he noticed the odd juxtaposition of religion and sex: 'Their hands caress the dough and candied fruits . . . They confide ancient recipes like love letters. They imitate forbidden fruits with a wonderful almond paste.'

What provoked such an indulgence in these sugary delights of the flesh? Some writers suggest it was an artistic outlet for the nuns—the only way to combat the austerity and monotony of their lives—while others think it was a means of maintaining legitimate contact with the outside world. Perhaps initially, given sugar's early use in Europe as a medicine, they might even have assumed they were piously attending to the sick. As the centuries passed, mind you, such sweet excess seemed guaranteed to actually *make* people sick. Giuseppe di Lampedusa in *The Leopard*, Sicily's most famous literary classic, describes a table weighed down with goodies at a reception: 'Huge sorrel babas, Mont Blancs snowy with whipped cream, cakes speckled with white almonds and green pistachio nuts, hillocks of chocolate-coloured pastry . . . pink ices, champagne ices . . . a melody in major of crystallised cherries, acid notes of yellow pineapple, and green pistachio paste of those cakes called Triumph of Gluttony . . .' And of course the 'shameless Virgin's cakes shaped like breasts' if you had any room left for more.

This all seems a bit impious, and wandering around the pastry shops of Siracusa I marvel that the creations inside could possibly have originated in convents. Rum and Cognac ooze from little pyramids of *dolcetti al liquore*, *bocconcini* glisten wickedly with sticky almond paste, deep-fried *cassateddi* burst with rich ricotta. There certainly isn't much emphasis on mortification of the flesh. Other pastries are filled to excess with preserved fruit and topped off with icing sugar and little silver balls. Piles of marzipan oranges and apples seduce customers from counter tops, reminding me that these too are convent inventions.

And then I find my virgin's breasts. They're on the menu of a café in the old quarter, listed like the services offered in a brothel: *minne di virgine* at three euros a grope. The café is small but cosy, with a floor of swirling patterned tiles and embedded bottle tops. Impossibly beautiful Italian models look seductively down from arty black and white photos on the walls, surrounded by out-of-focus fountains and pigeons. The café owner is, however, plain and dumpy, and wears a shapeless dress printed with scarlet hibiscus.

'I bet those aren't virgin's breasts,' Tina titters.

'They're monuments to Italian motherhood. She probably has ten children.'

Above her sagging flesh the woman's face is open and cheerful. She talks about the weather, asks me where I'm from, brings out glasses of water and doesn't bat an eyelid when I order virgin's breasts and a coffee. She nods and smiles.

Virgin's breasts might seem the most impious of all Sicilian pastries but in fact these titbits (excuse the pun) are associated with St Agatha, the patron saint of Catania, who lived in the third century. Her beauty attracted the eye of a local Roman consul named Quintian. She would have none of him, and in a fit of pique he forced her to enter a Catanian brothel where, however, Agatha managed to remain steadfast and virginal. Enraged, the consul had her breasts cut off with shears, but Agatha was healed in her prison cell after seeing a vision of St Peter. She finally expired after being rolled over hot coals and splintered glass. Later she became the patron saint of wet-nurses and bell-founders, and is invoked against eruptions by Mt Etna. In iconography St Agatha is often depicted carrying the shears that tortured her, and she nearly always holds a platter on which her severed breasts are piously displayed.

'And she looks just like a waitress carrying out a nippled cake,' I say to Tina happily. I'm delighted with my virgin's breast, which has a marzipan flavour to it and oozes fruit jam. Surely this is Sicily's ultimate symbol, uniting not only food and sex but death and religion as well.

'I'm sure the Marquis de Sade would've been amused,' says Tina. 'All that sexual violence. He had a very sweet tooth you know.' The way she looks at me I know she's making some kind of veiled criticism of my own sweet tooth. Maybe she thinks I'm a sexual pervert.

I nibble away on my sugary breast and tell Tina that people with a sweet tooth have very fulfilling sex lives. Sugar and sex! Americans call people they're attracted to 'sugar' and 'honey'; Italians say *zuccherino* (little sugar) and *biscottino* (little biscuit). I'm always a bit wary of people who don't like sweet things.

Tina snorts and rolls her eyes. 'You know what?' she says. 'Both the tongue and sexual organs have really sensitive nerve endings called "Krause's end bulbs". So there's your connection between sugar and sex.'

Hmm. I wonder how Tina knows these things. 'Krause's end bulbs? What an unappetising name.'

Tina ignores this, yawns like a cat and smirks. 'I guess that's why we *hunger* for someone's touch,' she says.

'Or *feast* our eyes on somebody,' I answer, as she runs her fingers through her tumbling hair and licks sugar off her lips.

What a dish!

Everyone in Sicily talks about Siracusa: its history, charming old town, picturesque location and bracing sea air. It sounds interesting. Certainly interesting things have happened in baths in Siracusa, starting in the third century BC with Archimedes. In the words of Plutarch: 'Oft times his servants got him against his will to the baths . . . And while they were anointing him with oils and sweet savours, with his fingers he drew lines upon his naked body, so far was he taken from himself, and brought into an ecstasy or trance, with the delight he had in the study of geometry.' Archimedes, of course, eventually solved a scientific puzzle while in one such trance, and leapt naked from his bath—or more accurately, from the baths—to run around the streets shouting *Eureka!* Then there is St Barbara, of course, who came to a sticky end thanks to the unsolicited renovations she made to her father's bathhouse. Later Emperor Constans, who briefly made Siracusa the capital of the Byzantine Empire, got whacked on the head with a soap dish by his chamberlain while he, too, was having a bath. The year was 668; the emperor's untimely bathroom assassination caused a rebellion over the succession, which Arab raiders exploited to their advantage, leaving the way open for the Islamic occupation.

These baths have long gone, of course, and much of what remains today of Greek Siracusa is boarded off. People have also failed to tell me that Siracusa is an industrial city and major port full of smoke stacks and apartment blocks. The air smells of rust and oil. Badly parked cars block half the pavements, and badly driven cars clog the narrow streets. Shabby concrete shopping blocks are decorated with metal shutters and peeling election posters, then festooned with sagging telegraph wires. It's only when I step inside these shops that I get a glimpse of the famed Italian sense of style: women's suits displayed among black marble and gilt mirrors, futuristic-looking household appliances, leather shoes arranged on polished wood shelves. I marvel at a pair of shoes with stiletto heels the length of kitchen knives.

'*Mamma mia!*' an elderly woman exclaims in my ear. 'I don't know how anyone can wear those. I even fell wearing these!'

I look down at her feet: she's wearing bedroom slippers.

Her face and lip are cut. She seems offended when I laugh in delight, but it's only because I've never actually heard an Italian say *Mamma mia* before.

Most of Siracusa is pretty battered too, especially the old town, which lies on a promontory known as Ortygia. This is an altogether delightful contrast to the modern town, a place of shadowy streets and piazzas wilting in the sun. Time-worn houses are exuberant with pot-bellied, wrought-iron balconies. The *gelaterie* and restaurants are full of middle-aged Germans in floppy white hats, while Frenchwomen wander the streets taking pictures of geranium pots. A policeman slumps inside his car in the main piazza smoking a cigarette, waiting wistfully for a crime. The only burst of energy is on the cathedral steps, where an anxious mother is straightening her daughter's long wedding veil and train.

Tina and I scurry around her and into the cathedral, where we sit in the shadows as the bride walks down the aisle. She's plump, with dyed blond hair fixed in ringlets down the side of her face. Two bridesmaids follow with orange roses in their hair. No one seems to be paying any attention to the triumphal march; half the guests are still straggling in behind the bride, gossiping in exaggerated whispers. They clatter into the pews, unheeding as the opening prayer is read out. A tall man in a suit is taking a video; the camera is almost stuck in the bride's face and a spotlight glares from the altar.

I glance around at the building. Siracusa's cathedral is the earliest church in western Christendom, constructed under Bishop Zosimus in the seventh century. The Christians were still nervous in those days; it looks like a fortress from the exterior. Inside the elegant ceiling of dark stone is studded with heraldic shields from which heavy metal chandeliers hang on massive chains. The floor is a pattern of inlaid stone. In front of the wedding pair an impressive altar of burnished silver glimmers in the dim surroundings.

The bride and groom kneel on red prayer stools. The groom is balding and sweating in a tight grey suit. His bride is younger and pretty and he looks as if he can't quite believe his luck. I feel unaccountably sad for the bride; her wedding seems like such a disorganised affair. There are so few guests in the vast emptiness of the massive cathedral, and I have an urge to rush around asking them to stop talking. Maybe all Sicilian weddings are like this, haphazard and convivial. When the bride walks back up the aisle she seems happy enough. The groom looks vaguely embarrassed but a lot more relaxed. After they step outside I can hear rice falling on a car roof and the sound of slamming doors.

Wandering around the interior of the cathedral, I find a side chapel displaying a bit of bone that was once part of the left arm of St Lucy. Her chapel is a bit of a shock, as if some mad architect plonked an ornate corner of Versailles down into the austerity of the cathedral. The ceiling is painted with prophets and angels, cherubs pop out of fluted columns, and a little balcony erupts in a baroque blossom from the wall, held up by bare-breasted women. Below, more respectfully dressed supplicants come and go, smudges of black kneeling in a sea of colour. A blaze of electric candles illuminates the silver casket that contains the fragment of holy bone. There's also a life-sized silver statue of St Lucy, which is carried around the town on her saint's day.

Lucy is the patron saint of sight, of Siracusa and of all

Sicily. I'm finding myself increasingly fascinated by the saintly side of Catholicism, with its bizarre blend of belief and fantasy. According to legend, Lucy, the daughter of a wealthy Siracusan merchant, took a vow of perpetual chastity after seeing a vision of St Agatha. Lucy was denounced to the authorities as a Christian, probably during the persecution by Diocletian in 304. She was condemned to confinement in a brothel, but by the intercession of the Virgin Mary her legs became locked and her virginity was preserved. The authorities attempted to burn her; the flames were repelled. Her eyes were gouged out and she was finally dispatched with a sword. St Lucy frequently appears in medieval paintings with her eyes displayed on a platter, much in the way St Agatha displays her breasts.

I can never really tell in Sicily where history and legend become woven together. After a while I realise it doesn't really matter. It's nice to think that Archimedes ran naked down the street, that St Agatha had miraculous breasts and Lucy locked legs. It's nice to think that Marcella's friend Maria went to meet her Maker with a smile on her face, bathed in a heavenly perfume. As with travel books, there's no such thing as fact, only interpretations.

Outside the cathedral my feet crunch over grains of raw rice, reminding me of the wedding. The bride and groom are probably in some restaurant feasting and laughing, and then they'll take a ship down at the harbour and go off to Malta for their honeymoon. They'll come back and live in a white villa surrounded by red geraniums and blue sea. They'll dine on potfuls of spaghetti and the house will smell deliciously of basil and tomatoes. That's Tina's interpretation anyway. The story of her own relationships is a litany of disaster but she's incurably romantic.

Who cares about the facts? I nod at Tina in agreement. I'm a bit of an incurable romantic myself.

It's nice to believe the married couple will live happily ever after.

There are peachy buttocks and magnificent bosoms everywhere in Noto. Naked saints with skin pink and glossy as icing swoon from church ceilings, and generous dollops of jam-coloured blood drip from their wounds. Roly-poly cherubs look as if they've been fashioned from marzipan: happy little boys with fat dimpled behinds and inadequate wings. Cavorting evangelists display surprisingly shapely thighs and chests and wear little skimpy togas of silk: Roman theme night in a gay bar. An angel bursts from behind great swirls of creamy clouds like a striptease dancer leaping from a birthday cake. Her wings are lovingly detailed and delicate as spun sugar and her robes billow out across the wall. A single breast is showing, perfectly rounded, as tempting as a Sicilian pastry.

The invention of sexy desserts in Sicily's nunneries doesn't seem so extraordinary when I come to Noto. Noto's churches are full of sensuality, and it strikes me that Sicily's confectionary was coming into its own at the same time as the baroque movement flourished. The richness of churches and pastry shops in Sicily is dazzling, sometimes nauseating, always extraordinary. In Siracusa I spot breads baked in the form both of crosses and phalluses. Now, here in Noto's churches, I come across the brittle bones of the dead in glass reliquaries, and they look no different from the sugar-dusted *ossi di morti* under the glass of a baker's counter. The churches in Noto could as well be designed by a confectioner as an architect; they're *pièces montées* on an extravagant scale. Creamy marble oozes from every pillar and cornice. Organs teeter like gigantic, cloying wedding cakes. Pillars twist around on themselves, striped in bright colours like rock candy at the seaside. There are virgin's breasts everywhere. The ceilings are painted in the cassata-colours so beloved of the baroque era, and are a study in debauchery: popping breasts, rude bums, pink nipples scarcely hidden behind transparent swathes of chiffon and richly draped silken robes.

It seems artificial, a bit camp, almost a joke. A church doesn't seem like quite the right place for eroticism, movement and sociability. It seems to me that religion is really about just the opposite: spirituality, stillness, confronting God alone.

'But Catholicism isn't just about religion,' says Tina. 'It's about politics and temporal power too. And it's about passion. You have to get over your British Protestant background.'

Tina follows me around Sicily and lets me scribble away in my notebook, page after page, and then devastates me with a pithy, insightful comment. Baroque doesn't seem to bother her at all. After some thinking I can see that Sicilians took to Spanish baroque in a big way precisely because it's such a gregarious art. They understand crowds and commotion; churches are very public places. And all those saints and miracles I've been hearing about everywhere are an accepted part of everyday life, not something separate from it. In

Montalto, Lucia, named after Siracusa's saint, calls on other saints for advice, while Marcella invokes the Virgin Mary to solve confirmation troubles. And so the martyrdom on the ceiling happens under the astonished gaze of a servant who just happens to be passing on her way to the market, and pauses open-mouthed at the sight. In Sicily religion is part of the day's business; you go in and mutter a prayer between your visit to the dentist and an early afternoon of sin.

A good many baroque churches in Sicily are cluttered and overblown, a few are quite simply superb. There's something delightful about the colourful excess, flamboyancy and sensuality of baroque: just at a moment in history when the Spaniards were dragging everything down, the Sicilians came up with another triumph. Still, I'll never quite get over the nudity and naughtiness, the almost ridiculous martyrdoms, the earthly distractions.

But this is only me. As I gaze at the ceiling a trio of women are kneeling in front of the altar, praying in muted voices.

Santa Maria, Madre de Dio . . .

Their whispers echo around the dome and side altars like the rustling of a hundred birds' wings.

Santa Maria, Madre de Dio . . .

They don't seem to see the odd juxtaposition of their simple prayers and the sensuous extravagance all around them. The women are dressed in humble black and keep their imploring voices low, deferent in the presence of God.

Up above them on the ceiling God is a figure lost among swooping angels, giggling *putti* and a flock of saints. His beard is fluffy and pink as candyfloss, his cheeks gaunt, and he looks hungry for a virgin's breast.

***

There's only one food that Tina is prepared to spend big money on, and that's ice cream. Tina is a careful shopper but something about Sicilian ice cream sends her scattering money like a Hong Kong millionaire in a casino. Tina has lived outside Sicily ever since she was eleven and the only food that she misses, that fires her imagination, is genuine gelato. One of her clearest memories of her childhood in Sicily is standing with a pistachio ice cream in the piazza in Messina staring up at the rearing facade of the cathedral as green sticky rivulets of ice cream ran down her wrist. Then her grandmother called her and she whirled around and the ice cream fell off the cone, *plop*, onto the ground. She cried.

Noto has a couple of *gelaterie* renowned for their ice cream and Tina is now making up for this minor tragedy of child-hood. In a fit of uncharacteristic extravagance she's ordered a *pezzi duri*. It's sliced off an enormous ice-cream cake in multi-coloured layers and includes strawberry and lemon ice cream as well as the pistachio that Tina particularly craves. *Pezzi duri* are becoming harder to find these days, because they aren't easy to make and are far more expensive than buying ice cream on a cone, but Tina seems oblivious to the fact that she's about to lose a couple of limbs at the cash register. Noto and Palermo are just about the only places still selling *pezzi duri*. Tina's is sprinkled with candied fruit peel and smothered in whipped cream.

I've resigned myself to a budget of granita, which suddenly seems a bit plain, although I'm having the unusual mandarin-orange granita for which Noto is famous. Gazing at the flamboyant dessert on Tina's plate I realise ice cream is a very baroque treat. For a start there's all that lurid colour. And like baroque art, it really is a rather clever invention; a lot of technical expertise is required to create it and the result is far more sophisticated than it appears. It doesn't surprise me at all that ice cream as we know it today was invented during the baroque era, for it was under the Spanish that the ices introduced by the Arabs became truly splendid. By the eighteenth century, Sicilians were munching their way through vast quantities of iced wine, iced coffee and chocolate, sorbets and ice creams whenever they could. Visitors to Sicily throughout the century commented on its universal appeal. Victor Amadeus of Savoy, briefly King of Sicily from 1713 to 1720, famously called the government in Palermo an 'ice cream parliament' in which the members appeared to do little but eat ice creams between parliamentary sessions. He wasn't amused.

Tina is more enthusiastic. She sups and sighs and licks a pistachio moustache from her face. Ice cream seems to bring out her abandoned side; even her unsweet tooth disappears in the face of this sublime junk food. In Siracusa I watch her devour a *bombe* packed with vanilla ice cream, whipped cream, meringue, crumbled macaroons, orange peel and candied cherries as if she hasn't eaten for a week. Everywhere we go she succumbs to cones topped with dizzying ziggurats of ice cream: pistachio, blushing strawberry, zippy lemon with a kick of vodka, comforting caramel. Even pseudo ice creams wheedle their way around her aversion to sugar. In the heat of Marsala Tina devours *gelo di melone* made from watermelon pulp thickened with cornstarch and sprinkled with chopped pistachio nuts, cinnamon and chocolate, all served up chilled and decorated with jasmine flowers: a homage to baroque beauty.

Sicilians have always loved their ice cream and it's a taste they carried to the rest of the world. A Sicilian called Procopio Coltelli brought the craze to France when he opened up a café in the heart of Paris, hung with crystal chandeliers and mirrors. Parisians went mad for the taste of *sorbetti* which, like coffee, was a novelty at the time. 'Ice cream is exquisite,' wrote Voltaire, a regular. 'What a pity it isn't illegal!'

Still, *sorbetti* wasn't exactly ice cream. The development of ice cream seems to have taken place around the 1750s, probably in France. The incorporation of cream, milk and eggs gave sorbets more boldness and body. Once ice cream could be moulded, anything was possible: coupes, parfaits, cakes, even (mercifully now out of fashion) ice-cream omelettes. Another novelty was the *bombe glacée*, a dessert of ice cream filled with custard and cake crumbs of the sort Tina devoured in Siracusa. For a while it became the fashion to serve a *bombe* at any celebratory dinner.

The *schiumone* of eastern Sicily, with a centre of frozen egg yolks whipped with sugar, is a local variation on the *bombe*, but such baroque extravaganzas aren't as common as they used to be. One of the few places left in Sicily where you can easily find them is down at the Marina on Palermo's waterfront. The Marina is another place haunted with a sense of the capital's former grandeur. Overlooked by rows of elegant mansions on the harbour and shaded by trees heavy with scarlet blossoms, the Marina has been celebrated in the letters and diaries of almost every historical visitor to Sicily's capital. In the good old days anybody who was anybody paraded up and down in the evenings and listened to the nightly concerts performed on the waterfront, but you need a fertile imagination to glimpse the Marina's glory these days. Half of Palermo's wartime rubble is dumped in the sea nearby, and its mansions are still scarred with bomb damage. The road itself is a humming highway with several lanes of traffic, the views over the sea are blocked by a tatty funfair. Tunisian immigrants sit out on the footpath hawking plastic buckets, rope, deckchairs, foam mattresses and garden tables.

Tina drags me down here every evening we're in Palermo so that I can empty my bank account into the coffers of the Marina's two surviving cafés. They're considered to serve the best ice cream in all of Palermo (which probably means the best in Sicily, if not the world) and will still go to the trouble of creating a *bombe* or frozen sponge if required. They serve *pezzi duri* too, just like in Noto, enticing customers with pastel shades and florid toppings of candied squash and crystallised flowers. Tina is in heaven.

'Talk about food and sex,' she says. 'This is better than sex!'

And she spoons another seductive dollop of mango ice cream into her mouth, moaning in delight. Choosing the right flavour has been a lingering process since there are so many of them. I've gone for a rather unusual jasmine ice cream subtly flavoured with a hint of cinnamon. I've already eyed up the lime and vodka and the pink promise of cherry and kirsch. The range of flavours suitable for ice cream must be one of the reasons for its success. Just about anything goes. The aristocracy in *War and Peace* eat carrot-flavoured ice cream, and in Sicily I've seen kiwi, pomegranate, mulberry, prickly pear and even rice ice cream. Recently *baci baci*, made from hazelnut chocolates, has taken the island by storm.

I sit down on the Marina with Tina eating my jasmine and cinnamon, and when I close my eyes against the dust and roar of traffic for a moment I fancy I hear the creak of carriage wheels and the rustle of silk. In the early twentieth century the carriages of half Europe's petty nobility stopped here on the waterfront, and ice cream was carried out to the occupants. (It was considered beneath one's dignity to sit at the pavement tables.) Like them, I think of ice cream as an aristocratic treat, no doubt a legacy of my continental upbringing. This is a sophisticated and elegant dessert throughout much of Europe, not the child's treat of Australia. Ice cream to me is Viennese cafés, a slender French glass beaded with condensation and filled with an extravagance of vanilla and melted chocolate, an Italian confection in green and pink served by a waiter in white. Ice cream is adult and sexy; advertisements on Italian television show couples romping in bed in a tumble of satin sheets, sculpted flesh and premium vanilla.

I have my comfort foods, but ice cream isn't one of them, despite my British culinary heritage and Australian home. Continental Europeans make the best ice cream but they consume it in relative moderation. Ice cream in Sicily certainly isn't childish and quite often has nothing at all to do with cream. It hints of urban glamour, not rural nostalgia. And, as Tina and I depart from the Marina every evening in a haze of ice cream pleasure, we discover it certainly isn't cheap. This is sophisticated eating that comes at a price; a clever creation that blends technology with culinary art.

The Marina is now one of the ugliest stretches of water in the world. Palermo's statues have all lost their arms and the buildings are battered. Noto is falling down and even the gargoyles are grimacing in despair. But the Sicilians have always kept their eye on the important things in life. Even the simplest scoop of ice cream is exotic and splendid: mellow mango deep as a summer sunset, mulberry dark as a bruise, watermelon pink and icy, tangy tangerine. The taste of jasmine lingers on my lips like a kiss.

Sicily isn't what it used to be, but its food is as stunning as ever.

We've arrived in Noto, Tina and I, after driving over from Siracusa, singing to pass the time. We drive down a steep wooded valley, across a river, through a citrus grove and past ugly slag heaps coughed up from asphalt mines. We stop to stretch our legs in Ávoca; more baroque glory and decay among streets shaded by leaning palm trees. Soon drystone walls and rocky uplands are left behind, giving way to vineyards and almond plantations. Farms of grey stone hunker under carob trees, surrounded by hedges of prickly pear. This is a rich area known for its market gardens, and is the source of some of Sicily's best aubergines, chillies, peas and celery. Tomatoes grown here, tinned or made into concentrate, end up in Britain and America. Noto's artichokes are also famous.

All this provincial baroque and bursting fertility is a long way from the melancholia of Palermo and the west coast, but even here in this cheerful region disaster and death have always been lurking. The same earthquake of 1693 that flattened Ragusa also destroyed Ávoca, Noto and most of the other towns hereabouts. Noto was hardest hit. 'Then came an earthquake so horrible, so ghastly that the soil undulated like the waves of a stormy sea, and the mountains danced as if drunk,' wrote a poetic eyewitness after the event, before adding: 'The city collapsed in one terrible moment, killing more than a thousand people.' So devastated was the town, and so unstable the land on which it stood, that rebuilding proved impossible.

The inhabitants were forced to move away and construct a new town from scratch: a remarkable opportunity amid disaster. Under the Spanish-Sicilian Duke of Camastra and a team of local architects, the citizens rose to the occasion, creating not just a new place to live but one of the world's masterpieces of baroque town planning. It's all still there. Three main streets run parallel to each other across the hillside, punctuated by three squares dominated by three main churches, all linked by grandiose flights of steps. Unusually, the lower end of town is reserved for the well heeled, while the top of the hill is designated for the poor. Here the grandeur of the baroque vision gives way to a maze of narrow lanes and tiny houses, some not more than a single room, jumbled around churches and convents. Everything glows magnificently in honey-coloured limestone. Noto is a triumph, an example of baroque architecture at its exhilarating and beautiful best, and one of the great achievements of this period in Sicilian history.

One day the glories of Noto will all come tumbling down. Churches are now closed, convents abandoned. Baroque buildings crack and crumble, and in 1996 the cupola of the cathedral imploded. A fraction of it still remains, held up by a cage of steel girders, and 'restoration' has been taking place ever since. Half of Noto is under scaffolding, but it looks more like a town that's being dismantled than renovated. We wander into the central piazza to find most of it barricaded off with corrugated iron covered in scruffy election posters, and the town hall boarded up and abandoned. Cars career through narrow streets, sending vibrations through the delicate buildings. Teenagers on mopeds roar back and forward trailing oily blue smoke. Noto's famous gargoyles have blackened faces and look a bit peeved.

And yet if Noto is tatty it's because the town is alive, a here-and-now sort of place. Noto isn't a baroque fossil polished up for the tourists. The town has the wilted but rather charming decadence of some old socialite who refuses to succumb to plastic surgery and just goes on living with the wrinkles. There's no sense of distance: people slap posters on old walls, congregate on marble steps as casually as they would in their living room, zoom honking along traffic-filled baroque roads. Under the grand Porta Reale a man casually stations a cart, brightly painted with characters from Sicilian folk tales: Roger the Norman and Saracens and Spanish knights. He's selling *passatempi* (literally 'pastimes' or nibbles): slices of *torrone*, salty pumpkin and sunflower seeds and roasted nuts. Teenagers buy cubed chunks of watermelon and coconut from a bed of ice and slurp them on the steps of the ruined cathedral.

The architecture and layout of most European cities is designed to impress and intimidate. Haussmann laid out the boulevards of Paris so that manoeuvring armies could control the masses; the Hapsburgs built a grandiose Vienna to cele-brate the glories of their empire. These aren't cities where

Italians would feel comfortable. Italian cities are intimate; they're celebrations of people and ideas, not politics. In the true sense of the word, Italian cities are public spaces. The flamboyant Pretoria fountain in Palermo is no different from a simple village well: people cluster around its rim, gossiping and splashing. In Noto, townsfolk gesticulate in stately squares, slurping ice cream and unbuttoning their collars to fan themselves in the evening heat, lingering indolently. They bustle into baroque churches the same way they visit the bank, for a quick transaction with God. There aren't any intimidating monuments or grand vistas—only intimate squares, underwear fluttering from balconies, lunch consumed at pavement tables, lovers' tiffs overheard by the neighbours.

We walk along a sleepy street, passing an old woman sitting on a stool outside the door of her house. She's lost most of her hair and teeth, and has so many wrinkles her eyes have almost disappeared. She's wearing a flowery, baggy dress, but her feet are proud in shiny gold high-heeled shoes. Her face is half in shadow, grey hair scraped back, as she watches the town collapse around her.

'Who died anyway?' she mumbles at us as we pass.

The old woman tells us that someone must have died because the church bells are tolling. Tina takes off her sunglasses with the elegance of a movie star confronted with a fan, and looks at the old woman as if deciding whether to answer.

'I've no idea,' Tina says finally.

'Because I have to know if it's a friend of mine. I'll have to bring something, won't I?' responds the woman anxiously.

'Yes, but I don't know who died,' retorts Tina sedately.

It's just a fleeting moment, a passing encounter. Yet after a while I forget the buildings and realise the people are the focus: people at windows and on balconies, people idling on doorsteps, milling in the piazza, joyous over food in cafés and jostling thigh-to-thigh in public buses.

I can't recall much about Noto's baroque beauty, but I can still remember the old woman in her high-heeled shoes, sitting on her doorstep wondering about death.

Sicilian food is glorious, rich in flavour and symbolism. Tuck into just about any foodstuff in Sicily and chances are you'll soon be encountering all of life's chief obsessions made flesh: religion, death—and of course, sex.

Tina and I are sitting in a field gazing at Mt Etna. The sun is moulting, scattering chips of burning colour across a hot landscape fit for Bacchus: voluptuous tangerine trees, grapes swelling golden on the vine, tomatoes sultry in the fields. The almonds are being picked. Squashes are hanging out to dry and will soon be made into sweet candied squares. The hot curves and flushed colours of the landscape are pure poetry, polished and sensual as a love sonnet. The air smells rich and fruity. The sky begins to stir restlessly, full of scudding clouds for the first time in ages, though it mightn't rain for weeks yet. The fig trees have ripened, plump with purple late-summer promise. We're picking them straight off the trees by the roadside, splitting them open and sucking out their pink flesh.

Fruit has always been very, very sexy, none more so than the fig. The word 'fig' is often used to describe both a fruit and the female genitals in various languages; in ancient Greek *sukon* has both meanings. The Greeks thought the fig was a sexy fruit. Here are a few lines from a play by Aristophanes: 'Now live splendidly together free from adversity. Pick figs. May his be large and hard, may hers be sweet.' Not very subtle, is it? No wonder just about every religious artist has used a fig leaf to cover up the naughty bits in their paintings: the choice was hardly made at random. In Sicily 'fig' is also vulgar slang for the female parts, as well as an obscene gesture. Perhaps this is why Sicilian-born Emperor Frederick II thought of figs after Milan's sullen citizens ignominiously drove his wife out of the city. The emperor had figs inserted into the backside of a mule and punished the offending Milanese by forcing them to suck the fruits out and eat them, or else be hanged forthwith.

Fresh figs are a far cry from the shrivelled-up, dried version of the fruit that you find pre-packaged in supermarkets. (Although fine dried figs are delicious too, and quite a different experience from the fresh ones.) Fresh figs have the same elegant shape as the dome on the Taj Mahal, striped purple-blue, and inside they are a burst of luscious red, moist and refreshing. You could try feeding them to someone drizzled with honey and a dollop of cream as a prelude to seduction. When Tina and I have finished gorging by the roadside we collect a few more figs in a brown paper bag to take back to Montalto with us, where we'll eat them with mascarpone, or goat's cheese and honey.

We're on our last short trip. The little town of Sávoca is our destination, but really that's just an excuse to spend the day skirting Mt Etna, which I want to see up close after weeks of spotting it at a distance. Recent volcanic activity has made climbing to the top impossible, but we can at least meander around its flanks. This is a dangerous place: fertile, fiery and beautiful. August is sliding imperceptibly into September as we meander the country roads. Etna's vast pyramid broods over a landscape of fertile farmland alternating with beach and pine forest, vineyards and tangerine groves. The fields are streaked with the scarlet of tomatoes drying in the sun; in the early days tomatoes were called 'love apples' and were considered an aphrodisiac. Up on the hillsides wild quince trees ripen with fruit. Often eaten at weddings, quinces symbolise fertility and beauty. The ancient Greeks and Romans dedicated the fruit to the goddess of love.

Late summer in Sicily is a place full of the most marvellous fruit, a sumptuous fertile sensual season. Peaches are piled in the markets, fleshy as church cherubs, and served up in cafés stuffed with crushed macaroons and syrup. Sicilians love fruit salad with a little sugar and lemon juice and maybe a dash of Marsala, bursting with baroque colour: purple figs, velvet plums, apricots orange as the summer sky in evening. The last of the wild summer strawberries are still to be found in the forests in little nuggets of scarlet flavour; incomparable when sprinkled with sugar and moistened with the juice of blood-oranges and lemons. *Fragolina* (little strawberry) is a term of endearment hereabouts. I'm not surprised, since strawberries are particularly sexy as fruit goes. Who can forget the scene in Roman Polanski's *Tess* in which Alec d'Urberville seduces Tess with roses and strawberries? The luxurious red fruit bursts in soft-focus against Nastassja Kinski's full red lips: an intimate and sensual moment trembling with symbolism.

This is the last moment of abundance; soon Sicily will

slide into a marmalade autumn of fading fertility and intima-
tions of death. It's death once more we've come to visit in
Sávoca, where thirty-five bodies are on display in the village's
Capuchin crypt. These mummies aren't as well known as
their cousins in Palermo, but I've been told they're better
preserved and have much more character. The first body was
displayed here in 1776 and soon the fashion caught on. When
a local aristocrat or other notable passed away their corpse
was taken to a room deep under the crypt known as a
colander. (Food and death are always intimately linked in
Sicily!) Here the bodies were eviscerated, sprinkled with salt
and left to strain for a year. It can't have been much different
from the way Sicilians make tomato preserve these days at
the end of summer, sprinkling the tomatoes with salt and
basil leaves and screwing them tightly into jars. Anyway, after
a year the corpses were cleaned with vinegar, taken outdoors
and set in a well-ventilated place for a while before being
dressed in all their finery.

There's no one about at the Capuchin crypt except a
youthful-looking monk who sells us our tickets and then
vanishes behind a pillar. We grope our way down a flight of
stairs that descends through a trapdoor in the floor of the
church. At the bottom seventeen corpses leer at us from niches
in the wall. A former lawyer stands in a long coat (stiff as
canvas now) buttoned to his ankles, but the coat has burst
open in the middle, exposing his ribcage. Nearby a deceased
doctor wears a natty lace waistcoat but has no hands and is
tipped to one side, arms akimbo as if dancing. A friar has a
cowl and rope belt; the village priest sports a faded red tricorn
hat and sash. His mouth is gaping open, and tucked into it is

what looks like a shrivelled clove of garlic. Perhaps this was part of a disinfecting process; since ancient times garlic has been used to disinfect corpses. Stuffing the mouth of the deceased with garlic cloves was also once thought to prevent them from turning into vampires. In Sicilian tradition, garlic is also placed in the bed of a woman in labour, and later in the cradle, as a way of warding off evil influences.

There's no evil feeling in the crypt, despite the skulls leering from a high ledge around the top of the walls; perhaps the garlic is working. Other bodies snuggle into coffins decorated with skulls, crossbones and heraldic shields. Some are glass-fronted and decked-out inside with cushions and tasselled fringes. One contains Michele Trimarchi, who lies with his legs crossed, his hands folded over his stomach. He wears a black suit and his jawbone has fallen down into his frilly white cravat.

'God, this is macabre!'

But I don't agree with Tina. These bodies resemble extras from Michael Jackson's *Thriller* video, with their tattered embroidered clothes and elegant cravats, their buckle shoes and velvet knickerbockers. This defiant attempt to clutch at the remnants of a former life seems a bit sad, yet strangely fascinating too, and a little amusing. Death is rarely sinister in Sicily; if anything it's sentimental. People used to come down into this crypt to visit their grandfathers, perhaps to chat to them just as Marcella chats to Maria lying in Montalto grave-yard. This ritual doesn't seem macabre to me but nostalgic and rather beautiful.

Sicily is like a Capuchin corpse: important once, now abandoned. Sávoca village, when we walk around it, hangs on to the hillside with bits dropping off it, slowly rotting away. The hill is crowned with a great Norman castle, later added to by the Spanish, and there are several large *palazzi* and half a dozen churches; this must have been a thriving place once. But the castle is overrun with weeds and sparrows and the *palazzi* are flaking into the street as if struck by some dreadful wasting disease. The choir and apse of the church disappeared into the valley during a landslide and parts of the town sit in heaps of earthquake rubble. In the middle of it all the landed gentry hold out like refugees in the piazza, dozing over cups of coffee and calling each other *Don*, just as they did in the days of the Spanish. I'm sure there are Trimarchis and Procopios among them, descendants of the folk in the crypt.

This is my last foray into Sicily. There's something about this island that has resonated in my soul: death, mad religion, passion, sensuality, decay, carnal art and artful carnage. We sit outside the Bar Vitelli, setting for some of the scenes in *The Godfather*, and gorge on figs and peaches and almonds and cream. Inside a fat old woman lurks behind a dusty counter surrounded by grocery boxes that look as if they were designed thirty years ago. There's a white Bakelite wireless and colonial cane chairs. I order coffee.

I feel drowsy, but I don't want to fall asleep in Sávoca; I might wake up to find my fingernails the length of shoe-horns, my hair around my knees. Sávoca looks as though it has slowly been winding down for the last few centuries, stopping altogether in 1950, retreating like a mythical village into cobwebs and crumbling stone.

Sicily is a place of fairytales and legends, an island of saints and bandits and sweet ravaged beauty. I smile at Tina across the table. We sip our coffee and finish off the figs.

Then we drive back to Montalto.

No sooner are we back in the village than we hear that Tina must make an appointment with the priest. Marcella reminds her cautiously that she has to confess before she acts as god-mother in this weekend's confirmation. Since we're all going to church tomorrow anyway for the annual village festival, this would be a good opportunity to speak to Padre Perrino.

Tina is suspiciously quiet when her mother relays this message to her. I hold my breath, waiting for her reply. The three of us are in the kitchen bottling sauce for the winter, surrounded by sackloads of soft ripe tomatoes bursting with summer juices. The tomatoes are big, the size of my clenched fist, far better for tomato sauces than any I can buy in my local supermarket in Sydney. Whenever Marcella gives me a recipe containing tomatoes I know I'll have to double the quantity back home in order to achieve the same rich abun-dance. The secret of a good tomato sauce, says Marcella, is to barely cook the tomatoes at all. Just a few minutes is enough to let the juices burst out and blend with the olive oil and whatever you have frying in the pan.

Tina is skinning tomatoes that have been boiled just long enough to allow the skins to come away from the flesh with ease. She concentrates in silence, but I can see her annoyance in the way she yanks at the skins. Tomato juice splatters across the table.

'I've already been to confession,' she finally says.

There's a disbelieving silence in the kitchen and I nearly slice off my finger with the knife I'm using to finely chop some celery stalks. The celery, along with carrot, onion and season-ings, is going into the pan of tomatoes and will be simmered into a purée. It says a lot about my growing confidence that I'm no longer worrying about how *much* celery and onion goes in. I just chop it up and throw it into the pan without even double-checking with Marcella, feeling triumphant.

'Yes, because of course I knew there wouldn't be time when I got back, and anyway I didn't want to talk to *our* priest. So I went to confession the other day. In Noto, as a matter of fact. We just happened to be passing a church, and so I popped in. Isn't that right, Brian?'

I scrape more celery into the frying pan. We were in a church in Noto all right, but I seem to remember we were ogling the breasts of the women on the ceiling. Fortunately, however, I'm spared an answer.

'You expect me to lie to Padre Perrino? How can I lie to my God?' Marcella cries, stabbing at a pile of tomatoes with a fork.

'Ma, you don't have to lie.'

'Oh, Holy Lady of Sorrows, what have I done to deserve such a daughter?'

Tina has finished her peeling. She pounds with unneces-sary fury at her skinless tomatoes with a potato-masher, glaring at them as if they might jump up and bite her. The ripe tomatoes smell glorious. Marcella's kitchen is infused with the rich scent as the sauce bubbles away on the stove, red as Etna lava. Marcella hovers over the saucepan with sea salt and pepper, sprinkling and tasting. Her demented energy is a way of relieving her annoyance, I think, and deflecting attention from the conversation.

'Oh, well,' says Marcella, putting a wealth of emotion into her words.

I suspect Marcella has had a lifetime of *Oh, wells*. I hover around the cooking and conversation helplessly, but fortunately at that moment Marcella decides the sauce has cooked enough and I throw myself into a bustle of bottling. The sauce smells rich and fruity and plops into the jars with a satisfying squelch.

Tina heaves another bag of tomatoes onto the table. The cooking lulls us: rich tomato steam rising from the stove, rhythmic chopping and peeling, the satisfaction of producing this rich summer sauce that will do Marcella and Giuseppe well into winter. Tina and Marcella have fallen into a dangerous silence. As if to rid herself of her irritation, Marcella flings herself into a frenzy of pasta making. She bangs away at the dough with her clenched fists, flipping it over and slapping and pressing it so that I can almost see her frustration ebb away into the mixture. I dust flour off my glasses and sit and crank the handle of the little Imperio until *tagliatelle* are draped all over the dining room like Christmas decorations. Marcella hovers over huge pots of steaming water, stirring and muttering, and takes sips of village wine.

I ask Marcella what kind of pasta we're having tonight.

'*Tagliatelle* with whore's sauce,' she answers, wiping down the table and laying out spoons and forks for dinner.

'It's spicy,' says Tina, as if sensing that I'm trying to find a neutral topic of discussion. 'And that risqué name! Maybe it's a baroque dish too.'

Whore's sauce is one of Marcella's favourites, and one of mine. It contains onion, garlic, capers, olives and chilli in a tomato sauce. Often anchovy oil and a few finely chopped anchovy fillets are used in preparing the sauce, adding a richness of taste without an overpowering fishy flavour. The result is a spicy dish full of temptation and delight—a little bit wicked, as its name suggests. *Pasta alla puttanesca!* Trust Sicilians to be so forthright with a name.

'I think that prostitutes ate it,' offers Marcella. 'You know, it's so quick to make, but it's rich and nourishing. They could have dinner quickly and then be back on the job, eh?' She looks at Tina and me with a twinkle in her eye. There's a moment of surprised stillness and then we all burst out laughing.

'Not what I heard,' says Tina. 'I heard it's a favourite of married women who are having affairs. You know, quick to make, but it has such a lingering smell. The poor husband thinks his wife has been slaving over a hot stove all afternoon.'

These observations put us all in high humour, and the tiff over Tina's confession seems to have been forgotten. If men did more cooking there would be less wars. There's something very intimate and almost meditative about cooking and eating together. We sit down at the table, twisting up our *pasta alla puttanesca* and sighing with satisfaction. When the meal is finished Tina leans over and gives her mother a kiss on the cheek. She'll go to confession first thing tomorrow, she says.

There might be passion in pasta, but apparently there's peace too.

Next day sees Tina demurely walking down to church to see Padre Perrino. I follow with Marcella half an hour later, and trail her into the Mother Church, Montalto's most important church, which I've not yet visited. Even here miracles have happened. Some fifty years after its founding in the sixteenth century the church was struck by lightning during a fierce storm. Much of the building was set ablaze, and the fire soon spread to the hangings and wooden cross of the central crucifix, which was the work of one of Sicily's finest sculptors, Frate Innoccenzo da Pietralia. Yet although the hangings were reduced to ashes and the cross was charred and blackened, the figure of Jesus itself remained miraculously unharmed. The Christ still hangs there to this day; it's a curious yellow colour, with a crown of thorns as disorderly as a crow's nest. Innards spew out of the wound in his side. As you walk in front of the figure the expression on its face is said to change from passion to agony to joy.

'See,' cries Marcella eagerly, dragging me to one side of the altar. 'It's the second miracle of the crucifix. First it's saved from the fire. Then the changing of the face. Look, from here you see the expression of his passion.' She grasps my arm and hauls me across the altar. 'Now here he's joyful.'

She crosses herself as I stand and look around. The church has fake marble and pink walls onto which concrete roses have been stuck. Slogans are painted across the arches of the nave like pronouncements of the Chinese communist party. *God is rich in mercy. God is great in love.* And the one in the middle: *Heart of Jesus, I trust in you.*

Two young acolytes, in white robes trimmed with red, shuffle up to the chairs behind the altar and sit down, rubbing sleepy eyelids. Tina walks down the aisle and joins us, silent on the subject of her confession. Padre Perrino enters and starts intoning into a crackling microphone. Then he sprawls back in a chair and waves imperiously at the villagers to be seated. Most of them are women; Lucia, as usual, is attached like a limpet to the salvation of the front pew.

I slip out the door just as the service begins. Outside in the piazza the menfolk are standing around in crotch-scratching groups that include members of the band and two policemen. Like most Sicilian policemen they have a slightly dissipated look: belts slung low beneath beer bellies, faces unshaven, bags under their eyes, sweaty patches under the arms. They loll against their patrol car, smoking and complaining.

We're all waiting for the grand parade that will start after the service, all part of an annual village festival. Time passes. Two young girls come along and strew the cobbles with oleander blossoms. An old woman totters out of the church and complains the service is taking too long. The bandsmen suddenly get tired of sitting around waiting and, stubbing out their cigarettes, pick up their instruments and burst into tune. Their uncertain hooting brings Padre Perrino rushing out of the church to hush them. The oleanders are trampled. Padre Perrino goes back inside. A little boy takes a drumstick off the drummer and beats people with it while his doting mother looks on in amusement.

There's such a hubbub I'm sure no one inside the church can hear mass. When it's over the worshippers stream out of the church doors and in a general muddle organise themselves for the procession. Then we all head up the street. The trumpets are farting away as the organist shouts prayers against the clanging of the church bells. Padre Perrino strides up at the front holding the Eucharist like a battering ram, a scowl on his face. An acolyte is holding a tasselled umbrella in yellow silk as little girls in white scurry about throwing petals.

I imagine the procession will only take about an hour, but I'm wrong. The Eucharist has to be carried through just about every street in the town, so the cortege will be wandering about for most of the afternoon and evening. Then there are the private altars that the villagers have set up by the roadside, at which the priest is obliged to halt and give a sermon. He stops at the first one, where a square of red carpet has been laid down on the cobblestones, surrounded by pots of geraniums and vases of carnations. There's a Jesus poster taped to the wall and a plastic Mary with a light winking from her brow. The priest starts to mumble. The family whose house the altar belongs to listens in rapt attention, but no one in the crowd appears to be interested. Everyone mills about, smoking and gossiping away. Then they regroup and off they go. The trumpets wail and burp to the out-of-tune tootling of clarinets.

Marcella is determined to follow the Eucharist until she drops, but Tina and I grow swiftly weary. Before we slip off Marcella makes us promise we'll fling open the windows of Aunt Rita's house in order to let in the light of the Eucharist and the priest's prayers for the coming year. We clatter through the echoing building, flinging open the shutters and letting bursts of late-afternoon sunlight into the unused and melancholy upper rooms, probably for the first time in years. I think of Aunt Rita and her casual generosity in lending her granny flat to me all these weeks. Sad yet kind, Aunt Rita must be the archetypal Sicilian.

I lean out of the window as the procession comes meandering down the hill. I put my arm around Tina's shoulders and we look down at Padre Perrino's bald head, the purple caps of the bandsmen and the big white hats of the little flower girls. I'm suddenly very happy, and sad that the confirmation is nearly upon us and soon we'll have to go home.

The tasselled umbrella vanishes down the street followed by Pietro the organist, the acolytes, the exhausted villagers. The trumpets give their final unconvincing honk and fall silent. We close the shutters and fumble our way down the stairs in the dark. Outside, the faint smell of crushed oleander blossoms sits in the air like a sigh.

8

LAST SUPPER

Montalto is an ugly little town, but the luminosity of Sicily makes it beautiful. It seems to have a perpetual glow that distracts from the peeling walls and uninspiring buildings: the air is sharp and crisp as lemons in the morning, thick and honeyed in the late afternoon. Even in the glare of midday the light is beautiful, dancing like Asti Spumante in the piazza. The main street is noisy with yelling kids and splut-tering Fiats, and then you step around a corner to find hushed somnolence in a canyon of walls wine-yellow and amber. Oleander blossoms fall onto the pavements, pale as the dripping wax of candles in churches. The Mediterranean light scribbles poetry at every corner.

These are hot days made for chilled wine watered down with lemonade. Marcella sits at the kitchen table with a big bowl of lemons at her elbow, slicing them into chunks and dropping them hissing into our drinks. Now that our holiday is drawing to a close Tina sits with us, close to her mother, as if wearied of warfare. They touch each other on the back of the hands and laugh and reminisce. The lemons in the bowl glow like a sultan's ransom and the sharp fizzy wine trickles down my throat with dangerous pleasure. I'm reminded of the lemons in the opening scene of Giuseppe Tornatore's *Cinema Paradiso*. At the start of the film an old Sicilian woman phones her son in Rome; he hasn't been back to the island for thirty years. His mother is convinced he'll remember his childhood hero, a film operator called Alfredo who has recently died, and she wants her son to come back to Sicily for his funeral. As she talks of the past, the camera focuses on a bowl of lemons that seem to be the old woman's memories made visible. You can almost smell the fruit, the sea that glitters beyond the window, the heat of the peeling shutters, the evocative pull of the south.

Tina has come back to Sicily too, but only briefly, and her memories are of America. Her relationship with her mother has a geographic as well as emotional dislocation. Marcella, despite thirty years in America, is still Sicilian to the core, filled with religion and death and thoughts of what could have been. As the lemon light of afternoon fades towards evening her thoughts grow weary. We sit out on the balcony as hot scented air stirs around the street corner. The night sky is like velvet, and the church blushes under dim spotlights. Ice cubes clink in our tall glasses. We drop halved apricots into them, leaving them to soak up the wine before fishing them out with our fingers and eating them. It's a night made for reminiscence, for sadness and regrets as bittersweet as lemon blossoms by moonlight.

Regrets? Marcella regrets not having done more for her daughters when they were young, regrets that their relationship is now inevitably difficult and emotionally fraught. She knows her daughters blame her for staying with an abusive father— how could she not know, when she blames herself too?

And so I sit on the balcony with Marcella and Tina as night falls over Montalto and the ice melts in our drinks. Marcella is an intelligent, observant and open-hearted woman, but she has let herself be crushed by life. She almost seems to welcome her sadness, displaying it with a proud stoicism almost religious in its fervour. I feel like shaking her and telling her it isn't too late, that she could live another twenty years. But it isn't really my business, and Marcella won't change now. Her soul has long ago surrendered to circumstance.

'Anyway,' says Tina to me one day. 'Don't listen to my mother's sob stories. She's not the Snow White of the piece either.'

Well, I'm sure Marcella has done things she's told me nothing about, but Tina is too consumed by her own bitterness to recognise the bitterness in her mother, the realisation of a life stunted. Abandoned dreams, violence, uncertainty, betrayal, fatalism: Sicily in microcosm is reflected in the lives of the Calascione family. Half a century ago Marcella set out for her job with a travel agent in Messina, dreaming of foreign destinations and languages and freedom. Now the only thing left for Marcella, when her husband is out, is to sit at home on her own and write poems and snatch moments of French conversation practice while she can.

Prompted by lemons and wine and Tina's signs of affection, Marcella tells us about her poems for the first time. She pulls out a red-backed notebook and rifles through it, exposing page after page of small, cramped writing. There are lines crossed out and others inserted, and notes scribbled in the margins; years of speculation in blue ink. When Marcella comes to the page she's looking for, she pauses and looks up at us. This poem is called 'Leaving New York' she says, and starts to translate. At the opening the character in the poem—Marcella herself—sits with a heavy heart at her window in the city, preparing to farewell America.

> *Now that the days of my life approach sunset,*
> *Like a siren song I hear my town calling me back*
> *To the nostalgic summers of Sicily.*
> *As my life ebbs away like a wave on the beach*
> *I whisper farewell to you, New York,*
> *City of splendid lights and heavy hearts*
> *Where I abandoned the beautiful years of my youth.*

The night is very quiet. In the distance a dog barks and then falls silent. Feet tip-tap along the street below and a door bangs. Marcella's voice wavers and then she continues with the second verse, translating hesitantly, sometimes backtracking when she finds a better phrase.

'It's so much better in Italian,' says Tina. 'It's so sad.'

Her eyes are full of tears: maybe she does recognise her mother's tragedy, even though she doesn't want to face its implications and isn't ready to forgive. I think of the Chinese legend in which an immortal gives a man a gift of wine which, when drunk, will make him forget the past. Happy wine, it's aptly called. There's no happy wine for Sicilians, no way for Tina and Marcella to forget the past. The past in Sicily is always harsh and never far away, and nobody ever forgets.

Marcella's tears are dripping onto the notebook, smearing the ink. I hold her hand and it feels cold and fragile. In a moment of grace Tina puts an arm around her mother's shoulders and pulls her close.

Marcella sits surrounded by lemons and poetry, weeping without a sound.

I like lemons. Who doesn't? The lemon is bold, sassy, sexy, beautiful and a bit dangerous—the Cleopatra of the kitchen. The lemon has a delightful shape and an eye-catching colour that might have been dreamed up in some hip graphic design studio. Lemons are cheerful things, especially in Sicily, where they're often enormous. I'm used to seeing commercial lemons in Sydney's supermarkets, picked when they're still green and immature, stored artificially and then ripened with ethylene gas; the fruit shrinks and the skin becomes thick and tough. Lemons left on the tree are large, full of juice and scented even before you cut them open. They're irresistible. Sicilian artist Renato Guttuso was so dazzled by them that he painted a canvas of lemons, full of blazing intensity and vitality. It was this painting that seduced Elizabeth David in the greyness of post-war England; after seeing it she decided to write a cookbook on Italy. Using words like 'lemon', 'apricot' and 'almond', and writing about the freshness of Mediterranean cuisine in the face of English culinary bleakness, she recalled afterwards, seemed almost indecent. Guttuso's painting appeared on the cover of the pioneering *Italian Food*. Elizabeth David ranks lemon juice second only to salt as a seasoning in the history of cooking. Funnily enough lemons are only mentioned twice (as a dressing for salad and an ingredient in granita) in her book, and most of Sicilian cuisine is entirely ignored.

The small, sweet variety of lemon known as *lumia*, often sprinkled with salt, is eaten raw as a snack in Sicily. (It tastes rather delicate and has none of the sharpness of a regular lemon.) Citrons are also greatly appreciated on the island. The fruit is larger than a lemon, with a thick lumpy skin, very thick pith and not much flesh. Both the pith and flesh are eaten together, since on its own the flesh is quite sour. Sicilians like to use citrons in salad, mixed with slices of crisp fennel and dressed in olive oil with a dash of salt and pepper. Oranges are also used in salads, often mixed with red onion and garnished with mint leaves, olives or a little chopped chilli.

The lemon is certainly a characteristic flavour of the Sicilian summer. It's frequently used in dressings, desserts and granita, and also accompanies fish and vegetable dishes. In Marsala, I drop wedges of lemon into cold mineral water to combat the heat, watching the sudden fizz of bubbles and the cloudy oiliness that swirls through the glass, then letting the sharp thirst-quenching flavour trickle down my throat. In Trápani I squeeze lemon over grilled tuna, amazed that something so simple could be so startlingly perfect. Marcella stuffs whole lemons into the cavity of a chicken, then roasts it in the oven to produce meat of marvellous tenderness and fragrance. In Palermo Tina and I succumb to the cold, clever tartness of lemon ice cream, its pale primrose colour concealing a flavour that sets my teeth on edge.

There's poetry in lemons. Pirandello wrote an entire play, *Le Lumie di Sicilia* (1910), based around a gift of lemons that a Sicilian carries to Milan for his childhood sweetheart, an opera singer. The vibrant colour, intense perfume and bitter qualities of the lemons all remind the opera singer of home as she sits in distant northern Italy. Lemons frequently appear in Sicilian literature as potent symbols of memory and nostalgia. Contemporary novelist Dacia Maraini says lemons remind her of her sunlit childhood near Palermo, and even the word 'lemon' gladdens her heart. She admits to an obsessive passion for the fruit, and always carries one in her handbag. Tina, I've noticed, nearly always has lemons in her fridge at home, or studding her fruit bowl like nuggets of gold.

My mother loves lemons, too. As a child I used to watch her make endless cups of lemon tea, squeezing a slice of lemon between her fingers into the cup of brew, where it left an oily trail, then dropping the lemon slice in after it. The spoon tinkled against the porcelain, releasing a perfumed steam of almost oriental richness. Afterwards, she'd pick the lemon out of the bottom of her cup, sodden but still with a sting, and suck the juices out of it, pulling the flesh off and leaving just a sliver of skin abandoned on the saucer. She would squint at me in mock horror at the bitterness, licking her lips.

Maybe it's Marcella, nostalgic and teary-eyed on her balcony, that makes me suddenly nostalgic. I think of the cheesecakes and meringue pies my mother made when I was a child, displayed with bland and creamy innocence in the centre of the table, but secretly loaded with lemon zest like a defiant shout against the ordinary. My mother stirred great pots of sticky lemon curd, yellow as a trumpet fanfare, which made my eyes water over the breakfast table. Another favourite was lime marmalade, lugged in suitcases from Britain and gleefully spread on toast. My mother would squeeze great quarters of lemon over freshly cooked pancakes. Grapefruits were hidden at the bottom of our Christmas stockings and pulled out as if they were treasures. Grapefruits always seemed very special, eaten halved for breakfast with undisguised pleasure with an added sprinkling of sugar, more for the gritty crunch than the sweetness.

My mother was captivated by the seduction of citrus. Now I am too. I see lemons everywhere in Sicily, and they are just another recognition, as I grow older, of how like my mother I really am.

I walk up to the graveyard once more with Tina and Marcella. The wreaths on Maria's grave are shrivelled and grotesque, the pile of soil still waiting for its marble slab. Maria's family has done well, Marcella explains, and she expects some impressive monument to be erected over her grave. Marcella seems happy that her friend has escaped the indignity of being placed in the wall that marks the eastern edge of the graveyard, with its row of little doors like an oversized filing cabinet, behind which the coffins of the poor are slotted.

Tina's relatives have also managed to avoid the ignominy of the filing cabinet; her family members rest under substantial marble slabs. Tina and I trail around after Marcella as she places fresh flowers on the graves of her cousins and aunts. Tina looks embarrassed at the ritual, but I'm rather touched by this communion with the dead. Marcella is standing at the grave of her uncle. 'I bless God with all my heart for the happiness you brought into my life,' she says. She sticks three of the roses she's carrying into the metal urn in front of the headstone.

'He was a brilliant musician. He could play any instrument, except with the mouth. You see what I mean? Not flute or something. Piano, violin, guitar. He died very young. You didn't know him, Concettina.'

We move on to the tomb of Tina's paternal grandparents, Federico Calascione and Anna Recupero. Two brass pots on the marble contain dehydrated chrysanthemums, only the faintest traces of yellow betraying their original colour. Tina pulls the flowers out angrily, so brittle they almost disintegrate in her hands.

'My grandfather was a bastard anyway.'

Marcella doesn't respond. She watches as Tina yanks up a few weeds that have sprouted around the edge of the plot. Tina recalls seeing her grandfather on visits to Sicily as a teenager. She was always terrified to go into his house, she tells me, because of his foul moods, his temper, the big brassy laugh that would set the dogs in the piazza barking. Her grandfather was a tall man, spindly and gaunt, who ate slices of melon off the end of a hunting knife and kicked his dogs. But anyway, Tina adds irrationally, as it turned out he was always quite nice to her.

Marcella doesn't seem to think so; I notice her father-in-law only gets a single rose. 'May the peace of the Holy Spirit always be at the centre of your heart,' Marcella mutters half-heartedly.

But over at her own mother's grave Marcella sits down and weeps a little.

'Your Nonna was very intelligent,' she says to Tina, who stares out crossly over the wall towards the village.

'Especially at maths.' Marcella turns to me. 'She taught herself, because her father refused to let her go to school. He was the village poet and postmaster,' she explains. She trails her fingers softly across the top of the headstone.

I see Tina isn't cross but on the verge of tears. She loved her grandmother. She says she can remember her grandmother doing this very same thing, wandering about putting flowers on tombs without batting an eyelid, and then when she got to her husband's grave sitting down and weeping her eyes out with loneliness, even though he'd been dead for ten years.

'Yes, my parents had a wonderful bond,' says Marcella quietly. For a moment she's silent. 'Afterwards, she was never the same. She was silent and remote, as if her energy went with my father into his grave. She was a lovely woman.'

Suddenly, unexpectedly, Marcella gives me a beaming smile. And here, she adds, is her own plot. She squints approvingly over the landscape. Her future resting-place has a view over the glittering sea as far as the hazy smudges of the Aeolian Islands on the horizon.

We wander on around the cemetery. The headstones are covered in brass lettering extolling the virtues of their occupants—this one hardworking, the other pious and simpatico—and deploring their demise. *Untimely taken from the bosom of his family. Called before her time into the arms of the Lord.* The comments seem grotesquely sentimental at first, but soon I realise they're all the same standard, hackneyed phrases used over and over again until they've become almost meaningless. Death for Sicilians is a ritual: the stock phrases, the obituary posters, the graves with their swooning angels, the flowers, the visits. And I suddenly realise that Sicilians, in spite of their reputation, are actually impressively organised: even the graves are neatly lined up in rows, brushed and cleaned. Death is, after all, just the last ritual of a carefully laid-out ceremony that starts with birth and baptism and moves on to confirmation and marriage. Just like the morning mass, the midday siesta and evening stroll. The *antipasti*, the pasta, the *secondo*, the fruit and coffee. You should only drink a cappuccino before midday. Have chickpea bread on the Feast of Santa Rosalia. Always eat macaroni at weddings. There's a charming, stereotypical anarchy to Sicilian public life, but private life is rigourously organised in a grid of expectations, traditions and rituals that is almost oriental in its complexity. Marcella's graveyard visit isn't just a whim: it's a duty.

Even duties can be heartfelt, something I think a resentful Tina sometimes can't perceive. We end up back at Maria's resting-place and I feel the poignancy of the moment. Marcella has given in to that fatal emotion of immigrants, nostalgia. After all these years she's returned to Sicily, only to discover everything has changed, that what she came back to find isn't there any more: here there are only the ghosts of her past. More tears trickle down Marcella's cheeks. She looks very old and defeated as she sticks the last of her roses into the soil.

'May the beautiful Mother of Jesus adorn your soul with flowers,' she whispers.

Nobody speaks as we drive back home.

***

It's nearly my last evening in Sicily and I want to take Tina out for dinner. She looks tired and melancholy and I decide a pizza might brighten her up; pizza is such a cheerful food. Giuseppe recommends a place down on the coast, and it doesn't take us more than ten minutes to drive there. From the outside the restaurant doesn't look very inspiring. It's a concrete block with dusty windows surmounted by a garish pink neon sign: *Pizzeria Boomerang*.

'You've got to be joking,' I say to Tina.

We soon discover that the chef, Antonio, inherited the name from the previous owner and isn't even sure what it means; he's certainly never been as far as Australia. The very thought seems to make him anxious. He's a little wisp of a man, fragile as a dandelion, with a big dandelion puff of grey hair and mournful eyes. He ushers us into the restaurant as if surprised to see us, flicking a cloth at the tabletops.

The interior of Pizzeria Boomerang isn't any more inspiring than its name. The wooden tabletops are pitted with knife marks and stained with purple wine rings, and 1970s tourist posters hang on the walls. In one corner a huge potted palm leans dangerously. We take a table nervously in its shadow. I tell myself that, if Giuseppe has recommended this place, it must be for good reason—after all, Giuseppe himself ran a pizza parlour in the Bronx. Besides, I'm reassured by the freshness of the toppings lined up in bowls along the counter: salted anchovies in brine, a mountain of capers, strips of artichoke glistening in olive oil, diced onion, sliced mushrooms, chopped garlic, shredded basil, grated cheese. Along the back wall on a wooden rack sit rows of *pagnotte*, the balls of dough from which pizza bases are made. As we settle in, Antonio dusts the bench with flour and plops a *pagnotta* on it, slapping it with his palm and fingers. His nervousness and fragility are suddenly gone: he looks like a man who enjoys his work.

'That's the right way to do it,' says Tina approvingly. 'An Italian pizza maker wouldn't be seen dead with a rolling pin, or flipping the dough in the air like that mad chef in the Muppets.'

I grunt in agreement. Italians can be as fussy about their pizzas as they are about pasta. The elite Associazione Verace Pizza Napoletana requires that the dough be shaped by hand, and include no other ingredients but flour, yeast, salt and water.

Antonio works the dough quickly and efficiently, although I don't see any sign up claiming he's a member of the prestigious association. But I'm sure Antonio knows that if he pokes and prods the dough too much it will lose the air bubbles that make it rise in the oven and keep it soft during cooking. No sooner has he flattened out the wheel of dough than he smears it with tomato purée, sprinkles oregano and garlic over it, and adds a handful of mozzarella and a few cubes of aubergine. I watch him as he cracks an egg onto the middle of the pizza and sprinkles *grattugiato* cheese over the top. With a flick of the wrist he douses the top in olive oil and shovels the pizza on a long wooden paddle into the little arched door of the oven.

The pizza oven squats hunchbacked in the corner, decorated with yellow and blue glazed tiles. It's a miracle of art and technology and nothing like a regular oven; more like the sort Hansel and Gretel were threatened with in the picture books of my childhood. A true pizza oven is heated with wood, and the fire is never completely extinguished but remains overnight in an ashy heap and is then stoked up towards evening (few pizzerias are open at lunchtime) with stout lengths of wood. When the bricks that line the interior turn paler in colour the oven is ready to use. The best bricks for a pizza oven come from Santa Maria near Salerno on the Italian mainland, and are set with clay and insulated with sand. The floor of the oven supports large tiles on a bed of river sand and sea salt, which is able to endure daily heating and cooling without expanding, shrinking or shifting. The heat is intense (at least 400°C), since a pizza must be cooked through in a couple of minutes. A pizza's glory lies in its speed of cooking.

Antonio has only taken twenty seconds to create the topping on the pizza he's making, and minutes later he's pulling it out of the oven. He spins it down on a customer's table together with a flagon of house wine, cold and red and given away by the litre for a few euros. Tina is waiting in delighted anticipation: she misses Italian pizzas. Pizza outside Italy, she says, is a travesty. Pizza, she tells me (jabbing at me with her fork) isn't a stodgy lump of dough onto which gut-bursting mounds of cheese and vegetables are shovelled. Nor can pizza possibly be cooked in an electric oven and then be served up congealing on a plate. It should be cooked over a wood fire in a traditional brick oven, which is why most self-respecting Italians go out for pizza. A pizza should be practically flat when it comes out, the topping bubbling and still too hot to eat when it arrives at the table.

The crust must be blackened and puffed up, both chewy and yet deliciously crunchy.

'The first oven-fired pizza I had was on the evening I graduated from secondary school,' I tell Tina, 'in a little Italian pizza place down by the lake in Geneva. I had a four seasons.'

A four seasons pizza is hard to get right, I now realise, because the various toppings cook at different speeds. The prosciutto in particular has a tendency to dry up and shrivel, curling and cracking at the edges like old vinyl. That evening, as I sat enveloped in celebration and a sad sense of a passing era, the pizza was perfect: ham crisp and juicy, cheese chewy, pulling out in unctuous strings as I cut bite-sized morsels. I remember digging into the slightly burnt crust and thinking it was heaven. Before then, I'd only ever had pizza cooked in an electric oven in the La Siesta pizzeria. Still, even that pizza had been a treat. My parents didn't have much money in those days, and a trip to La Siesta was a grand outing. It was a cheap and honest place, the sort with red-chequered table-cloths and empty Chianti bottles for decoration. Old copper pizza shovels and woven baskets hung on the walls, and little mullioned windows of yellow glass gave jaundiced glimpses of the street. We ate pizza and drank Coke, feeling warm and cosy as we watched people wrapped up against the cold hurry along the pavement. These days I eat pizza fairly often, but it still seems like a treat to me, something warm and special. Pizza with a light green salad and a glass of wine is a proper meal to be savoured and enjoyed. Pizza reminds me of my mother and father, and how they contrived to give me a happy childhood.

'God, you guys were like the Brady bunch,' says Tina.

Tina always says this when I talk about my family. Her tone is faintly mocking with an edge of wistfulness. This is how Tina would like to have grown up, in a *normal* family of Easter eggs and homemade lemon curd, a family that went out to a pizzeria as if it was an adventure.

Antonio brings out a *pizza margherita*, wondrous in its simplicity. It smells rich and fragrant. According to tradition this pizza was invented in 1889 by a chef named Raffaele Esposito on the occasion of a visit to Naples by Queen Margherita of Italy. Several pizzas were presented to the queen, who declared her favourite to be the one with tomato, mozzarella and basil. Since the pizza had the same three colours as the flag of the recently unified Italy this was perhaps a choice of political tact rather than personal taste. Esposito had been tactful also; he replaced the traditional garlic with mozzarella in deference to the royal breath. Think of how little anyone knows about Italian queens and you'll see Margherita was lucky to be immortalised, even if only in the kitchen.

It doesn't take Tina and me long to scoff our *margherita* between us, and soon we're hunting the menu for another pizza. The *margherita* is the basis for most Italian pizzas in concept, and others are created by swapping or adding ingredients. Take off the cheese and you have a *marinara*, which has nothing to do with seafood but was once eaten on long sea voyages, during which cheese couldn't be kept fresh. Take off the tomatoes and you have a *bianca* or white pizza, often referred to as *alla napoletana* everywhere but Naples, where confusingly it's *alla romana*. A traditional Roman pizza in Rome is also lacking in tomato, but is made with oil and onion. In Apulia they favour finely chopped onion, oregano and pecorino cheese (*alla pugliese*). One of the reasons for the popularity of pizza is that you can add just about any topping you desire: coconut if you're Costa Rican; red herring or salmon and onion if you're Russian; eel or squid if you're Japanese. The Hawaiians supposedly like ham and pineapple, although Italians think putting pineapple on pizza is sacrilege. I've seen just about everything in fancy overseas pizzerias: smoked kangaroo, tofu, broccoli, Indian butter chicken.

Antonio hasn't fallen into such foolishness; his menu is sensibly unadventurous. After a bit of good-natured bickering with Tina we settle on an old-fashioned *pizza siciliana*.

'My dad is right, these pizzas are *so* good,' says Tina. 'I never missed Italian food much but when I lived in America I used to long for a real Italian pizza. That was before my Dad started a pizzeria himself, of course. Most of the pizzas in America are so *gross*, it's hard to believe they come from Italy.'

But they did come from Italy, thanks to the Italian immigrants who flocked to America. The first pizzeria, it's claimed, was opened in Spring Street in New York in 1905 by an immigrant called Gennaro Lombardi. But pizza remained an ethnic food until the 1950s, when it suddenly burst into the general American consciousness thanks to returning World War servicemen and pizza's connection with celebrities such as Frank Sinatra and Joe DiMaggio. 'When the moon hits your eye like a big pizza pie, that's *amore*,' sang Dean Martin. *Amore* it has remained: seventeen percent of all restaurants in America serve pizza and millions more are consumed at home.

'So pizza these days is as much an American food as an Italian one,' I suggest.

'But American pizzas are so *gross* and no one even notices because they eat them in front of the TV. It's junk food and junk programs,' says Tina in disgust. The truth is that the two are oddly linked. The TV show that produces the most orders for pizza deliveries used to be *Melrose Place*; orders rose fifteen percent when Heather Locklear became a cast member. (Proving perhaps that food and sex really go together like ham and pineapple?) But the biggest pizza ordering frenzy of all time took place during the hour when O. J. Simpson was speeding down the Los Angeles freeway, live on television— apparently an event so riveting that few could be bothered to make their own dinner.

'Jesus, it's the end of civilisation as we know it,' says Tina in mock horror.

'Or the triumph of pizza!'

'Hm. *This* is the triumph of pizza,' says Tina as she lifts another slice of *siciliana*.

The *siciliana* is indeed an excellent little pizza. The top is smeared with tomato and decorated with anchovy fillets and olives. Capers hide deep in the tomato, producing little hidden explosions of taste, and the olives are sharp and juicy. This is a slice of Sicily, full of unexpected little bursts of flavour.

'You see?' Tina repeats happily. 'A triumph!' She waves a slice of *siciliana* in the air and I know that the house wine we've been knocking back is beginning to take its toll. 'Those American pizzas have about as much similarity to *real* Italian pizzas as pornography has to making love.'

Mm. Food and sex again, there we go. When we're finished Tina suggests we should just pass on desserts and order another pizza, maybe just a small one. A *parmigiana* perhaps?

When Antonio brings it to the table minutes later it's another triumph: fresh creamy mozzarella (nothing like the industrial rubber I buy in the supermarket in Sydney), flavoursome plum tomatoes, aubergine in crisp, blackened wheels. Pizza may be quick and simple, but cooking it to perfection is an art. The surface of the pizza is flecked with black pepper and the red tomato and yellow oil is bubbling nicely. The crust is raised and browned, with speckles of black; the slight charring has been created by the addition of handfuls of wooden shavings to the oven, causing the flames to momentarily flare up. As I cut into it, the crust crackles and splits. The cheese pulls off in thin strings, curling around my fork.

This is definitely not pornography, I tell Tina. It isn't even making love.

This is a grand passion.

Confirmation day dawns bright and clear. After a quick breakfast we're ready to head off. Tina is wearing a short, sleeveless black dress and dark sunglasses. Her hair is fluffed out in abundant waves. To my even greater surprise, Claudia is wearing black too: a short skirt and jacket, high heels, sunglasses. Her hair is gelled up into perky spikes and she's wearing her usual vivid lipstick, even more startling against the sobriety of her clothes. Together, Claudia and Tina look like a pair of glamorous young widows off to celebrate the demise of their wealthy husbands.

We head in convoy to Messina. The cathedral looks onto

a large piazza which, unusually for Sicily, isn't being used as a car park. It has benches and shady trees, even a café in one corner. We're much too early for the service—no one wanted to risk being late at this stage!—and there's still plenty of time to settle down at an outdoor table for coffee and *cannoli*, a favourite indulgence of mine. Its chief ingredient is sweetened ricotta, sometimes with a little candied fruit or flakes of chocolate incorporated into it. The filling is served inside a deep-fried tube of pastry made with sugar, cinnamon, egg yolk and Marsala wine, and sometimes a dash of cocoa. Many commentators have noted the phallic symbolism of the *cannoli* and its oozing white filling. Like many other former products of the nunneries, it teases with sexual connotations.

I crunch up my *cannoli*, sip my *latte* and gaze at the square's extravagant Renaissance fountain, topped by Orion and depicting various myths associated with water and rivers in a hopelessly quirky muddle. Sprites, old river gods with long beards and sagging stomachs, women on galloping horses, giggling *putti* and voluptuous naked naiads with long flowing tresses adorn the upper levels. Underneath *tritoni* recline with arms stretched above their heads, fishy tails entwined, great pendulous testicles casually displayed. They have ugly popping eyes and straggling forked wisps of hair on their chins.

'Never mind that,' says Tina. 'Check out the tower behind you.'

The cathedral's campanile over my shoulder is another study in extravagance and whimsy. A huge lion prances near the summit, rearing on hind legs and clutching a red battle standard in its forepaws. There's a golden rooster, two fierce-looking women poised to strike enormous green bells, some robed saints, chariots pulled by dragons, and knights in armour revolving around a Grim Reaper. These are all distractions from the world's largest astronomical clock, replete with dials displaying hours, days, months, the movement of the planets and religious festivals.

'It's almost noon,' says Giuseppe. 'Every day at noon the cock is crew. And the lion roaring.'

As the clock strikes the hour, angels and animals start parading across the clock face. A golden cockerel does indeed crow, and a lion gives an unexpected mechanical roar, almost causing me to choke on my second *cannoli*. Little human figures trundle in and out, all to the accompaniment of 'Ave Maria' in a distorted bellow. Its midday, and time for the confirmation.

With moustaches of milk and flecks of pastry on our Sunday clothes we flock into the cathedral. It was first built by the Normans in the eleventh century and saw the marriage of Princess Joanna, sister of Richard the Lionheart, to the Norman King William II. Most of it was toppled in the 1908 earthquake and then reconstructed. Much of the sculpture around the main portico is original, representing the usual saints, angels and prophets and, with a particularly Sicilian touch, some naughty stone boys climbing up a huge vine to pluck bunches of grapes.

The cathedral is almost full. People mill about greeting each other with extravagant kisses and hugs accompanied by vigourous backslapping. I can't see many of the demure girls in white I expected at a confirmation: most are dressed to kill in high heels and miniskirts, with broad Moschino belts and Gucci handbags. Coltish, stockinged legs and tanned cleavages are everywhere.

'If it wasn't for an absence of drinks and canapés, I'd think I was at a cocktail party,' I mutter to Tina as we settle down in our pews. Giuseppe and Marcella are along the pew from me, Claudia's family behind. Tina is beside me, with Claudia on her other side.

Tina giggles. She's been looking a bit tense and preoccupied all morning, but the comment seems to relax her. 'They all missed out on confirmation when they were twelve. Probably they haven't been inside a church for years, and suddenly they remember they need a confirmation certificate to get married.'

The congregation rises to its feet. The bishop enters from a side door, followed by his acolytes. He lumbers up the aisle and collapses onto a throne. He has resplendent white robes, white hair, and a chest like a pouter pigeon—a sort of albino Friar Tuck, though he looks far from merry. He launches into the service. The congregation sways and stands, sways and sits, rippling like a field of ripe Sicilian wheat. Their responses whisper around the walls of the cathedral in gusts. *Holy Mary, Mother of God, pray for us sinners, now and at the hour of our death* . . . Tina's lips are moving vaguely but no sound is coming out, and I realise she no more knows the responses than I do.

It's rather startling to observe this chic, chattering crowd suddenly listening to talk about sin and death. *O my Jesus, forgive us our sins, save us from the fires of Hell* . . . The bishop slumps back in his throne and launches into an indifferent sermon addressed to those about to be confirmed. I wonder what Claudia, sitting beside me, really makes of all the responses she has so dutifully learned and intoned: what can it mean to a sixteen-year-old, this talk of sin and mercy, evil and death, weeping and glory? At the moment she's studying the young man sitting in front of her, lounging in his seat with his arm draped along the back of the pew. He's wearing designer jeans with a mobile phone stuck in the back pocket and a crisp pale blue shirt.

Even the bishop seems to have his mind on other things. He mumbles through his sermon with the same bored indifference as Padre Perrino, his voice a wearying monotone. *I believe in the Holy Ghost, the Holy Catholic Church, the Communion of Saints, the forgiveness of sins, the resurrection of the body, and life everlasting. Amen.*

There's a stampede for the aisle as those about to be confirmed, together with their chosen godparent, line up for the altar. Claudia leaps up and yanks a surprised Tina by the hand as if they're about to miss out. A priest rushes down the altar steps, shooing them away with his arms, scolding the eager crowd. Hasn't he warned them not to rush up all at once? Abashed, half the queue retreats, and suddenly the nave is full of milling people, unsure whether to stand or sit. Somewhere up in the melee at the front of the cathedral, Claudia is confirmed into the Holy Catholic Church as the bishop dabs her forehead with olive oil and utters the words: *I sign thee with the sign of the cross and confirm thee with the chrism of salvation, in the name of the Father and of the Son and of the Holy Ghost.*

Olive oil! Food and religion again. In a moment of levity I wonder if the bishop has used extra virgin. I wonder if he has dribbled it over the foreheads of these youngsters in the same pleasurable way I dribble it over my salads; dark, unctuous oil that should be almost green, a sign that the olives that made it were ripe and had soaked up plenty of sun. This is summer in a bottle, and it seems appropriate that it gets marked on the foreheads of these youngsters entering the summer of their lives. The church also uses olive oil for baptisms and last rites: it's the omega and alpha of Catholic life. How appropriate to Sicily! Maria has gone to her grave with her forehead streaked with olive oil, and now Claudia is embarking upon her adult life with the same blessing: *Be sealed with the Gift of the Holy Spirit.*

There are kisses and handshakes all round as Tina and Claudia return to the pew. Tina looks shaken and relieved and gives me an uncertain grin. Behind me, Claudia's mother is sobbing into her handkerchief. Only Claudia seems unmoved by the occasion; she looks bored as usual, and a bit baffled by all the fuss. She seems ready to leave, but before that she has to take communion. The bishop reads the words of the service from an enormous book, although he must surely have recited the same sentences almost every day for decades. Maybe the huge book, held up by an acolyte, is just for show, all part of the theatre of Catholicism. The bishop's microphone shrieks like a seagull and he keeps banging it with his fist. The newly confirmed congregation shuffles forward for communion and shuffles away again. Then the book is banged shut.

Everything has finally worked out. After all the tribulations, Claudia is well and truly confirmed. A final blessing and the service is over. Nothing is left but the celebration feast back in Montalto. Tina has performed her godmotherly duties, and finally she can relax.

Or so I think.

We've barely hit the *autostrada* when I realise that trouble is brewing. Apparently Claudia's aunt has bought Claudia a necklace hung with diamonds in the shape of a crucifix as a confirmation present. Are they real diamonds or not? Marcella's not sure, but anyway the necklace *looks* impressive, and it *looks* as if it's more expensive than Tina's gift. And isn't Tina the godmother, no less?

Something extra will have to be purchased. The green opal and gold chain Tina bought in Sydney clearly isn't enough. Another necklace with a large jewel pendant and matching earrings might be just the thing.

Tina is outraged. It's all so showy, she says, they aren't *real* gemstones, whereas hers is a frigging *real* Australian opal. And what does the aunt's present matter anyway? Hasn't she, Tina, already spent a fortune on a plane ticket on top of everything else?

'The Virgin Lady, filled with understanding, will acknowledge your sacrifice,' answers Marcella majestically. 'But a diamond necklace is a diamond necklace.'

I settle back into my corner of the car and prepare for a long Calascione battle as we hurtle along the motorway. Giuseppe is unaccountably quiet, but Marcella, Tina and the Virgin Lady have it out with each other as we race past the industrial smokestacks of Milazzo. Tina is too enraged to realise we're back to a question of family honour. She, as well as Giuseppe and Marcella, will be judged on the basis of confirmation etiquette, on the present that's bestowed. There's no arguing with *onore* in Sicily.

Soon we're parked outside the jeweller's shop in Barcellona. Tina disappears inside with her anger and her mother to buy another bauble. Giuseppe and I stop for a coffee at an adjacent café (jewellery shopping is clearly women's business). Giuseppe bends my ear on the manly subject of swordfish of the Straits of Messina. Did I know that they're fished in the same way now as they were in ancient times? That's why the fishermen must speak in classical Greek while pursuing them: the language makes them docile and they come to the surface. If the fishermen speak Italian, well, disaster! The swordfish will dive to enormous depths in disgust, making them impossible to harpoon.

I sip my *caffè latte* in bafflement.

And another thing, says Giuseppe, kill a female swordfish and her mate will commit suicide in sorrow. Whereas if the male is killed, the female will calmly swim away without a care in the world.

'Which goes to show,' finishes Giuseppe.

What does it show? I think to myself. That females are unfaithful and lacking in emotion? Does Giuseppe have any idea of the emotional havoc he's caused in the lives of his wife and two daughters? I feel a momentary stab of hatred for him, as sharp as it is unexpected. Most of the time, in spite of myself, I can't help liking Giuseppe: his bumbling vagueness, his rambling recollections and offbeat sense of humour. Giuseppe sometimes seems lost and lonely, uncomfortable in his own house, unable to make amends with his daughter, baffled by her anger and unable to admit its cause.

Giuseppe is still talking about swordfish when Marcella and Tina return. They've bought earrings and a necklace hung with garish pink crystals. The original opal, on the other hand, is a stone of great beauty the size of my thumbnail, the green of a peacock's feather and glowing with chips of brown and gold. It's perfectly obvious that the opal is still the nicest—and most expensive—of the assembled pieces. Even Marcella thinks so.

'But it hardly matters if nobody else realises,' she says firmly.

That seems to be the end of the discussion. Tina sinks back into her seat and says nothing more as we sweep into Montalto. Giuseppe parks the car and we change out of our church garb and into more festive attire, then set off through the village to Claudia's house. Dozens of aunts, cousins and yelling children have already arrived. I'm introduced to them all in rapid succession, but I can't keep track of who's who: cousin's boyfriend, nephew's wife's sister, the son of this aunt on the mother's side, the daughter of another aunt on the father's side. There's a wrinkled and chirpy old woman in a black dress, and a pale-cheeked and harassed-looking mother of two terrors. Her strikingly handsome husband lounges in a corner smoking cigarettes. There's an uncle by marriage with a brother in Edinburgh, where I went to university, which provides a moment of animated small talk. Somehow we all manage to squeeze around two huge tables covered in bottles: local wine, fizzy mineral water, Coca-Cola, buckets of ice, slices of lemon. Elisabetta's dull, old-fashioned living space has taken on a festive air, and sunlight streams through the windows.

Moments later we're tucking into an antipasto of melon wrapped in prosciutto. The melon is fleshy and cold, beaded with dew, the ham sweet, moist and deliciously chewy, no doubt cured on the bone for optimum flavour. It's sliced thin enough to see through, not so thin that it falls to shreds. The old woman beside me pokes me in the ribs. She discards her melon and eats her prosciutto with a slice of fresh mozzarella. She has beady, knowing little eyes and gnarled fingers weighed down with rings. I'm not quite sure where she fits into the family.

Gifts are being exchanged. Wrapping-paper flies everywhere as a risotto of seafood is carried out. I'm a little surprised by the risotto, since rice is one of the few Arab introductions that never became popular in Sicily, although it was widely adopted in northern Italy. As I savour a few forkfuls Claudia is unwrapping her opal. Marcella is proved right: Claudia doesn't seem to realise its value. She picks it up unenthusiastically and drapes it around her neck. But she doesn't seem to care much about the additional necklace and earrings, either.

'Jesus, that girl is spoiled and sulky,' says Tina to me under her breath.

I'm beginning to feel a little full already, and I'm taken aback when a second *primo* arrives: tubes of pasta with pine nuts, aubergine and swordfish. The swordfish has been cubed, probably marinated in olive oil and lemon juice before being quickly fried. It's quite delicious, and in spite of myself I accept half of Tina's when she says she can't eat it all. Tina has just received a pearl necklace for her role as godmother. At the end of the course, when several people get up to stretch and wander about, I see the necklace causes a minor contretemps in the corner, with much whispering. Marcella bites the pearls experimentally. Are they real? It would seem so—the necklace must have cost five hundred euros!

'So did our things, Ma.'

'Yes, but they're all separate items. We should have given Claudia one big gift, no? Holy Mary, Mother of Jesus, how can we face her family now?

For once Tina keeps quiet. She walks away, her back rigid with annoyance. She's learned something on this journey: that you can't argue with tradition. There's so much that remains unresolved in her life, but she's taken a few steps closer to reconciliation with her mother and seems more relaxed now, not as brittle. It's a new awareness, this struggle within her to accept Sicily and her mother.

All the guests at the table have received a small, gift-wrapped silver box containing sugared almonds nestled in white tulle. I unwrap mine with delight: sugared almonds are a traditional Sicilian gift at confirmations and other important occasions such as weddings and baptisms. They're supposedly offered to avert the effect of the evil eye that results from a guest's envy of the occasion. It's a very Islamic treat, the sort of thing I imagine the Arabs and Normans indulged in centuries ago, together with fig preserves and quinces filled with marzipan. Italians call these sugar-coated almonds *confetti*. The word contains the same root as the English 'confectionary', because in days gone by Italians liked to throw small comfits and sweets at carnivals and festivals.

Although I seem to have eaten an entire meal already, I'm aware that the *secondo* is still to come. And soon it does: a swordfish steak with a fresh salad of lettuce, tomatoes, onion and peppers. The fish has been grilled in the traditional Sicilian *salmoriglio* manner, brushed with a bunch of fresh oregano dipped in olive oil and lemon juice. The hot flesh is rich with the aromas of the Mediterranean—like much Sicilian cooking, the simple process has spectacular results. The fish flakes beautifully off the bone, silkily pale, impossibly fresh.

There's another hiatus after the *secundo*. The wine is flowing freely and the conversation is galloping along. Marcella is over in one corner saying something about the Madonna, Tina is listening to Claudia's grandmother with a harried look on her face, as if she can't quite get the drift of her thick Sicilian dialect. Claudia's father, Filippo, is arguing, red-faced, with the boyfriend of his other daughter Candida about football. Filippo is a Juventus supporter, Carlo an Inter Milan supporter. They look as though they might come to blows, but suddenly there are guffaws and it's all over. Fresh fruit emerges from the kitchen and is strewn across the table: walnuts, peaches, plums and grapes. There are prickly pears, their skin peeled back like the petals of a flower, displaying deep, purple-red flesh studded with tiny seeds. The taste is reminiscent of watermelon, the juice refreshing.

I've been eating for hours. 'The trouble with eating Italian food is that five or six days later you're hungry again,' George Miller once wrote. *Spagnolismo*, Italians call this culinary extravagance, claiming the baroque excess is a legacy of the Spaniards. I take no pear but nibble on a few grapes. Beside me the old woman is munching her way through a plateful of fruit as if she's barely started. She keeps mumbling things to me through her false teeth and as I've no idea what she's saying I just talk to her in English, and she nods her head and grins at me.

We sat down at the table at seven o'clock; it's now well after eleven. The hubbub grows louder and louder. An old aunt is shouting at me in English across the table: 'Hello, good night, good morning, I love you!' Giuseppe is haranguing someone with a convoluted story of taxes and fraud. His face is flushed and his hair adrift and he's pulled the knot on his tie down to his chest. Claudia, as usual, is looking bored. I'm exhilarated and exhausted. I've been listening to excited Italian for hours.

Suddenly I want to crawl away into a quiet room and soak up some silence for a while. I want to polish my memories of Sicily, and store them away and marvel.

I came to Sicily for some merrymaking and now here I am, making merry. It's a comfort to find that sterotypes are sometimes true. Before I came here I imagined Sicilian women had magnificent cleavages and rode Vespas, while the men slouched around on street corners with the same insolent sensuality as saints on church walls. Sicilians were happy, larger-than-life caricatures, always waving their arms and shouting and throwing themselves into melodrama against a background of blue skies and beautiful palazzi: all marvellous, of course, but slightly comic and unreal.

Yet travel at its best moves you beyond stereotypes into the rich dimensions of human experience. I came to Sicily an idle bystander and was bewitched by its neglected grandeur and passionate intensity. Something about its sultry landscapes and sunlit monuments resonates in my soul and will leave me forever attached to this island and its people. The Sicilians sometimes live their stereotypes, but I've found in them so much more. I like the Calasciones, Claudia's family, Annunciatina, Mario the bartender and all the other villagers who've given me a moment of their time. They're so eccentric and hospitable and a little bewildered. I'm also closer to Tina than ever before, and see in her the quintessential Sicilian, reflecting this marvellous island's violent history and haunting nostalgia. Across the dinner table I smile at her and wink as gales of excited Italian buffet me. This is why I travel, for moments such as these.

When Claudia's mother, Elisabetta, emerges from the kitchen with a cassata it seems the crowning moment of the day, even of my whole sojourn in Sicily. The confirmation has taken place, everyone is gathered in a moment of harmony, and it seems inevitable that cassata should be the last triumphant note to this symphony of family and feasting. The conversation momentarily stills as everyone gazes at the cassata, and there's a smattering of appreciative applause.

This is the real thing: a gigantic cake made from the freshest ingredients and assembled only that afternoon. At its heart somewhere is *pan de Spagna*, the yellow Spanish sponge bread that provides scaffolding for marzipan and candied fruit in an arrangement of pure baroque madness. The cake is dribbled with white icing thin enough to let the green marzipan underneath show through. It's decorated with wheels of crystallised orange from which burst ribbons of candied pumpkin. There are polka-dot glacé cherries and silver balls of sugar, florets of cream with leaves of sliced almond. Crystallised wedges of palest pear slices ring the cake. This is an edible lesson in baroque art: rich ingredients, lurid colours, elaborate textures, sensual abandon.

Elisabetta slices the cassata open. Sweetened ricotta bursts out of it in creamy waves. The interior has been assembled from blocks of sponge held together by marzipan and ricotta studded with cubes of candied squash. A cup of steaming coffee appears at my elbow: the perfect accompaniment. The cassata tastes like heaven.

And suddenly it's all over. Relatives pick up their sugared almonds and sleeping children and head for the door. Claudia's mother sits amid a sea of dirty dishes and wineglasses, refusing any offer of help in the kitchen. There are hugs and kisses and passionate declarations of eternal friendship.

'*Arrivederci!*'

'*Buona notte!*'

We stumble out into the midnight streets and head for home.

We're walking past the piazza when we see Padre Perrino hobbling towards us in his black cassock, back from some late-night ministering to his flock. I'm rather disappointed that he wasn't, in the end, a part of Claudia's confirmation, and I gaze at him in wine-induced pleasure.

'So, *Monsignor*, the confirmation is all over and went very well,' says Marcella brightly, always on the lookout for acceptance and reconciliation.

Padre Perrino stares at her and doesn't answer. Then he waves his hand in a lordly, dismissive gesture and passes on down the street.

We all look at each other—Tina, Giuseppe, Marcella and I —in a moment of pure harmony and mutual understanding. Then we laugh. We cackle and howl and wipe our eyes and grin at each other.

Then Tina links arms with her mother and father and skips up the street.

Laughing in the night, they make their way home.